The Quest for the Real Jesus

Biblical Interpretation Series

Editors in Chief
Paul Anderson
Yvonne Sherwood

Editorial Advisory Board
Akma Adam – Roland Boer – Musa Dube
Jennifer L. Koosed – Vernon Robbins
Annette Schellenberg – Carolyn J. Sharp
Johanna Stiebert – Duane Watson
Ruben Zimmermann

VOLUME 120

The titles published in this series are listed at brill.com/bins

The Quest for the Real Jesus

Radboud Prestige Lectures by Prof. Dr. Michael Wolter

Edited by
Jan van der Watt

BRILL

LEIDEN • BOSTON
2013

Library of Congress Cataloging-in-Publication Data

Wolter, Michael.
 The quest for the real Jesus : Radboud Prestige lectures by Prof. Dr. Michael Wolter / edited by Jan van der Watt.
   pages cm. — (Biblical interpretation series ; VOLUME 120)
   ISBN 978-90-04-23578-6 (hardback : alk. paper) — ISBN 978-90-04-25480-0 (e-book)
 1. Jesus Christ—Historicity. I. Watt, Jan G. van der. II. Title.

 BT303.2.W65 2013
 232.9'08—dc23

2013018719

This publication has been typeset in the multilingual "Brill" typeface. With over 5,100 characters covering Latin, IPA, Greek, and Cyrillic, this typeface is especially suitable for use in the humanities. For more information, please see www.brill.com/brill-typeface.

ISSN 0928-0731
ISBN 978-90-04-23578-6 (hardback)
ISBN 978-90-04-25480-0 (e-book)

Copyright 2013 by Koninklijke Brill NV, Leiden, The Netherlands.
Koninklijke Brill NV incorporates the imprints Brill, Global Oriental, Hotei Publishing,
IDC Publishers and Martinus Nijhoff Publishers.

All rights reserved. No part of this publication may be reproduced, translated, stored in
a retrieval system, or transmitted in any form or by any means, electronic, mechanical,
photocopying, recording or otherwise, without prior written permission from the publisher.

Authorization to photocopy items for internal or personal use is granted by Koninklijke Brill NV
provided that the appropriate fees are paid directly to The Copyright Clearance Center,
222 Rosewood Drive, Suite 910, Danvers, MA 01923, USA.
Fees are subject to change.

This book is printed on acid-free paper.

CONTENTS

List of Contributors vii

Abbreviations ix

Preface xi
Jan van der Watt

Which Jesus is the Real Jesus? 1
Michael Wolter

From Mark's Son of God to Jesus of Nazareth—*un cul-de-sac?* 19
Cilliers Breytenbach

The Remembered Jesus 57
James D.G. Dunn

Contours of the Historical Jesus 67
R. Alan Culpepper

Jesus as Savior and Protector—Before Easter and After 87
Craig A. Evans

A New Starting Point in Historical Jesus Research:
The Easter Event 99
Michael R. Licona

Theological Hermeneutics and the Historical Jesus:
A Critical Evaluation of Gadamerian Approaches
and a New Methodological Proposal 129
Christopher M. Hays

Historical Jesus Research as New Testament Theology 159
Robert Morgan

In Which Sense has the Conviction that Jesus was Resurrected
the "Certainty of Fact"? 185
Notger Slenczka

vi CONTENTS

Im Glauben zum ‚wirklichen' Jesus? Überlegungen zu
Michael Wolters Umgang mit der historischen Jesusfrage 205
Martin Laube

Academic Curriculum Vitae 223
Michael Wolter

List of Publications 225
Prof. Dr. Michael Walter

Index of Authors 233

LIST OF CONTRIBUTORS

Cilliers Breytenbach is Professor of Literature, History and Religion of Early Christianity at Humboldt-University, Berlin, Germany and also Extraordinary Professor of New Testament and Classics at University of Stellenbosch, South Africa.

R. Alan Culpepper is Dean of McAfee School of Theology at Mercer University, Atlanta, GA, USA.

James D.G. Dunn is Emeritus Lightfoot Professor of Divinity at Durham University, United Kingdom.

Craig A. Evans is Payzant Distinguished Professor of New Testament at Divinity College, Acadia University, in Nova Scotia, Canada.

Christopher M. Hays is a British Academy Postdoctoral Fellow of Keble College and the Faculty of Theology and Religion at University of Oxford, United Kingdom and also a Research Associate in the Department of New Testament at University of Pretoria, South Africa.

Martin Laube is Professor of Systematic Theology and Reformed Theology at Georg-August-University Gottingen, Germany.

Michael R. Licona is Associate Professor in Theology at Houston Baptist University, TX, USA as well as guest researcher at North-West University, South Africa.

Robert Morgan is Fellow of Linacre College, Oxford.

Notger Slenczka is Professor for Systematic Theology/Dogmatics, Faculty of Theology, at Humboldt-University Berlin, Germany.

Jan G. van der Watt is Professor of Source Texts of Christianity at Radboud University Nijmegen, Nijmegen, Netherlands as well as Extraordinary Professor, Research Institute for Theology and Religion, University of South Africa.

Michael Wolter is Professor of New Testament, Faculty of Protestant Theology, at University of Bonn, Germany as well as Honorary Professor, Faculty of Theology, at University of Pretoria, South Africa.

ABBREVIATIONS

AB	The Anchor Bible
ABD	D.N. Freedman et al., eds., *The Anchor Bible Dictionary* (6 vols.; New York: Doubleday, 1992)
ABRL	The Anchor Bible Reference Library
AJT	*Asia Journal of Theology*
ATANT	Abhandlungen zur Theologie des Alten und Neuen Testaments
BAR	*Biblical Archaeology Review*
BETL	Bibliotheca Ephemeridum Theologicarum Lovaniensium
BEvT	Beiträge zur evangelischen Theologie
Bib.	*Biblica*
BSOAS	*Bulletin of the School of Oriental and African Studies*
BTB	*Biblical Theology Bulletin*
CBQ	*Catholic Biblical Quarterly*
ExpTim	*The Expository Times*
FRLANT	Forschungen zur Religion und Literatur des Alten und Neuen Testaments
HeyJ	*The Heythrop Journal*
HTR	*Harvard Theological Review*
HTKNT	Herders Theologischer Kommentar zum Neuen Testament
JPOS	*Journal of the Palestine Oriental Society*
JR	*Journal of Religion*
JSNT	*Journal for the Study of the New Testament*
JSNTSup	*Journal for the Study of the New Testament.* Supplements
JTC	*Journal for Theology and the Church*
JTS	*Journal of Theological Studies*
KuD	*Kerygma und Dogma*
LNTS	Library of New Testament Studies
Neot.	*Neotestamentica*
NIGTC	The New International Greek Testament Commentary
NovTSup	*Novum Testamentum.* Supplements
NRSV	New Revised Standard Version
NTD	Das Neue Testament deutsch
NTL	New Testament Library
NTOA	Novum testamentum et orbis antiquus
NTS	*New Testament Studies*

NZSTh	*Neue Zeitschrift für Systematische Theologie und Religions-philosophie*
OLP	*Orientalia Lovaniensia periodica*
PGM	K. Preisendanz, ed., *Papyri Graecae Magicae: Die Griechischen Zauberpapyri* (ed. A. Henrichs; 2 vols.; Leipzig: Teubner, 1928–1931; repr. Munich and Leipzig: Saur, 2001)
PRSt	*Perspectives in Religious Studies*
SBL	Society of Biblical Literature
SBLRBS	SBL Resources for Biblical Study
SBS	Stuttgarter Bibelstudien
SBT	Studies in Biblical Theology
stw	Suhrkamp Taschenbuch Wissenschaft
SEÅ	*Svensk Exegetisk Årsbok*
TANZ	Texte und Arbeiten zum neutestamentlichen Zeitalter
TLZ	*Theologische Literaturzeitung*
TRu	*Theologische Rundschau*
TS	*Theological Studies*
TSAJ	Texte und Studien zum Antiken Judentum = Texts and Studies in Ancient Judaism
TTKi	*Tidsskrift for Teologi og Kirke*
WMANT	Wissenschaftliche Monographien zum Alten und Neuen Testament
WUNT	Wissenschaftliche Untersuchungen zum Neuen Testament
ZNT	*Zeitschrift für Neues Testament*
ZNW	*Zeitschrift für die neutestamentliche Wissenschaft und die Kunde der älteren Kirche*
ZTK	*Zeitschrift für Theologie und Kirche*

PREFACE

The first series of lectures that formed a part of the *Radboud Prestige Lectures in New Testament* were held in December 2011 at the Radboud University Nijmegen. They were presented by Prof. Dr. Michael Wolter of the University of Bonn, Germany. His main prestige lecture focused on the important question of the quest for the historical Jesus.

The aim of the *Radboud Prestige Lectures in New Testament* is to stimulate high level academic discussion, not only in the Netherlands, but also wider afield. In addition these lectures acknowledge the outstanding work of internationally recognized scholars. The esteemed scholars that are invited to participate in these lectures are widely regarded as leaders in their respective fields in the New Testament. Each one shares their wealth of knowledge and experience on topics of their own choosing. While the series of lectures are held at the Radboud University Nijmegen, publication of the lectures stimulates further academic research and discussion on the respective topics. The project is done in co-operation with Brill Publishers, who kindly undertake the publication of the lecture series.

The format of this volume is somewhat unique and provocative. Prof. Wolter offered his main prestige lecture on the quest for the historical Jesus. In this lecture he challenged many of the current views within the historical Jesus research by critically evaluating the approaches in various categories. This lecture was then presented to a variety of scholars from different disciplines (i.e. New Testament studies and systematic theology) who approach the problem from a number of different perspectives, thus bring a rich texture of insights. The aim was not only to get an overview from some of the important players in the field, but also to provide insights into the current standing of the research on this problem. Systematic theologians and New Testament scholars were jointly invited to participate in the debate by way of response to Prof. Wolter's paper. In this way one can appreciate the role the quest for the historical Jesus plays within a wider framework. This resulted in interesting articles that not only deal with historical, but also with philosophical and hermeneutical issues. Hopefully, these different approaches would serve as further stimulation within this debate.

Two things were asked of the contributors. Firstly, they were asked to respond to Prof. Wolter's lecture. Although there is, of course, agreement with much of what Prof. Wolter maintains, his views are nevertheless discussed critically and at times there are some difference among the scholars on crucial points. This is the advantage of these contributions – it introduces the reader to the finer nuances of the debate. Secondly, the contributors were asked to present their own views. The articles therefore do not only critically engage with Wolter's views, but also offer alternative views, which obviously broaden the scope of these discussions.

Consideration was given to the possibility of writing an extended introduction as well as asking Prof. Wolter to respond to the different contributions. It was eventually felt that neither option should be followed in this volume. Firstly, Prof. Wolter's contribution already serves as introduction to, and focus of, the volume. Another introduction would be superfluous. Secondly, in consultation with Prof. Wolter, it was decided for several reasons not to add another chapter with Prof. Wolter's reactions, since his response would no doubt stimulate further responses from the other contributors, thus leading to an endless debate. Rather, such debate and discussion should form part of the debate following this volume. It was felt that the readers, being emerged into the many views and perspectives in the volume, would, in a manner of speaking, write their own 'conclusion'.

Our thanks go not only to Prof. Wolter and the other contributors for their willingness to participate in this volume of the *Radboud Prestige Lectures in New Testament* but also to Brill for their willingness to support the lecture series. We are looking forward to the next series of prestige lectures that will be held in April 2013 by Prof. Dr. Alan Culpepper, Mercer University, Atlanta, USA, on the ethics of John.

November 2012

Jan van der Watt
Radboud University Nijmegen

WHICH JESUS IS THE REAL JESUS?

Michael Wolter

I.

1. What is the similarity between Jesus of Nazareth and—let's say—Alexander the Great, Martin Luther, or Winston Churchill? All were great people. Biographies and historical books have been written about all of them.

The problem is, however, that Jesus of Nazareth was, on the one hand, a historical figure, but on the other hand, we know that for Christians he was and is more than just a historical figure like Alexander the Great, or Martin Luther, or Winston Churchill. We would certainly not claim that any of these aforementioned men was God's son, that they rose from the dead and that God's salvation is available through one of them.

At the same time, however, we also know that not everyone believes these things about Jesus. Here we face an intriguing question: anyone can write a book about the teaching and actions and fate of Jesus of Nazareth. To do this, one does not have to believe that Jesus was God's Son, that he is risen from the dead or that God's salvation is made available through him. One does not even have to believe in God. To write a good book about Jesus, one must merely be able to apply historical methods critically and honestly. One can surely write about Jesus in the same manner that one would write about Alexander or Luther or Churchill.

The question is whether this is the Jesus in whom Christians believe? Do we believe in *that* Jesus who is reconstructed for us by historians? Of course, nobody does. To mention God in relation to this Jesus is entirely optional since this particular Jesus can be reconstructed in an entirely secular form.

Moreover there are theologians who write such books about Jesus. They reconstruct a fully historical Jesus, they put him into his cultural environment, depicting a person who is no different from any other person in history. Therefore the theological impact of their results is equivalent to—in the words of Dale Allison—"a list of the U. S. Presidents and their dates".[1]

However since they are theologians this enterprise leads to two interesting questions:

– Is there a difference between a book about Jesus that has been written by a historian who is not a theologian and a book about Jesus written by a theologian who does serious historical work?
– How important is this Jesus, reconstructed by means of historical analysis, for Christian faith?

2. In light of this tension the theological significance of the inquiry into the historical Jesus has existed since the publication of Martin Kähler's lecture *The So-called Historical Jesus and the Historic, Biblical Christ* in 1892.[2] Kähler addresses the so-called "life of Jesus research", which is commonly cited as beginning in the eighteenth century with Hermann Samuel Reimarus.[3] And although Reimarus had already made a similar distinction to that later made by Kähler,[4] it led him to quite different conclusions. Reimarus presented Jesus essentially as an ethical teacher who belonged entirely to Judaism, and who, with his teaching, wanted "to improve men in their inner disposition and all their heart".[5] In contrast, Jesus' resurrection and exaltation, his messianic status and his being the Son of God were the apostles' inventions after Jesus' death, as were the idea of the salvific significance of his death, the expectation of his return, and much more.

---

[1] D.C. Allison, *The Historical Christ and the Theological Jesus* (Grand Rapids and Cambridge: Eerdmans, 2009), 10.

[2] M. Kähler, *The So-called Historical Jesus and the Historic, Biblical Christ* (German ed. 1892, 2nd ed. 1896), trans., ed. and with an introduction by C.E. Braaten (Philadelphia: Fortress, 1988; all quotations are taken from this edition).

[3] Cf. in that sense the subtitle in Albert Schweitzer's *The Quest of the Historical Jesus: A Critical Study of Its Progress from Reimarus to Wrede* (London: Adam and Charles Black, 1910). This subtitle is omitted from Schweitzer's expanded second edition (1913) with its new title, and therefore absent from John Bowden's translation (London: SCM, 2000), even though Bowden retains the 1910 English title.

[4] In his essay "On the Intention of Jesus and His Disciples" which was originally published by Gotthold Ephraim Lessing in connection with the subtitle "Another Fragment of the Wolffenbüttel Unknown" in 1784 Reimarus demanded "to separate completely what the apostles say in their own writings from that which Jesus himself actually said and taught" (*Reimarus: Fragments*, ed. C.H. Talbert, trans. R.S. Fraser [London: SMC, 1971], 64).

[5] Ibid., 69–70.

Unlike Reimarus, Kähler believed that the historical Jesus behind the texts of the Gospels is not accessible. He ascribes the impossibility of the endeavour of reconstructing the historical Jesus to the fact that the Gospels are not historical reports, but rather proclamations. For him the "so-called historical Jesus" as he is historically reconstructed, can be nothing other than "a modern example of human creativity".[6] This Jesus is irrelevant for Christian faith because he is only a creation of "modern authors" and "conceals from us the living Christ".[7] This "historic, biblical Christ", Kähler wrote, is "the real Christ", who was proclaimed by the apostles, died for our sins, was raised from the dead on the third day, "whom with the eyes of faith and in our prayers we meet at the right hand of God",[8] "Christ the Lord".[9]

3. The positions of Hermann Samuel Reimarus and Martin Kähler establish a framework, which clarifies the question of the historical Jesus and its theological significance or insignificance right down to the present day. How does the "historical Jesus" of Hermann Samuel Reimarus relate to the "theological Christ" of Martin Kähler? Even the title of the recently published book by Dale Allison, which I mentioned above, is focused on this very difference. Interestingly enough he exchanged the adjectives: The title of his book reads *The Historical Christ and the Theological Jesus*. This interchange tells us that the author of this book is keenly engaged in trying to overcome the division between Reimarus and Kähler and that his endeavour is a rather desperate attempt.

In my opinion three ways of dealing with the issue are possible:

a) We can follow the path that Martin Kähler has indicated, which was also taken, most notably, by Rudolf Bultmann. The reasoning Bultmann gave for his choice is well known:

First, the character of the Gospels as evidence of the faith of the post-Easter communities prevents them from giving access to the historical

---

[6] Kähler, *Jesus* (n. 2), 43.
[7] Ibid., 43.
[8] Ibid., 61.
[9] Ibid., 64.

4 MICHAEL WOLTER

Jesus because "they do not intend to be read as historical reports, but as a portion of proclamation".[10]

Second, also for *theological* reasons, it is not appropriate to make the historical Jesus the object of faith, because only the Christ of the *kerygma* can be that.[11] There is thus a historical continuity between the historical Jesus and the proclamation of early Christianity, but not between the historical Jesus and Jesus Christ, because, as Bultmann has written: "The Christ of the kerygma is not a historical figure which could enjoy continuity with the historical Jesus."[12] It is only theologically important—Bultmann writes, as famously and controversially—*that* Jesus existed: "The decisive thing is simply the 'that'", not the "what" and the "how" of the historical Jesus.[13] Following along this same path we primarily find students of Bultmann (with the well-known exception of Ernst Käsemann)[14] and—on the other side of the ocean—Luke Timothy Johnson.[15]

b) The other possibility is to follow the path of Hermann Samuel Reimarus. On this path one would encounter, in particular, the early representatives of the so-called "Third Quest for the historical Jesus".[16]

---

[10] R. Bultmann, "The Primitive Christian Kerygma and the Historical Jesus", in C.E. Braaten and R.A. Harrisville, eds., *The Historical Jesus and the Kerygmatic Christ: Essays on the New Quest of the Historical Jesus* (New York and Nashville: Abingdon, 1964), 15–53, here 21.

[11] Ibid., 17.

[12] Ibid., 18.

[13] Ibid., 20, 21; cf. also p. 20: From the historical Jesus the *kerygma* only needs "the 'that' of his history".

[14] The so-called "New Quest of the historical Jesus" (see below n. 16) originated from him. This debate was initiated by Ernst Käsemann's essay "The Problem of the Historical Jesus", in idem, *Essays on New Testament Themes* (SBT 41; London: SCM, 1964), 15–47. For him "[t]he question of the historical Jesus is, in its legitimate form, the question of the continuity of the Gospel within the discontinuity of the times and within the variation of the kerygma" (46). In the synoptic Gospels' apparent efforts "to cleave firmly to history" he sees one way of giving expression to the "*extra nos* of salvation" (33).

[15] L.T. Johnson, *The Real Jesus: The Misguided Quest for the Historical Jesus and the Truth of the Traditional Gospels* (New York: HarperSanFrancisco, 1996). Cf. ibid., 134: "Christianity in its classic form has not based itself on the ministry of Jesus but on the resurrection of Jesus, the claim that after his crucifixion and burial Jesus entered into the powerful life of God, and shares that life (whose symbol is the Holy Spirit) with those who can receive it."

[16] This label originates from the English translation of Albert Schweitzer's *Geschichte der Leben-Jesu-Forschung* as *The Quest of the Historical Jesus*. Accordingly the Life-of-Jesus research was counted as the "First Quest". Afterwards the discussion that was initiated by Ernst Käsemann (see n. 14) was called the "New Quest" (cf. J.M. Robinson, *A New Quest of the Historical Jesus* [London: SCM, 1959]), and the new interest in the historical Jesus

This line started in the United States, but then spread to Europe and elsewhere, and has since been differentiated into a wide variety of successive strands.[17] It is supported by a dedicated interest in the socio-historical description and explanation of the appearance of Jesus. Furthermore, it anchors the historical Jesus decidedly in his Jewish environment.

The fact that the "Third Quest" follows the path that Reimarus pioneered, can be exemplified by the approach of John Dominic Crossan.[18] In an earlier book on Jesus, his "Prologue" (programmatically entitled "From Christ to Jesus") suggests that the reader, "move behind the screen of creedal interpretation and ... give an accurate but impartial account of the historical Jesus as distinct from the confessional Christ".[19] In the "Epilogue" of the same book—complementary to the prologue—entitled "From Jesus to Christ", the historical Jesus is characterized as a peasant Jewish Cynic[20] whose "ecstatic vision and social program sought to rebuild a society upward from its grass roots, but on principles of religious and economic egalitarianism".[21] It is *this* Jesus to whom Crossan ascribes theological significance: "I argue, above all, that the structure of Christianity will always be: *this is how we see Jesus—then as Christ—now.* Christianity must repeatedly, generation after generation, make its best historical judgment about who *Jesus was then* and, on that basis, decide what that reconstruction means as *Christ now*."[22]

---

that cropped up initially in the 1980s in the United States was named the "Third Quest". According to G. Theissen and A. Merz, *The Historical Jesus* (London: SCM, 1998), 10, n. 25, this designation was used for the first time by S. Neill and N.T. Wright, *The Interpretation of the New Testament 1861–1986* (Oxford: Oxford University Press, 1988), 379.

[17] Cf. the overviews by M.J. Borg, "Portraits of Jesus in Contemporary North American Scholarship", *HTR* 84 (1991): 1–22; J.P. Meier, "The Present State of the 'Third Quest' for the Historical Jesus: Loss and Gain", *Bib.* 80 (1999): 459–487.

[18] To J.D. Crossan we owe two Jesus books: *The Historical Jesus: The Life of a Mediterranean Jewish Peasant* (San Francisco: HarperSanFrancisco, 1991), and *Jesus: A Revolutionary Biography* (San Francisco: Harper & Row, 1994).

[19] Crossan, *Jesus: A Revolutionary Biography* (n. 18), XI.—Cf. in this sense also Meier, "Present State" (n. 17), 463, who demands a "purely empirical, historical quest for Jesus that prescinds from or brackets what is known by faith", and even more explicit E.P. Sanders, *Jesus and Judaism* (London: SCM, 1985), 2: "I am interested in the debate about the significance of the historical Jesus for theology in the way one is interested in something that he once found fascinating", and finally at the end of his book (333): "I have been engaged for some years in the effort to free history and exegesis from the control of theology."

[20] Crossan, *Historical Jesus* (n. 18), 198; Crossan considers them as "hippies in a world of Augustan yuppies" (ibid., 421).

[21] Ibid., 196.

[22] *Jesus: A Revolutionary Biography* (n. 18), 200.

MICHAEL WOLTER

c) The third possibility is to tread another path. This path lies somewhere between the other two. A characteristic of this path is that it avoids both Reimarus' "historical Jesus" as a short-cut for the "Christ of faith" as well as Kähler's explanation of the works of Jesus of Nazareth in word and deed as theologically insignificant to the Christian faith. The object of Kähler's Jesus of Nazareth can only ever be the kerygmatic Christ.

The label that appropriately characterizes this third way is, "the story of Jesus in the light of the Easter faith".[23] With this label, inquiry into the historical Jesus obtains a perspective that not only allows it to become a theological question, but also allows its distinctive feature of the inquiry into the question of the historical Jesus to stand out in regard to the other questions put by the other two paths.[24]

In contrast to Kähler, the question of the historical Jesus as specified by the Easter faith makes a generally neglected aspect of the Christian Easter confession visible. Stated more clearly, it is not some random person of whom the Christian faith tells, saying that God raised him from the dead (Rom 10:9 and elsewhere) placing him in the heavenly, sovereign, position of his Son (Rom 1:4), giving him the "name above every name" (Phil 2:9, where the title "Kyrios"—"Lord"—is meant, see verse 11). Rather, he is a specific, historically unique person, whose words and deeds God "vindicated" (ἐδικαιώθη), as expressed in 1Tim 3:16. This situation leaves the Christian faith almost no choice but to ask what it was that this man had truly said and done in his life. It is therefore, primarily the historical inquiry into the pre-Easter Jesus of Nazareth that leads the Christian faith away from Bultmann's "that-character" and provides its substantial definiteness.

Compared with Reimarus' path, this perspective makes the distinctiveness of the historical inquiry into the ministry of Jesus of Nazareth much clearer. Of course the quest for the historical Jesus can be approached without regard to the Christian faith of Easter, and that is often done—

---

[23] R. Hoppe, *Jesus: Von der Krippe an den Galgen* (Stuttgart: Katholisches Bibelwerk, 1996), 19.

[24] A decade ago M. Kreplin had dealt with this problem in monographic length (*Das Selbstverständnis Jesu: Hermeneutische und christologische Reflexion: Historisch-kritische Analyse* [WUNT 2/141; Tübingen: Mohr Siebeck 2001]). We are meeting also with him on one of these "third ways". In opposition to the Reimarus way he states "that the historical Jesus cannot be the only and sufficient legitimation for the Christian testimony of faith" (41). In opposition to the Kähler way he justifies the quest for the historical Jesus with the statement: "It would be highly problematic if post-Easter interpretations of the identity of Jesus Christ would contradict the self-conception of the historical Jesus" (54).

by non-Christians and Christians alike. Such questions do not differ in principle from depictions of the lives of other people in the past, such as Alexander the Great or Napoleon. Therefore, similar research into Jesus of Nazareth can only produce results which are historically interesting at best, but nothing more. Moreover if one ascribes—as Reimarus and many others after him have done—an authoritative and guiding role to Jesus of Nazareth only because he was an outstanding ethical teacher and not because God has raised Him from the dead, one would be doing nothing less than making one's own values and norms—and thus oneself—the moral measure.

On the other hand, for this third way it holds that the question of the historical Jesus of Nazareth according to the Easter confession must share an essential characteristic with all other historical inquiries: In terms of *methodology* there are no principles or requirements, even for theologically oriented historical investigations, other than those that are commonly applied by the guild of the historians in any other historical inquiry into any other figure of the past.

It is much more difficult to identify the manner of the historical search for Jesus of Nazareth, which makes this inquiry a theological one, even though it is *methodologically* quite atheological.[25] What characterizes such an investigation since it is not pursued purely out of historical interest, but also aims at *theological* cognition? In what way do these issues coincide?[26]

---

[25] In his review of James D.G. Dunn's Jesus book *Jesus Remembered* (vol. 1 of *Christianity in the Making*; Grand Rapids and Cambridge: Eerdmans, 2003) Robert Morgan had discussed the question: "There are two different kinds of historical pictures of the first-century Jew Jesus, those of New Testament theology, written from a Christian standpoint and presenting a historical biblical Jesus, and those (equally legitimate) written (by Christians or non-Christians) from a non-biblical and non-Christian standpoint" (*ExpTim* 116, no. 7 [2005]: 217–223, here 220). Therefore he proposes to distinguish "confessional" from "non-confessional" quests of the historical Jesus (ibid.).

[26] A proposal to answer this question was recently made by Christof Landmesser. He demands not only to integrate "Jesus' teaching and his actions" into the quest for Jesus, but also "incarnation, soteriology, and resurrection" as "historically reconstructable" ("Der gegenwärtige Jesus: Moderne Jesusbilder und die Christologie des Neuen Testaments", *KuD* 56 [2010]: 96–120, here 115). He is right in so far as the elements mentioned can be historically reconstructed as *theological interpretations* since as such they go back to distinct human beings to whom we can ascribe in the way of historical reconstruction a certain time and a certain place. In fact they are "interpretaments which are given later" (ibid.) which *as such*, i.e. as fictions, can be described historically, but not as facts.

8   MICHAEL WOLTER

II.

We can get a step closer to answering the question we ended with in
the last section, if we first make ourselves aware that on every level of
our investigation only certain *images* of Jesus are available to us, and that
we can always *produce* only certain images of Jesus. In addition—as Dale
Allison has demonstrated[27]—from Reimarus to Crossan it has frequently
been the faces of the particular authors that are reflected by the images
of Jesus they reconstructed in their books.

We can distinguish a whole series of such images typologically. These
will be presented in the following section with the aid of a short overview.
They have the character of ideal types in a Weberian sense, i.e., they deal
with constructions of thought. We can distinguish seven different types,
which could be presented by proceeding chronologically from the present
back into the past:

1. First, there is the person we call "the historical Jesus". He appears as
the result of historical inquiry into Jesus of Nazareth. It would be quite
improper if we mistook this "historical" Jesus, as he is mediated by scholarly, historical criticism for something other than a historiographical
fiction. In keeping ourselves from such a fallacy, the recent historical-
theoretical discourse has once again made us aware that there is no
written history that reconstructs the past as it was in a real or factual
sense.[28] Through the selection and arrangement of the historical material, and simply through the transport of what is depicted in its own representative language, the "facts"—and there must have been facts (for it
has never been that nothing has happened)—become "fictions" and the
alleged "re-constructions" become "constructions". The historical Jesus is
a creation of historians.[29] The "historical Jesus" is therefore nothing more
than a figure drawn in printer's ink on paper: It is the image that the

---

[27] Allison, *Historical Christ* (n. 1), 15–22.

[28] Cf., e.g. H. White, "The Fictions of Factual Representation", in idem, *Tropics of Discourse: Essays in Cultural Criticism* (Baltimore and London: Johns Hopkins University Press,
1978), 121–134; H. J. Goertz, *Umgang mit Geschichte: Eine Einführung in die Geschichtstheorie*
(Reinbek bei Hamburg: Rowohlt, 1995); C. Lorenz, *Konstruktion der Vergangenheit: Eine
Einführung in die Geschichtstheorie* (Cologne et al.: Boehlau, 1997).—With respect to the
quest for the historical Jesus, cf. J. Schröter, *Jesus und die Anfänge der Christologie* (Biblisch-theologische Studien 47; Neukirchen-Vluyn: Neukirchener Verlag, 2001), 6–36.

[29] O. Vossler, *Geschichte als Sinn* (Frankfurt on Main: Suhrkamp, 1979), 9–23. Therefore
for the historical Jesus it holds true what Vossler, ibid., 23, writes about history as such: He
is "real only as activity, as thinking, nowhere else".

researchers of the historical Jesus conceptualize in their books on him. Therefore there is not only one historical Jesus, there are many. Every historian creates his own, and the images of these historical Jesuses are as diverse as the historians themselves are.

2. The second type is what I would like to call "Jesus Christ". In his time Martin Kähler called it "the historic, biblical Christ" who was contrasted with the "so-called historical Jesus". Elsewhere Kähler speaks of the "living Christ" and the "real Christ".[30] Again, Kähler's "Jesus Christ" and Bultmann's "kerygmatic Christ" are of course images. They are images, by which the Christian faith characterizes Jesus. These images exist solely in the confession of the Christian faith. They are unattainable by the methods of pure historical investigation since such investigations can also be conducted by non-Christians who do *not* share the Christian confession, which is a critical aspect of this method. Stated more directly, the outcomes of this method presuppose access to the certainty of Christian faith. The expression "Jesus Christ" cannot be invoked in a scientific study that focuses solely on the historical Jesus. Rather, it finds its truest expression within a historical framework that is shaped by Christian theology.

3. The third image or type can, with some restrictions, be seen as a combination of the first two. It could be called "the earthly Christ". This is the image of Jesus as it is conceptualized in the Gospels. This is an image that the sources themselves provide. This source based image is used for the construction of "the historical Jesus" in contemporary research.[31] The designation expressly states that in this image there is a presupposition of belief in the "Jesus Christ" of subsection 2. In addition it offers insight into the life and works of Jesus of Nazareth in the language of the Christian faith. Implied in the adjective "earthly" is its semantic opposition, "heavenly", and with this characterization it should be made clear

---

[30] Kähler, *Historical Jesus* (n. 2), 43.

[31] Among these are of course the Gospels, the canonical and the apocryphal. Some of the exponents of the "Third Quest" even prefer the latter (cf. in this respect especially J.D. Crossan, *Historical Jesus* [1991]; idem, *Jesus* [1994]; see n. 18). However, this position is also controversial within the "Third Quest" itself; it is explicitly contradicted, e.g., by J.P. Meier, *A Marginal Jew: Rethinking the Historical Jesus*, vol. 2: *Mentor, Message, and Miracles* (New York et al.: Doubleday, 1994), 140. The few non-Christian references to Jesus (cf. the compilation and discussion in G. Theissen and A. Merz, *The Historical Jesus* [n. 16], 63–89) contain nothing that is historically valuable and that adds anything to the image of Jesus depicted by the Christian tradition. Almost every non-Christian testimony is based on knowledge mediated by Christians.

that this is the retrospective image of the earthly ministry of the risen Son of God. In the case of Luke's story of Jesus we can perhaps even say that his representation of the image of the "earthly Christ" also employs historiographical methods. Its difference from the representations of the "historical Jesus" by modern historians lies in the fact that the latter end with Jesus' death, whereas for the Gospel writers, the works and fate of the "earthly Christ" are only the pre-history for the proclamation of "Jesus Christ" after Easter. This is expressed clearly in the title of Mark's Gospel ("The beginning of the Gospel of Jesus Christ, the Son of God", Mark 1:1) and also in the fact that Luke's account of Jesus continues in Acts, and that Matthew and John end their Gospels with the commissioning of the disciples (Matt 28:18–20; John 20:21–23).

4. "Jesus Christ remembered" is another type among the images of Jesus. I borrow this term, with some minor variations, from James D.G. Dunn, who has recently pointed out again that there existed an image that could be called the image of "Jesus Remembered".[32]

Dunn is referring to what he calls the "impact" that Jesus left on his disciples.[33] This category takes into account the fact that the Jesus tradition was originally passed on by people who, in contrast to the authors of the

---

[32] Cf. esp. J.D.G. Dunn, "Altering the Default Setting: Re-envisaging the Early Transmission of the Jesus Tradition", *NTS* 49 (2003): 139–175; idem, *Jesus Remembered* (n. 25), 130–132; idem, "Remembering Jesus", *ZNT* 10, no. 20 (2007): 54–59; C. Claussen, "Vom historischen zum erinnerten Jesus: Der erinnerte Jesus als neues Paradigma der Jesusforschung", *ZNT* 10, no. 20 (2007): 2–17; C. Strecker, "Der erinnerte Jesus aus kulturwissenschaftlicher Perspektive", *ZNT* 10, no. 20 (2007): 18–27. Of course J.D.G. Dunn is not the first to use this category; cf. apart from those mentioned by himself (*Jesus Remembered*, 131, n. 111), for instance, J. Gnilka, *Jesus of Nazareth* (Peabody: Hendrickson, 1997), 249. The same category is also used by Schröter, *Jesus und die Anfänge der Christologie* (n. 28), 65–67, although he uses it with a rather different meaning than Dunn. For him it does not refer to the memories of the disciples in the forefield of the first-time literalization of the Jesus tradition in the first century C.E., but to the "envisioned Jesus" as he is "the result of a contemporary portrayal of Jesus ... from a specific perspective at the beginning of the 21st century" (idem, *Jesus von Nazareth: Jude aus Galiläa—Retter der Welt* [Leipzig: Evangelische Verlagsanstalt, 2006], 22). His interpretation is based on an understanding of memory taken from a cultural anthropological point of view as it has been unfolded by A. Assmann, *Zeit und Tradition: Kulturelle Strategien der Dauer* (Cologne et al.: Böhlau, 1999), 63–90, and J. Assmann, *Religion and Cultural Memory* (Stanford: Stanford University Press, 2006), 31–45.

[33] Cf. Dunn, *Jesus Remembered* (n. 25), 130: "The Synoptic tradition provides evidence not so much for what Jesus did or said in itself, but for what Jesus was *remembered* as doing or saying by his first disciples, or as we might say, for the *impact* of what he did and said on his first disciples."

Gospels,[34] had been eye-witnesses of Jesus' ministry. The following three elements are salient for this image:

First, this is a post-Easter image of Jesus. Although it has roots that go back to the days of the life of Jesus of Nazareth, this category can only describe an overall picture of the person, and this can only be done in hindsight when the whole of the completed actions and the fate of Jesus are considered. This denotation not only has to do with the memory of single sets of words or deeds of Jesus, but with the post-Easter commemoration of the totality of his teaching and acting as well as his fate.

Second, the understanding of these images of Jesus should be reserved with the Easter faith from where the memory of the work and fate of Jesus carries on. Of course, there are those who do not share this belief, and yet have a "memory" of Jesus after his death.[35] However, their memory contains a different interpretation of Jesus' words, actions and conditions from those who look back in the light of their Easter faith. "Jesus Christ remembered" is thus marked by those who, like the ones who represent the "earthly Jesus" of subsection 3, remember Jesus in the light of the Easter faith. The difference is therefore a rather medial one: the Jesus whom we have called "the earthly Christ" is a literary figure; "Jesus Christ remembered" is only one non-literary part of the identity shaping knowledge of those who remember him.

Thirdly, it should not be forgotten that "Jesus Christ remembered" is also an ideal type. This category involves not only *one* or even *one specific* image, but just as with the "historical Jesus" and "earthly Christ", it deals with a variety of different images of memory. In fact, there are as many "remembered" images of Jesus Christ as there are Christians who remember his words and deeds and his fate.

5. "Jesus from Nazareth" is what I would like to call the type or image that people who were involved with him during his ministry made of Jesus. These include his addressees or eye-witnesses of his deeds as well as members of groups critically opposed to Jesus. These images could refer to public opinion about Jesus as in Luke 7:34, paralleled in Matt 11:19: "A glutton and a drunkard, a friend of tax collectors and sinners", or those

---

[34] With the probable exception of John's Gospel, if—as it is said in John 21:24—the author of its first edition was in fact the beloved disciple and if this person has in fact joined Jesus in Jerusalem.

[35] This memory corresponds to the image of Jesus illustrated in subsection 5.

who met him favourably and believed,[36] even Pilate, who had obviously pictured Jesus in a manner that allowed him to crucify Jesus. Not unlike the images sketched in the previous subsection, this is also a type that is differentiated into a large number of various singular images. Thus we can also expect just as many images of Jesus as there are people who had met Jesus. This image is the result of a very ordinary process, which happens not only with those who had met Jesus, but everywhere where people meet and communicate with each other: that they perceive each other in a certain way and attribute an identity to their respective other. This type of image of Jesus, which owes itself to external perception, is contrasted with the next point.

6. "Jesus' self-interpretation" refers to, as it were, a complementary correspondence with the image described in the previous subsection because the external perceptions of a person by his contemporaries and his self-perception always differ from one another. In the research of Jesus this type of image is already very familiar. Here it is called, for example, "Jesus' self-understanding"[37] or "the Christology of Jesus".[38] It is not just important but absolutely vital that this type of 'Jesus' is also regarded as an image: the image that Jesus had of himself, of the meaning and significance of his teaching and actions. From this type of image, only one single specimen exists since it is produced by only one person: by Jesus himself.

7. *One* question finally remains open: Is there something akin to a figure we could call "the real Jesus"? Is there a "real Jesus" as an ontic reality beyond the images that people have been making of him since the time he lived—and also beyond the image he had of himself?

In the literature, this predicate is found astonishingly frequently. Martin Kähler had already called his "historic, biblical Christ" the "real Christ",[39] and more than 100 years later he is followed by Luke Timothy Johnson,

---

[36] As to that J. Schröter, *Jesus von Nazareth* (n. 32), 265–266.

[37] This is the headline of part four of Dunn's *Jesus Remembered* (n. 25), 613; see also L. Goppelt, *Theology of the New Testament*, vol. 1 (Grand Rapids: Eerdmans, 1981), 159, and the same-named articles by N.T. Wright, in S.T. Davis, D. Kendall and G. O'Collins, eds., *The Incarnation* (Oxford: Oxford University Press, 2002), 47–61, and by M. Kreplin, in T. Holmén and S.E. Porter, eds., *Handbook for the Study of the Historical Jesus*, vol. 3: *The Historical Jesus* (Leiden and Boston: Brill, 2011), 2473–2516.

[38] This is the title of the book by B. Witherington (Minneapolis: Fortress, 1990); Schröter, *Jesus von Nazareth* (n. 32), 243, distinguishes between "Jesus' self-understanding" as "internal perspective" and the "judgement of his contemporaries" as "external perspective".

[39] Kähler, *Jesus* (n. 2), 43.

according to whom the real Jesus is none other than the risen Christ who is proclaimed in the New Testament and throughout the history of Christianity and is, as such, present in faith.[40] Benedict XVI also identifies the church's representation of Jesus as the "real Jesus". For him it is "the People of God—the Church" (xxi); "actually the deeper 'author' " (xxi) of the Gospels, whose Jesus is "the real, 'historical' Jesus in the strict sense of the word" (xxii), which has to be distinguished from the images of Jesus produced by historical research about Jesus.[41] By the latter formulation— "the 'historical Jesus' in the strict sense of the word"—Benedict XVI brings attention to an important distinction: This "real Jesus" must by no means be confused with the "historical Jesus" as it is (re)constructed by the historians according to subsection II.1, although this confusion is wide-spread.

On the other hand, it is obvious that Martin Kähler, Luke Johnson and Benedict XVI commit one and the same mistake: They simply identify a particular image of Jesus that human beings create with the "real Jesus" for whom we are asking.

The question of whether there is such a Jesus who is initially not more than, in fact, an ideal object[42] or theoretical construct can be answered in different ways.

In light of the historical-theoretical debate briefly mentioned above about the possibilities of representing historical events,[43] this should certainly be answered by saying: Yes, the "real Jesus" definitely exists in the sense of ontic reality, but we cannot really say anything about him, because every linguistic description and even every perception of such a reality is always contaminated with particular *interpretations*.

This interpretation integrates the data designated through the medium of language into the paradigm of the symbolic universe which the user of its symbols inhabits. Moreover, not only can we state nothing definitively about this Jesus, but we can never recognize the "real Jesus" as such. The reason for this is that there is no knowledge without a simultaneous integration into the cultural encyclopedia that is available to the recognizing person.

---

[40] Cf. Johnson, *Jesus* (n. 15), 166 and passim.

[41] J. Ratzinger (Pope Benedict XVI), *Jesus of Nazareth: From the Baptism in the Jordan to the Transfiguration* (trans. A.J. Walker; London: Bloomsbury, 2007), xxi, xxii.

[42] Schröter, "Jesus im Kontext: Die hermeneutische Relevanz der Frage nach dem historischen Jesus in der gegenwärtigen Diskussion", *TLZ* 134 (2009): 905–928, here 905, n. 1.

[43] See above p. 8.

14 MICHAEL WOLTER

This skepticism derives from the epistemological insights of constructivism. According to Hans Fischer, knowledge can never represent a "reality independent of cognitive consciousness",[44] but it is, without exception, "primarily, a *self-referential* process". "The subject has knowledge only insofar as it has been produced through a cognitive extension of his *own operations.*"[45]

Any historian who asks about Jesus and wants to remain honest, must admit that "the real Jesus" is not accessible to him. He will not deny that there has been some kind of 'real' Jesus, but he must be aware of the fact that he can neither know nor even describe him. It is also important that what is being said goes not only for Jesus and for knowledge of the past, but also for any kind of knowledge—also for 'knowledge' of our own identity and the identities of our contemporaries.

The Christian theologian will come to no other result if, concerning the "real Jesus", he posits this question as a historian: He (the real Jesus) existed, but no one can know him as such or even make statements about him.

However, he—the theologian—can go one step further than the historian who happens not to be a theologian. The theologian's understanding of reality is always characterized in his bringing the reality, which is the object of his knowledge, into a relationship with God—as interpreted always and only in faith, that is, *as a particular reality determined by God as a specific reality.*[46]

It does *not* follow for our question concerning the "real Jesus" that we can say, with recourse to a vulgar theological concept of God's omniscience, that no one but God knows him. That would fall far too short, because God's knowledge is categorically different from human knowledge. His knowledge relates almost in an opposite way: While human knowledge remains deprived of ontic reality, it is only through the knowledge of God

---

[44] H.R. Fischer, "Abschied von der Hinterwelt? Zur Einführung in den Radikalen Konstruktivismus", in idem, ed., *Die Wirklichkeit des Konstruktivismus: Zur Auseinandersetzung um ein neues Paradigma* (Heidelberg: Carl-Auer-Systeme, 1995), 11–34, here 19.—Cf. in this sense also the statement given by Otto Vossler quoted in n. 29.

[45] Ibid., 19–20 (italics his).

[46] Cf. in this sense W. Härle, *Dogmatik* (Berlin and New York: Walter de Gruyter, 1995), 216, on the relation between the world and God: "'World' is not and does not embrace 'God', on the other hand 'world' is not conceivable without 'God' but only as *determined* by Him" (italics his). Here Härle adopts Rudolf Bultmann's well-known definition, according to which "God is the Almighty; in other words, God is the reality determining all else" (R. Bultmann, "What does it mean to speak of God?", in: idem, *Faith and Understanding*, vol. 1 [ed. with an introduction by R.W. Funk; London: SCM, 1969], 53–65, here 53).

in the first place that anything is constituted as reality. In other words, the Christian faith's understanding of reality assumes that the reality of God's knowledge is not independent of him (as is the case with human knowledge), but that it is firstly created as such through being known by God, and that it is *this* reality that is pre-given for human cognition, but which it never grasps entirely. Who or what people 'really' are, is therefore determined—beyond all human self-ascriptions and ascriptions of the other—by who and what God knows them to be. Correspondingly, for Christians, the 'real' author of this contribution is not the person as he is considered to be by himself or his contemporaries, but only by God. If it were not so, God would not be God.

For our question about the "real Jesus", it follows that even here the Christian understanding of reality also deals with an *image*: the image that God has of Jesus. The "real Jesus" beyond the images that people have made of him in his own time and since then is, therefore, none other than the Jesus as God knows him, whose identity came into being through God's knowing him.

III.

The questions we have formulated in our title and at the end of the first section find their answer in the meaning of Christian Easter faith.

Christian Easter faith has its origin in the visionary experiences of Peter, James and Paul and the others named in 1Cor 15:5–8, who perceived Jesus as a figure appearing to them from heaven.[47] These experiences were interpreted by them in a certain way. For all those who have not enjoyed such an experience, including ourselves—Christian Easter faith consists in accepting the interpretation these witnesses provided by their visionary experiences.

The first inference was obvious: If a person whom everybody knew had been crucified as a criminal has appeared from heaven, then God must have raised him from the dead and exalted him into his heavenly glory. Although there was nobody who had witnessed the resurrection of

---

[47] This conclusion is allowed by the use of the Greek expression ὤφθη + dative in 1Cor 15:5–8; Luke 24:34 and 1Tim 3:16. The Septuagint uses this expression as a technical term to describe theophanies. It denotes appearance from heaven, especially of God himself (e.g., Gen 12:7; 17:1; 18:1; 1Kgs 3:5), of an angel (e.g., Exod 3:2; Judg 6:12; Tob 12:22) or of God's glory (e.g., Exod 16:10; Lev 9:23; Num 14:10).

16   MICHAEL WOLTER

Jesus and although the certitude that God has raised Jesus from the dead
was from the very first moment on only an interpretation drawn from
the visionary experiences mentioned above, this certitude has always
been regarded as a *certitude of fact* within a Christian concept of reality.[48]
Therefore there can be no Christian faith, whose concept of reality does
not contain certainty about the fact of the resurrection of Jesus. We can
refer to what Paul expresses in 1Thess 4:14 when he says that "we [the
Christians] believe that Jesus died and rose again". He asserts here that,
for him, the resurrection of Jesus is just as 'real' as his death.

Furthermore, the interpretations of the early Christian Easter experience include the claim that God had legitimated and vindicated the teaching and the actions of Jesus contrary to the appearance of disproof given
by the cross on which he was executed as a criminal. This aspect was
briefly brought into view in 1Tim 3:16: "He was vindicated (ἐδικαιώθη) by
the Spirit." A text such as *T. Ash.* 6:4 may function like a lens that makes
the theological profile of this interpretation even clearer, which—when
read with a view to the crucifixion of Jesus—needs no additional explanation; especially since here, as in 1Tim 3:16 "justice" is mentioned. According to *T. Ash.* 6:4 it was common knowledge that "the end of a man's life
demonstrates his righteousness" (τὰ τέλη τῶν ἀνθρώπων δεικνύουσι τὴν
δικαιοσύνην αὐτῶν). Normally the end of the life of a person is his death.
Christian faith assumes that it is the resurrection which marks the end of
Jesus' life on earth.

If we apply our interpretation of the above-mentioned visionary experiences to the typology of images of Jesus, which we have developed in the
previous section, their theological significance is obvious: it suggests that
God, because he resurrected Jesus and raised him up to heaven, also vindicated Jesus' own self-interpretation.[49] Furthermore, it stipulates that the

---

[48] Cf. in this respect especially 1Thess 4:14a (εἰ γὰρ πιστεύομεν ὅτι Ἰησοῦς ἀπέθανεν καὶ
ἀνέστη): the real conditional clause εἰ + indicative present represents not a condition in
the strict sense of the word, but bears a *causal* meaning. Sentences like this one indicate a presupposition that is not doubted (cf. also Rom 5:15; 8:11; Col 3:1, and F. Blass and
A. Debrunner, *A Greek Grammar of the New Testament and Other Early Christian Literature:
A Translation and Revision of the 9th/10th German Edition* by R.W. Funk [Chicago: University of Chicago Press, 1961], § 372: "εἰ with the indicative of reality"). Therefore the Pauline
text quoted above should be translated causally ("*because* we believe that..." or "*since* we
believe that..."). When Paul parallels ἀπέθανεν and ἀνέστη and makes both verbs dependent on πιστεύομεν (the first person plural denotes the Christians), he makes it clear that
for him Jesus' resurrection is as real as his death.

[49] Cf. above p. 12.

"real Jesus", in the sense presented above,[50] is none other than how Jesus understood himself, or, in other words, that the "real Jesus", as constituted by the judgement of God, had taken a concrete form in the self-interpretation of Jesus within the human life-world. It can only be said of Jesus and of no other human being—and this too is part of the Easter faith—that his self-understanding is identical to the image that God has of him.

A further aspect includes the fact that the Easter visions alone would certainly not have been enough to reach the interpretation that Jesus has been placed by God in the heavenly, sovereign position of the Son of God (Rom 1:4), and did so with the *Kyrios* title of the "Name above all names" (Phil 2:9–11). This cannot be explained unless it had a corresponding basis in Jesus' own self-interpretation. Jesus must thus have understood his work not merely as that of a prophet, announcing the imminent coming of the Kingdom of God, but as an integral part of the eschatological carrying out of God's universal reign on earth, so that the salvation of God promised to Israel could already be *selectively* experienced and authoritatively interpreted through him as God's authentic representative.

What are the implications for the theological character of historical enquiry into Jesus of Nazareth? Of course, the point of such an investigation, which sees itself as part of a *theological* question, is not to justify the Easter faith. It can do this no more than a historical inquiry that is decidedly *atheological* can disprove it. In methodological terms, the same principles apply for both, and either way, the result can only be a historiographical construct. In both cases, one and the same question is asked—namely: "Who was Jesus really?" The historians—be they theologians or not—can only confess that they don't know—at least if they are honest. The theological historians furthermore know that this question will be answered by the self-interpretation of Jesus. It is here where the focus of their theological interest will always rest, although they know that they could always only produce ephemeral historical Jesuses.

---

[50] Cf. above pp. 14–15.

FROM MARK'S SON OF GOD TO JESUS OF NAZARETH—
*UN CUL-DE-SAC?**

Cilliers Breytenbach

Thy glass will show thee how thy beauties wear,
Thy dial how thy precious minutes waste,
These vacant leaves thy mind's imprint will bear,
And of this book, this learning mayst thou taste.
The wrinkles which thy glass will truly show,
Of mouthed graves will give thee memory,
Thou by thy dial's shady stealth mayst know,
Time's thievish progress to eternity.
Look what thy memory cannot contain,
Commit to these waste blanks, and thou shalt find
Those children nursed, delivered from thy brain,
To take a new acquaintance of thy mind.

These offices, so oft as thou wilt look,
Shall profit thee, and much enrich thy book.

Shakespeare, 77th Sonnet

1. TRAVELOGUE: AN ACCOUNT OF SEVERAL JOURNEYS

1.1   *The First Journey's End in the Wredestraße*

After Reimarus had drawn the map, critical New Testament scholarship
set out on its journey to find the historical Jesus behind the dogmatic
Christ of the Gospels.[1] They thought they could travel undisturbed to and

---

* Paper read at the Third Session of the Princeton–Prague Biennale for Jesus Research,
Prague, April 22–24, 2009. Preliminary drafts of this paper were read at the New Testament
research seminar at the University of Stellenbosch and the Colloquium at the Institute
for Christianity and Antiquity in Berlin. I thank the participants, especially Bernard C.
Lategan, for their comments. Since the publication of the Prague papers has been delayed,
I thank Jan van der Watt for the opportunity to publish a first version of my essay in the
current context. For this purpose, section 5 has been added.

[1] Up to a great extent the rise of the historical critical method had the urge to find
the "real" Jesus as its catalyst. Intertwined with the reconstruction of the best manuscript
tradition to replace Erasmus' *textus receptus*, scholars like Lachmann laid the foundation
of source criticism. This resulted in the recognition of the priority of the Gospel according
to Mark by Wilke (cf. Schmithals 1985:66–173). After Weisse's source critical hypothesis

fro from Mark to Jesus. And then, coherently and brilliantly argued, that great scholar of the turn of the century, William Wrede (1901), blew up their imagined bridge. He took Mark's narrative seriously. From Wrede we learnt that the Gospel according to Mark is a story about Jesus, structured around the so called "Messianic Secret".[2]

Not only Wrede's razor sharp argument that Mark no longer had any "Anschauung" of the life of Jesus led to the demise of his Gospel as primary source for reconstructing the life of Jesus. In his Berlin "*Habilitationsschrift*" *Der Rahmen der Geschichte Jesu,* Karl Ludwig Schmidt (1919) contributed decisively to the debate as well. Schmidt argued that the Gospels consisted of individual scenes which had been transmitted without fixed chronological or topographical markers. He led the way to the general opinion that the overarching temporal and geographical framework of the Gospel narratives is secondary and cannot be utilised for the reconstruction of the life of Jesus.[3]

In the years following Wrede, Adolf Harnack (1907:8) chose to travel from another base to find Jesus, namely from the second primary source called Q. Whatever Q was perceived to be, Mark was set aside for it. "Jesus research" ventured to set sail from a hypothetical harbour that first had to

---

on a second source for Matthew and Luke had gained ground and Holtzmann had established the two source hypothesis (cf. Schmithals 1985:182–197), scholars threw themselves on Mark, using it as the primary source for the reconstruction of the vita of Jesus of Nazareth.

[2] Albeit that it is more appropriate to speak about the "Secret of God's Son" as one of the central aspects of the plot of the Gospel, Wrede's monograph gave the fatal blow to the staggering "First Quest" to find the historical Jesus. Within the frame of his topic, he illustrated that as far as the Messianic Secret is concerned, it is impossible to regard Mark's account of Jesus' actions as a reflection of what happened in the life of Jesus. The devastating impact of Wrede's challenge to the historicity of the life of Jesus research based on the Gospel of Mark can be grasped if one reads through § 19 of Schweitzer's (1913) masterly written account. For this reason the first edition (1906) was aptly entitled: *Von Reimarus zu Wrede.*

[3] "Vieles, was chronologisch und topographisch aussieht, ist nur der Rahmen, der zu den einzelnen Bildern hinzukam" (Schmidt 1919:V). So far so good. But does the secondary nature of the topographical and temporal remarks really disqualify them for historical (re-)construction? In many cases one has to confirm Schmidt's opinion that special and temporal markers in Mark's narrative cannot successfully be plotted unto the coherent journeys and stringent timelines in the life of Jesus. But is this really the question? That Mark did not intend to recapture movements of Jesus from A to B to C and back in his narrative needs no arguing. He neither tried to give a continuous report of days, weeks or a year in Jesus' life. When historians want to come up with such constructions they do get lost in the topographically unmarked spaces and discontinuities in Mark's narrative world. But does this mean that Mark does not at all contribute to our picture of the places and spaces, the days and the times of Jesus' ministry?

FROM MARK'S SON OF GOD TO JESUS OF NAZARETH—*UN CUL-DE-SAC?*

be plotted on the map. It goes without saying that the travellers had little chance of landing their ships all at the same isle of the blessed, unless they had reached consensus on their point of departure before setting sail. Holding firm on to the Markan map, we will rather travel on land.[4]

1.2   *Käsemann's Departure*

Nevertheless, even before Willi Marxsen's *Der Evangelist Markus* (1956), Ernst Käsemann reintroduced the importance of the narrative character of the Gospels. In his now famous critique of the position of Bultmann, "Das Problem des historischen Jesus" (1954), he drew attention to the fact that access to the past is mediated through narrative. "So sind wir vergangener Geschichte gegenüber auf das Erzählen angewiesen, wenn wir Kunde von ihr erhalten wollen. Alle Historie wird uns nur durch Tradition zugänglich und durch Interpretation verständlich" ([1954]/1960:190). For Käsemann it was significant, that the Gospels convey the Christian message within the framework of the life of the earthly Jesus (192–193).[5] For those who

---

[4] Wrede's mistrust in Mark led to the approach chosen by Rudolf Bultmann in his booklet on Jesus (1926). We note famous voices dissenting from Wrede. In his commentary on Mark published in 1933, Julius Schniewind noted that in depicting typical scenes, locations and opponents of Jesus in a vivid manner, Mark kept the picture of Jesus' ministry alive (1933:37–38). In his *Galiläa und Jerusalem* Lohmeyer highlighted Mark's theological conception that Jesus started and concentrated his ministry which fulfilled eschatological expectation in the holy, elected land of Galilee juxtaposing it with his final journey into death to the unbelieving Jerusalem. According to Lohmeyer this basic concept had primarily theological, but nevertheless also historical roots (1936:35). But at this time the impact of Wrede's and Schmidt's blows on the Gospel according to Mark had considerably diminished trust in its reliability to map the road to the Jesus of history (cf. 1936:28). Lohmeyer thus focussed his attention on the theological conception of the evangelist. In the vein of form criticism which tried to illuminate the history of the synoptic tradition (cf. Bultmann 1921/1931), Bultmann (1926) focussed on the teaching of Jesus, largely ignoring the biographical information entailed by the Gospel narratives. Of course Bultmann took Wrede seriously, but as far as Mark was concerned, the focus shifted from the entire narrative to the kerygmatic intention of individual episodes in the pre-synoptic phase. Even Lightfoot (1934), who attested Mark a greater mastery over his material as did Bultmann, regarded him as an arranger of individual episodes into contrasting and threefold patterns. Somewhere between the great wars Wrede's narrator was slain by divergent forces of form criticism. The rise of redaction criticism took place within a framework which regarded the Gospels as collections of pre-synoptic proclamation, preaching reflecting the situation of the evangelist and his congregation. "Am Anfang war das Kerygma." Many roads behind Mark were indicated, but most of them were said to lead to the pre-Markan Hellenistic congregation, some of them were claimed to reach a little further into a life setting within the Palestinian "Urgemeinde" and almost none were regarded to lead back to Jesus of Nazareth.

[5] The early church's belief that Jesus is the Son of God is part of the faith they had since Easter. Why did they hold on to the earthly Jesus? Why did they cast their contemporary

22   CILLIERS BREYTENBACH

were devoted to the resurrected Jesus, revelation was inextricably connected to the "irdische Leiblichkeit" (202). Käsemann was of the opinion
that the quest for the historical Jesus must start from the connection and
tension between the preaching of Jesus and that of his congregation (213).
As an instrument to discern Jesus' message from that of the early church,
he formulated his now (in)famous criterion of dissimilarity (205),[6] his
major tool in an effort to construct the road between the Gospel tradition
and Jesus.

In his rejoinder on Bultmann's self-defence, Käsemann correctly
noted that the real bone of contention lies in the understanding of history (1964:52).[7] He countered mainly by asking why—if early Christianity were not interested in the life of the earthly Jesus—it still did clad
the *"kerygma"* in a narrative about Jesus as late as the Gospel of John

---

faith in the resurrected Lord into the life of the pre-Easter Jesus? Because they believed
that God's eschatological revelation was tied up with this Nazarene, Palestine and the
concrete time and circumstances (Käsemann [1954]/1960:200). The first Christians were of
the opinion that the understanding of the earthly Jesus presupposes Easter and that Easter
cannot be understood adequately without the earthly Jesus (196).

[6] On this see Theißen and Winter 1997.

[7] In his self-defence submitted to the Heidelberg academy in 1960, Bultmann disregarded the possible positive aspects of the tension between Jesus and the early church
and rather underlined that the mythical Son of God replaced the historical person Jesus
(1967:446). It might be that Bultmann favoured a theory of substitution because he juxta-
posed Wrede's construction of the supernatural Markan Son of God with his own idea of
the historical Jesus. He denied that the synoptic Gospels present us with an image of the
person of Jesus, his internal development or that they allow historical research to reconstruct his life (451) or the meaning he attached to his death (455). For Bultmann, there
was no factual continuity between the *kerygma* which moulded the Gospels and Jesus as
historical figure. He would thus not set out on the journey to find the historical Jesus. In
answering the question whether the life and effect of the historical Jesus are entailed in the
"kerygma", Bultmann could for four reasons not find factual continuity between them. In
the first instance, the nature of his *"kerygma"* is determined by Pauline and Johannine theology (446–447). To keep to his term, the "kerygmatic" dimension of the Gospels mediating
the authority ("Vollmachtsbewusstsein"—452) of Jesus of Nazareth through narration into
the present is not overlooked (468). It is however subjected to a fuzzy "Christ-*kerygma*"
claimed to be Pauline and Johannine. According to Bultmann, the voice of the exalted
Lord resounds in the *"kerygma"*, not that of the Jesus of history (458). Secondly, he defines
the Gospels as sermons (450–451). In the light of his own remark that "echte Geschichts-
Interpretation das damalige Jetzt zum heutigen macht" (465), one can ask if it is really
inevitable to redefine the narrative interpretation of Jesus in the synoptics in terms of the
Pauline *"kerygma"* in order to honour its impact on human self-understanding. Thirdly
he adheres to Wrede's thesis that the Messianic Secret in the Gospels serves to legitimate
the unmessianic life of Jesus, "indem sie sie in das Licht der kerygmatischen Christologie stellt" (455). Finally, Bultmann, as Käsemann noted in his reply (1964:59–65), claims
that the *"kerygma"* presupposes a form of personal faith in Jesus as coming Son of Man
(Bultmann 1967:465), which is simply not present in the earliest synoptic tradition.

FROM MARK'S SON OF GOD TO JESUS OF NAZARETH—*UN CUL-DE-SAC?*   23

(Käsemann 1964:47).[8] The proclamation of the Gospels is determined by the past, not the present, they are not sermons as Bultmann claimed, albeit that they are not historical, they are "Berichte"—reports—about the past.[9] That Jesus had been, made it possible for the evangelists to remember him and to include his history in the Gospels.

For Käsemann there had to be a road from the Gospels to Jesus, and he challenged New Testament studies to chart it.[10] He set out on a new journey to the historical Jesus, but he never led the scholarly community to the promised land. His point of departure though, that the narrative form of the Gospels has implications for the historical question, stays valid. As in many cases, Käsemann vigorously slashed a path through the undergrowth, leaving it to others to thrash out the road through the forest.

1.3   *Driving in the Forest*

Unfortunately, in redaction criticism Käsemann's voice was ignored.[11] Come the rise of narrative criticism, Wrede's insight that the Gospel

---

[8] One has to explain the fact that the evangelists embedded the "*kerygma*" in a historical frame (54). This argument has a precursor in the work of Schniewind (1930:159–160).

[9] Käsemann challenged us to explain why, given the high christology of e.g. the Hymn in Philippians, early Christian proclamation took up the form of a report ("Bericht"): "sie (verbinden) historische Tendenzen mit dem Kerygma und bedienen sich einer historisierenden Darstellungsweise" (1964:54). "Wie konnte es von der Doxologie des Verkündigten nochmals zur Erzählung vom Verkündiger kommen, und zwar im Rahmen des Kerygmas?" (66). One does not need to accept Käsemann's own answer to his question in detail to acknowledge the validity of his statement that the recourse on the earthly Jesus became a criterion for post Easter theology. It documents "das Prae des Christus vor den Seinigen, das Extra nos der Botschaft.... Die Vergangenheit gab der Gegenwart die Kriterien zur Prüfung der Geister" (67).

[10] In 1970, Güttgemanns candidly questioned Käsemann's view of the central christological relevance of the narrative form of the Gospels. Güttgemanns sharply criticised the connection Käsemann made between the narrative form and history. According to him, Käsemann implies that history must be narrated if it is to remain history (1970:29). With reference to myths and fairy tales Güttgemanns correctly maintained that the narrative form itself does not imply adequate reason to acknowledge the historical value of a text (30). Although well informed about developments in narratology, especially on fictional narratives, up till the late sixties, Güttgemanns was unaware of the fact that within the theoretical discussion amongst historians, the fundamental importance of narration for historical discourse has well been established since the work of Droysen (1977) in the middle of the nineteenth century. Because he failed to take the vital relation between history and narration into account, Güttgemanns' critique of Käsemann can be neglected. He did, however, give an important impetus to help the rise of narrative criticism, cf. his influence on Vorster (1977; 1980 and 1998).

[11] Even more recent contributions to the discussion tend to overlook Käsemann's contribution to the role of narrative in this respect; e.g. Schröter 2001:17–18; 2007:107. But see du Toit 2006:20–21. From Marxsen onwards Mark was read as a sermon, depicting the

according to Mark is a narrative was rediscovered (cf. Breytenbach 1984: 47–68). But by then some New Testament scholars were so enchanted by the spell of New Literary Criticism that they declared the Gospels auto-semantic forms, each referring intra-textually to its own story world. Travelling within the text, narrative criticism came up with valuable insights, but fell short of utilizing reference to extra-textual entities for historical questions (cf. Vorster 1977; 1980; 1998:137–138).[12] With the exception of the initial innovative studies which took us on scenic drives with truly panoramic views on the Markan story world,[13] narrative criticism made mere small inroads into the text of the Gospel. These roads that wind through Mark's story world helped us to explore the narrative. But as roads in a relatively small national park, they lead nowhere, but through the forest.

Nevertheless there is some sense in driving within the park and getting to know it.[14] But where does the narrative road exploring the Gospel

---

relationship between the present exalted Lord and the disciples as a model for the Markan congregation. For almost twenty years Markan research did mirror its own constructions of alleged conflicts between Mark and his tradition or between groups in Mark's congregation within the text of Mark, travelling to and fro between the interpreter and the alleged sermon of Mark.

[12] Following the line of argumentation of Güttgemanns, Willem Vorster argues that "the narration character of the gospel genre calls into question both kerygma and history as distinctive characteristics of the gospel genre" (cf. Vorster 1983:91). He argues that the Gospels as narratives are determined by narrative characteristics and that the historical question is inappropriate in connection with this narrative genre (cf. 1983:92). It is, however, wrong to turn history and narration into alternatives (cf. below and Breytenbach 1984:83–84). The first reason why Vorster does this is because he operates with an already outdated concept of "fiction". Secondly he adheres to the dogma that literary works are autonomous, referring intra-textually. In the light of the ongoing discussion on fiction it became problematic to classify the Gospels as fictional texts or to isolate the text world from the reality it narrates. The other reason why Vorster manages to see narration and history as unrelated is because he is ignorant of developments in the theory of history. Since Johann Gustav Droysen ([1857–1883] 1977:282–299) it has been argued that narration is a fundamental way of presenting the past.

[13] E.g. the development of the Markan Jesus as literary character, the relation between him and his disciples, the women followers, central themes like the theology, the eschatology and Christology of the second Gospel (cf. the reviews in Rhoads and Syreeni 1999 and by Dormeyer 2005 and Scholtissek 2005).

[14] In an early essay, Lategan (1979:132) underlined how important it is to realise that Jesus' life has always been interpreted, positively by his followers, negatively by his opponents. Thus even the so-called eye-witnesses do not give access to the *bruta facta* of his life, but present us, as far as available, with interpretations of his life: "from their very inception these facts are placed within a specific existing frame of reference, are they interpreted from a distinctive perspective" (1979:132). Mark, our first available interpreter, calls his interpretation the good news about Jesus Christ (the Son of God). There is no way in which we can move behind his interpretation, back to the bare, uninterpreted life of Jesus. To think, that we can move from the linguistic mediation of the life of Jesus through interpreting narrative, back through the text to the facts of Jesus' life behind the text, as

FROM MARK'S SON OF GOD TO JESUS OF NAZARETH—*UN CUL-DE-SAC?*   25

according to Mark lead us? Taking the narrative road and roaming across the Markan text world would help the reader to construct the implied or model author as Lategan has argued (1984).[15] But it also enables the reader to construct the model auditors of Mark's story. In defining the role of the implied audience of Mark's Gospel, the modern critic can infer which knowledge is presupposed and which type of references to the extra-textual world the implied author intended his model auditors to make during the public reading of the text, or which information they had to add on to the information the discourse conveys.[16]

1.4   *Travelling off Road*

It is not possible or necessary to touch on all aspects of historical enquiry treated so lucidly by James Dunn in the learned introduction to his *Jesus Remembered* (2003).[17] For Dunn, the Gospels consist of an oral Jesus tradition which was marked by the impact Jesus made on his disciples: "the original impulse behind these records was . . . *sayings of Jesus as heard and received, and actions of Jesus as witnessed and retained in the memory . . . and as reflected on thereafter*" (129). According to Dunn the synoptic tradition gives access to "the memories of the first disciples—not Jesus himself, but the remembered Jesus" (131). Consequently, Dunn set out to portray Jesus as seen through the eyes and heard through the ears of the disciples. The roots of the synoptic tradition thus reach back into the pre-Easter period. Without abandoning the two source hypothesis, he regarded the variant synoptic narratives and teachings of Jesus as the result of literary re-performances of the Markan or Q-tradition in the light of the ongoing stream of oral tradition. The thrust of this ongoing process of re-performance is that the living Jesus tradition was remembered consistently

---

some New Testament scholars do, is a severe referential fallacy in which those scholars betray their positivistic epistemology inherited from historicism. A quarter of a century later (2004:145–146), Lategan could still aptly illustrate this in his discussion of the work of Theißen and Merz (1996).

[15] I prefer to use Eco's (1979) notion of the model author.

[16] For this important link between the reception of and reference to a text, cf. Lategan 1984:69.

[17] It is however important to note that Dunn, having taken the linguistic turn, avoiding referential and intentional fallacy, recognising the creative role of the reader, well informed about the postmodern debate, stressed that the primary task of historical interpretation is listening to the text. He rightly maintained that texts had a plain meaning rooted in their "originating" contexts of communication. Amongst skilled modern interpreters, consensus can be reached about the plain meaning of historical texts (cf. Dunn 2003:115–117), provided they are open to be addressed by the text in a real dialogue (124).

because of the impact Jesus made on his disciples (224, 238). Dunn did not want to get back at Jesus himself, but merely to the earliest impact Jesus made. "All we have are the impressions Jesus made, the remembered Jesus" (329).[18]

In developing his concept of remembering Jesus within the mode of living oral tradition, Dunn concentrated on the individual episodes in the synoptic Gospels. In these stories and teachings his mission was remembered. Dunn thus left the narrative tarmac of the Wrede road. Disregarding the transformative impact made by scripturisation on oral tradition (cf. Breytenbach 1986), he travelled with his own Freelander through the highlands of the synoptic tradition on vague form critical trails, claiming to follow Jesus' impact in these imprints (cf. Dunn 2003:332). In his reconceptualisation of the synoptic tradition as a continuous performance of narratives and teachings within an ongoing living oral tradition (334), he drew heavily on previous research on orality by his guild (especially Bailey 1991), but did not take cognisance of discussions in performative studies beyond New Testament studies. Performance studies illustrated that continuity between repetitive performances cannot be presupposed (cf. Joubert 2004; Kelber 2005, 2005a). As far as his central concept of "remembering" is concerned, research by the guild is scarce.[19] Referring to Nils Dahl and C.H. Dodd, Dunn settled for Jens Schröter's notion of remembrance (Dunn 2003:130, 178). Not taking into account available insights from cultural anthropology (Halbwachs 1950/1992; J. Assmann 1992; A. Assmann 1999), phenomenology (Casey 1987/2000; Ricœur 1998; 2002; 2004), cognitive psychology (van Dijk and Kintsch 1983; Schacter 2001) and narratology, Dunn's casual concept of remembering lets the wheels come off during his cross country drive, unable to reach highlands from where it would be possible to spot Jesus as seen through the eyes and heard through the ears of the disciples.

---

[18] As Schröter has noted in his dialogue with Dunn (2007a:51), the impact Jesus made on his followers cannot be grasped without taking into account their belief in his resurrection and exaltation. This is of decisive importance, since neither Q (in LukeQ 7:9// MattQ 8:10; LukeQ 17:6//MattQ 17:20 the object of πίστις is God's power) nor the Gospel according to Mark (cf. du Toit 2006:91–93) testifies that those who accompanied him had a pre-Easter faith in Jesus. As Wrede illustrated, the Markan Jesus is misunderstood by his disciples till the end.

[19] Gerhardsson's (1961) conception of memory presupposes fixed oral texts as if they were inscribed. For an alternative view cf. Breytenbach (1986; 1992; 1992a) and Kelber (2002:59–62).

FROM MARK'S SON OF GOD TO JESUS OF NAZARETH—*UN CUL-DE-SAC?* 27

1.5 *Circling the Entrance*

Following Dunn (2003:111), Jens Schröter underlined that historical Jesus research is indebted to the past of Jesus and the present of the researcher (2006:21, 34). In the effort to determine the meaning of Jesus for the construction of reality, historical Jesus research combines the past and the present from the perspective of the modern researcher. "Die Frage, wer Jesus *war*, kann deshalb von derjenigen, wer er heute *ist*, nicht getrennt werden" (2006:23). Not only the ever changing belief of the researcher but also the varying pictures of Jesus and plausible historical contexts presupposed by different scholars, determine the abstractions they make on the basis of the available ancient sources.

Schröter, who implemented a notion of cultural memory (1997:462–464) originally from Maurice Halbwachs via the reception by the Egyptologist Jan Assmann (1992)[20] is sympathetic towards Bultmann in insisting that it is impossible for historical research to tunnel through Christian belief in order to reach the "real" Jesus. He does not however juxtapose *kerygma* with history in the way Bultmann did (cf. Schröter 2007:120–121).[21] The narrative form of the Gospels mediates between mission and fate of Jesus and the interpretation thereof in earliest Christianity.

Within this broader hermeneutical frame Schröter noted that recent developments in the quest for Jesus proposed a more positive assessment of the Gospels as testimony to the mission and fate of Jesus (2007:106).[22] He supported a new look at the Gospels as historical sources whilst maintaining that, like all historical sources, the Gospel narratives must be subjected to scrutiny by the modern critical historical mind (110). When Schröter demanded that the current Jesus research has to clarify the relation between the Jesus event and interpretation in the Gospels,[23] it is a pity that he did not explicate his notion of historical memory. When he maintained that the Gospels contained memories of places, persons, opponents and political and social circumstances (121), one may ask what the status of literary conserved memories could be. What does it mean

---

[20] Assmann's notion of cultural memory draws on the work of Halbwachs (1950/1992).

[21] He regarded the tendency from Strauss via Wrede up till Bultmann to stress the divergence between the life and teachings of Jesus and alleged later over-layers of post-Easter Christian faith as misleading.

[22] In particular Charlesworth, Evans and Ellis regard the Gospels as historical sources.

[23] Even though it is possible to recognise the contours of the person of Jesus within a concrete context behind the conceptions of the Gospels (2006:28, 67), Schröter underlined, that historical research was obliged to explain why early Christianity interpreted the historical events in a specific manner (10, 30).

28   CILLIERS BREYTENBACH

that they are "historisch erinnernde Entwürfe" (126)? One needs to differentiate between memories which are contained within the frames of scenes of the individual episodes[24] and Schröter's thesis that as macro-texts, the Gospels are historical narratives. Does the classification of the Gospels as "historical Jesus narratives" really fit the complex relation between individual episodes and their emplotment into a macro, albeit episodical, narrative and between episodical memory and historiography in the form of an historical narrative?[25] Even though Schröter acknowledges that the Gospels combine historical memory and myth (144),[26] several questions remain unanswered.

With this classification Schröter takes the Wrede road that Mark is a narrative, but it is just not quite clear where he is taking us. Taking up Paul Ricœur's notion that the historical narrative represents the past, Schröter argued that the Gospels, through their narrative refiguration of the events, stood in for the person of Jesus (130). But for Ricœur a historical narrative claims to convey truth about the past and is based upon a refiguration of documented memory of prior events and circumstances. For Schröter, Jesus research, even when closely moulded on the Gospels as "historical Jesus narratives" and other sources, leads not to a reconstruction but a construction of Jesus (2007:108) in front of the sources and not to a historical Jesus behind them (2006:34; cf. 2001:54–55, 59–60). In several instances Schröter, in his popular but noteworthy book on Jesus (2007) evades judging the trustworthiness of how Jesus was remembered in

---

[24] "Die Evangelien stellen die Person Jesus vielmehr gerade so dar, dass die auf ihn angewandten Deutungskategorien *angesichts* seines Wirkens und Geschicks transformiert und mit neuem Inhalt gefüllt werden. Die deutenden Erzählungen sind also durch historische Erinnerungen veranlasst und stehen deshalb in Verbindung zu Jesu Wirken" (Schröter 2007:119).

[25] Against newer Jesus research based mainly on Q and in line with earlier researchers like Schniewind (1933), Lohmeyer (1936) and Dodd (1932), Schröter wants such aspects of the Markan narrative frame to be taken into account in an historical representation of the mission of Jesus (2007:136, 143). The historical plausibility of Mark's narrative sequence that Jesus was baptised by John and that Jesus' ministry was, by all difference, connected to that of John the Baptist, is confirmed by Q. As a "historical Jesus narrative" (144), Mark contextualises Jesus' ministry mainly in Galilee, confines it to archaeologically describable villages like Capernaum, avoiding the cities, and addresses his teaching to the rural population. For Schröter it is not appropriate to strip Jesus' teaching from the narrative Gospel frames. They contain memory on the localities of Jesus' mission, the types of audience he addressed (123). He thus subjected the information on localities, figures and events in the narrative framework and narrated episodes of Mark and Q to historical critical analysis to probe the historical plausibility of such information (131).

[26] Immediately the question arises, whether one should retain the rather dated concept of "myth", which Daniel Friedrich Strauss introduced into Jesus research.

the Gospel tradition, because this would mean driving the wedge between the Jesus of Nazareth and Jesus as he was remembered by early Christianity. Historical research, especially when based on narrative sources, has to engage in "Gedächtniskritik" (Fried 2004:48), for historiography should be based upon trustworthy memory about the past. Can historiography refrain from establishing the trustworthiness of its sources? Even if a construction of how Jesus was remembered is epistemologically spoken, "in front of" the Gospels, it must be argued in such a way that it becomes possible to imagine that it could stand in as a construction of Jesus "behind" the Gospels. When the right of the construction "in front of" the Gospels to stand in as trustworthy memory of the past "behind" the Gospels is not substantiated in every single case, we are merely driving around on the huge parking space in front of the arena in which the synoptic games were played imagining the game. Isn't it time to realise that since 2,000 years the game is over and we could merely go home and watch the recordings from the perspective of the Markan camera team and the replays and additions from Matthew and Luke?

1.6   *The Wredestraße as Main Road*

We have to realise that, as Norman Perrin (1966) expressed it: "The Wredestraße becomes the Hauptstraße." Mark is a narrative and, if I may add, an episodical narrative (cf. Breytenbach 1985). It must be treated as a narrative. Against this background I suggest we take up two insights from our predecessors. In the first instance, there is in this narrative, as Käsemann has noted, some tension between the earthly Jesus—about whom the narrative is—and the position of the narrator who presents him as the Son of God. We have to explore this tension.

Secondly, as Lategan (1984 and 2004) suggested, the road we have to take leads through our construction of the model author and model auditors. We have to gather all information in the narrative, which implies knowledge about the model author or auditors. This of course means that as readers our exit from the text is on the reception side, in the slip stream of our construct of the model audience. We are getting out on the side we got in when we started travelling through the forest. There is no way in which we could have driven through the text and exited on Jesus' side. We now know much more. Having slipped into the role of the intended audience our minds are enriched by the references and connections they could have and probably would have made to the extra textual-world.

CILLIERS BREYTENBACH

So let us continue our journey in two phases, addressing the mentioned issues in an inverted order: We first shall drive within the text world of the Gospel according to Mark (3.1). Then we will explore the tracks that might lead us behind the text (3.2). After we have travelled so far, I hope that the examples might illustrate if there is a road from Mark's narrative leading to Jesus or if I have led you up a dead end street (4). Before setting out on this journey into a text from the past, there is a need to make a detour in order to clarify what is meant by the past, memory and historiography (2).[27] There is an urgent need for a very brief clarification of such issues before travelling any further—unless one doesn't mind getting into one of those "hot rods" wildly driven around historicism's course during the so called "Third Quest".

2. Down Memory's Lane

2.1   *The Past: A "Has Been" That Is No More*

Mark's Son of God and Jesus of Nazareth are both figures of the past. One of the basic things about the past is that it was. Now it is over. We have to take Ricœur's warning seriously that it is inappropriate to treat the past as an entity, as a place where forgotten memories are stored and whence they can be uncovered by memory. Since an object or event from the past has gone by, it is lost. The past has thus a dual character: It *is no* more, but it *was* (Ricœur 1998:23–28). What remains of the past? *Inter alia*, memory!

2.2   *Memories Are Made of This*

2.2.1   *Memory and the Past*
Our journey down memory's lane sets out from individual memory, since memory is rooted in the individual. Aristotle reminds us that memory is of the past, ἡ δὲ μνήμη τοῦ γενομένου (Arist., περὶ μνήμης 449b). When an individual remembers a past event, memory entails an action in the present (remembering) and an "object", "action" or "event" from the past (memory). The relation to the past is thus crucial. When we claim that something occurred, we draw on our memory of the past. According to

---

[27] Due to time constraints on this paper, the question of the modalities of oral tradition cannot be treated here.

FROM MARK'S SON OF GOD TO JESUS OF NAZARETH—*UN CUL-DE-SAC?* 31

Aristotle we have to distinguish evocation (μνήμη) from search (ἀνάμνησις). Μνήμη, the presence of memory, designates a pathos, in which suddenly we remember this or that. Memory needs to be wakened, recalled; we "experience" a memory (Ricœur 1998:26; Fried 2004:49). What had been perceived, experienced, learned earlier and was absent is now present again. Ἀνάμνησις, the recollection of memory, is somewhat different. It is based on search. It returns to, retakes, recovers that which had been seen, experienced or learnt earlier. It is obvious that in the following we will concentrate on the recollection of memory, on remembering that.

When the initial memory of a temporal object or event has disappeared[28] it can be brought back through "re-presentation" in the act of remembering. There is however an important difference between this recollection and initial memory. If something is stored in memory, memorised, certain mnemo-techniques can be used (cf. A. Assmann 1999:28).[29] But when the object or event is recalled, then this is done at a specific occasion for a specific purpose. "Gedächtnis ist ein kommunikativer Akt" (Fried 2004:49). The act of remembering is reconstructive, it is guided by the reasons why someone remembers and is thus not merely an act of repetition (cf. A. Assmann 1999:29).

Representation, being a mode of imagination, does not bring the object or event back, at best the past can be recognised in it (Ricœur 2004:35–36).[30] The event or object is not here, it is still absent, but when we remember,

---

[28] With Husserl, Ricœur distinguishes between the retention of initial, immediate memory and reproduction or recollection of memory (2004:31). When we perceive an object, experience an event, we do it in time and space. In the flow of time and at a certain place the ever new now appears constantly and the now slips into the past. But we are able to retain something of the object we perceived or the event that took place in our immediate memory. In this retention the object or event is not refigured as an image in our imagination, but still present in a modified form of perception. We hold unto a perceived object or an experienced event for a duration of time as long as the retention lasts. After then the object or event removes itself, it is really past.

[29] The Gospel of Mark does give us the impression that the sayings of Jesus in 9:48–50 were connected by using the catchwords "fire" and "salt". The growth parables in chapter four might have been kept together in memory because of their thematic coherence (seed, field, sowing, growth).

[30] We have to distinguish memory from habit. Both are from the past, both become part of the living present. In the case of habit, however, we do not any longer highlight that the action is from the past, in the case of memory, we do (cf. Ricœur 2004:24–25). Memory that repeats (habit) is a representation memory, a remembering how. Without the effort of learning again, it re-acts a specific event from the past. Memory that imagines calls up an image from the past, it is remembering something. Fried (2004:82) distinguishes between habitual implicit memory which does not express itself in words (non-declarative), goal-orientated procedural prospective memory and explicit, declarative memory. It is the latter that concerns us.

we recollect the object or event by reproducing an image of it in our memory. In this image the event or object emanates from the past.[31]

2.2.2 *Memory, Imagination, Fantasy, Fiction or Hallucination?*

How do we distinguish memory's image from imagination, fantasy, fiction or hallucination? Memory, to highlight the most fundamental difference, has the benefit of recognition. At this point it becomes clear that memory can transcend the individual. Anyone who has been at a reunion of his final school class will understand this. After some discussion in the group about an incident or a teacher, a kind of communal agreement arises: "Yes this is the way it was, this is how we were." Memory distinguishes itself from imagination because in the image that is remembered the past can be recognised. The image refers to the past. "The cognitive dimension of memory, its character of knowing, lies in this reference. It is by virtue of this feature that memory can be held untrustworthy or not..." (Ricœur 2004:27). In memory the image that is remembered is recognised as being in accordance with the object or event that it remembers. It is by its "trustworthiness" that we are able to differentiate between memory and fantasy or fiction.

2.2.3 *Memory, Time and Space*

Memory is without the thing remembered, but it is with time (Ricœur 2002:732), it has the imprimatur of "before" and "after".[32] Memory is also with space. It is bound to those who were involved in the action and to the places and spaces where events happened, and objects were located. It is thus temporally and locally limited and confined to those who shared the experience, be it as participants or as onlookers. Although time and place cannot remember, they have importance for the construction of memory. They ground the remembered event or object by giving it a topos (cf. A. Assmann 1999:298–299) within the life span of those who remember their experience. Consequently declarative, recollective memory, i.e. "remembering that", is episodical, autobiographical or both (cf. Fried 2004:82).

---

[31] "And it is as other, emanating from a past as other that it is recognized as being the same as... The small miracle of recognition, however, is to coat with presence the otherness of that which is over and gone. In this memory is re-presentation, in the twofold sense of re-: turning back, anew" (Ricœur 2004:39).

[32] The "thing" remembered is *anterior* to its present evocation (Ricœur 2004:27). To put it with a term of Husserl, it is "Vergegenwärtigung" (presentification) which has to do with time (Ricœur 2004:45). "All memory is with time" (Arist., περὶ μνήμης 449b).

FROM MARK'S SON OF GOD TO JESUS OF NAZARETH—*UN CUL-DE-SAC?*   33

That memory is only there when recalled, has an important consequence. If we want to know something about a past event or lost object, we have to find those who still have a memory of it, those who actively partook in the said event or who were onlookers. We have to share time and space with them, in order to hear their testimony. Their testimony though is given in a narrative form which form and content in itself are determined by the number and density of the events experienced, the grade of involvement of those giving testimony in the events (participants or onlookers), how, given their own expectations and modes of perception, they personally experienced and interpreted the events and which aspects they choose to mediate in culturally determined forms of presentation (for more detail see Fried 2004:50–51).

For us however, it is not possible to share time and space with those upon whom Jesus made an impact to hear their testimony. With the death of the followers of Jesus, their memory died. The basic question however is, if there is a kind of memory transcending individual memory, some kind of "collective" memory.

2.3   *More Than One Can Remember*

2.3.1   *Memory beyond the Individual*

Even if direct experience is individual, individuals can entrust their remembrance of experience to the collective, to the group, allowing it to participate in the mediated remembrance of the individual (cf. Fried 2004:83). Through communication memory transcends the individual. Memory is thus retained in the individual mind but can be recalled and communicated to extend beyond the individual. In the act of communicating his or her remembrance, the individual re-presents experience impressed on his or her memory by recasting it into a medium, thus reconstructing it (cf. A. Assmann 2002:109). Language, but also other communal semiotic systems enable inter-individual communication and exchange of recollected memory (cf. Fried 2004:84–85, 130). In the extension of memory beyond the individual, its "excarnation", the spoken word, plays a decisive role: ἡ σὰρξ ἐγένετο λόγος. Those who can recall ought to tell. Children are introduced through their families into communal memory, people help each other to remember shared events or knowledge, the memory of one person serves as a reminder for the memory of the other one (cf. Keppler 2002). "Do you remember when we were,... when you were?" This illustrates that individual memory interacts with the memory of other individuals. People help each other to remember and they contribute to the

34   CILLIERS BREYTENBACH

shared memory which helps to mould the identity of the group.[33] Individual memory must be mediated to become group memory, since the latter is a collective phenomenon which "only manifests itself in the actions and statements of individuals" (Kansteiner 2002:180).[34] Memory is thus reconstructed and mediated, passed on. In this process of transfer, narration plays a decisive role (Ricœur 1998:789; Keppler 2002:139; Fried 2004:50). The most common "genre of communication" (Keppler 2002:142) is the anecdote, which can be repeated at random (A. Assmann 2002:103). It is typical for recalled, reconstructed, mediated memory that it can be repeated by others. It becomes memory of the second order.

2.3.2 *Remembrance and Medium*

Members of families and larger social groups contribute to their common memory by communicating what they remembered about their past at specific occasions. During such occasions episodic stories about shared times, spaces, places and experiences contribute to the common identity of the group (cf. Keppler 2002:147). Is there a way to "store" recalled memory as long as the community remembering the past together still exists? To store memory, you need a medium,[35] but there is more than that. The ability to store memory and the way in which the remembered is recalled are also determined by the patterns of perception individuals adapt

---

[33] Even though the memory of a group is not to be equated with the collection of individual memories, it is inappropriate to divorce this memory from its roots in individual memory. This danger looms in the reflections of Kirk and Thatcher (2005:40) on remembering Jesus in early Christian tradition. Memory of the individual and his or her future expectations steadily interact with communal images of the past and the common hope. On the other hand, the expectations communities have are shaped by the communal memory of their experiences and they remember their past in the light of their prospects. This polarity of individual and collective consciousness roots in being together in time and place and permits interaction between individual and communal memory. Is the social memory of a group organised as private memory of an individual? Does that what has been said about reflexive, individual memory and the past, imagination and recollection also apply to collective memory? In his critique of the work of Maurice Halbwachs (1950/1992), Paul Ricœur has argued convincingly that this is not the case. The need to distinguish between memory rooted in the experience of individuals and a secondary form of communal memory has serious repercussions for recent New Testament studies about remembering Jesus. Although Ricœur raised this critique (1998:79–80) soon after the publication of his *Temps et récit*, neither Schröter nor Dunn took cognisance of this.

[34] "Jeder Transfer muß die Hürde zwischen dem individuellen Erfahren und der Wissensaufnahme durch andere und durch ganze Kollektive, die Hürde also der 'Entäußerung' und Kollektivierung überwinden, um in das 'kulturelle Gedächtnis' Eingang zu finden" (Fried 2004:85).

[35] Simonides would not have been the famous founder of mnemo-technique, but for his legend transmitted by Cicero (*De oratione* 2.86.352–354).

FROM MARK'S SON OF GOD TO JESUS OF NAZARETH—*UN CUL-DE-SAC?*   35

during their socialisation (cf. van Dijk 1987; A. Assmann 2002:113–134; Fried 2004:55, 82) and the contemporary collective frame which organises the act of remembrance at a specific moment in time. "All memories, even the memories of eyewitnesses, only assume collective relevance when they are structured, represented and used in a social context" (Kansteiner 2002:190). Though memory can be stored in places, symbols and rituals,[36] writing is one of the most important media to store memory. With writing as extra-corporeal medium of transmission, the boundaries of an oral culture of memory are transcended.[37] In writing, places, buildings, people and their actions survive, whilst the land itself became waste, houses ruined, bodies decayed and deeds forgotten.

Aleida Assmann (1999:15) correctly reminds us, "daß das Erfahrungsgedächtnis der Zeitzeugen, wenn es in Zukunft nicht verlorengehen soll, in ein kulturelles Gedächtnis der Nachwelt übersetzt werden muß. Das lebendige Gedächtnis weicht damit einem mediengestützten Gedächtnis". When the above mentioned witnesses of the second order transfer the collective narrative from the oral mode to the written mode, two major shifts occur. The randomly repeated episodes are put into a narrative sequence (cf. Breytenbach 1985) and the second order memory is archived; it becomes a document (Ricœur 1998:119) and opens up the possibility for historiography. But one must always remember, in the case of the Gospel of Mark it was not the testimony of the individuals who experienced the events which was given to protocol, but the secondary memory of the community which had already been turned into oral narratives which crossed the Rubicon of literacy.

2.3.3   *Remembering and Historiography*

The persons affected by past events have to recall their memory as image of such events and testify to what has taken place. They report what they saw, heard, experienced. The crucial question is, whether this testimony is regarded as trustworthy by the listeners,[38] for only when reliable, it allows those listening to the testimony to participate in remembering what

---

[36] It is not difficult to imagine that in addition to the weekly "breaking of the bread", the first Christians commemorated Jesus' crucifixion during the annual Passover and the story about his passion in Jerusalem was told.

[37] "Das Potential der Schrift besteht in der Kodierung und Speicherung von Informationen jenseits lebendiger Träger und unabhängig von der Aktualisierung in kollektiven Inszenierungen" (A. Assmann 1999:137).

[38] "To memory is tied an ambition, a claim—that of being faithful to the past" (Ricœur 2004:21).

happened (cf. Ricœur 1998:33). Being exposed to the impact of the remembered events or persons which are mediated by the witnesses, the listeners themselves become witnesses of the second order, provided they trust the testimony as being truthful. Where testimonies refer to the same person or event the community of course checks the reports before they integrate the narratives of others into the communal memory. Such communal memory, as we have argued, is in continuity with and belongs to human consciousness which is still present. It is the recollection of experienced past events. In recollected memory the lived past is re-presented. But "collective memory is not history, though it is sometimes made from similar material" (Kansteiner 2002:180).

Being dependent on memory, the historical narrative, which by the definition of Ricœur is a narrative refiguration of the past, belongs to historiography. Like memory, it can also stand in for the past. The difference however is that the image that is recalled during remembering can be recognised as being a trustworthy representation of the past. Memory has the advantage of recognising its recollection of the past as that which has been. A historical narrative cannot share in this miracle of recognition. The re-presentation of the past in a historical narrative presupposes the recollected memory's claim to give trustworthy testimony to the past. Memory therefore comes before historiography.

The narrative recollection of memory, however, does not flow undisturbed into historiography. Neglecting this discussion and the substantiating empirical data of how humans actually remember, recent Jesus researchers naively reintroduced the category of the "eye-witnesses" (cf. Bauckham 2006; Baum 2008). Memories needn't be true, but they can be authentic (cf. A. Assmann 2002). Knowing the "Seven Sins of Memory" (Schacter 2001), transience, absent-mindedness, blocking, misattribution, suggestibility, bias and persistence, historical research has to engage in criticism of memory (Fried 2004:48). Notwithstanding the element of recognition and the commitment to be trustworthy, memory is recalled for a purpose. The act of remembering is thus reconstructive and determined by the present and the future of the individual who remembers (cf. also Kelber 2002:56–57) and the social context in which and those for whom s/he recalls his or her memory (cf. Keppler 2002:137–138). Historiography on the other hand disregards the present and the future and focuses its attention on the past, producing a historical narrative which claims to convey true knowledge about the past. It can take a critical stance towards memory, discerning trustworthy testimony from false report. It decides what memory it will use as documents. It asks whose testimonies might

FROM MARK'S SON OF GOD TO JESUS OF NAZARETH—*UN CUL-DE-SAC?* 37

have been suppressed and whose reports could be forged. Going beyond memory, historiography follows the logic of probability, striving to explain the causes and consequences of events and to understand the motives of human action.

2.4 *Where Do We Go from Here?*

It might be surprising that we distinguished memory, both individual and collective, on the one hand, and historical narrative on the other. Both, Dunn and Schröter, travel up and down both tracks, as if they were the north- and southbound lanes of the same highway. This is not the case (cf. Kansteiner 2002:185–187). In our context the interesting question arises if the text which came down to us as the Gospel according to Mark allows the conclusion that it is a narrative that still entails enough of the testimony of those who could recall their memories of the teaching and actions of Jesus of Nazareth for us to regard it as trustworthy memory or to call it an historical Jesus narrative.

3. TRAVELLING THROUGH, IN AND BEHIND THE TEXT OF THE GOSPEL ACCORDING TO MARK

In early Christian times, those who witnessed the teaching, actions and fate of Jesus selectively remembered his words, deeds, passion and death. Changing times and circumstances selected and shaped their memories of the teaching and other actions of Jesus. Sharing experience and having common expectations, they did tell one another their stories about Jesus and created a kind of a communal consensus about the past with Jesus that was fundamental to their own present identity and future expectations. Theory on cultural memory suggests that in second degree memory common macro-narratives would structure the memory of individuals. Such narrated memory is functional, selecting and combining elements from collective acts of remembering, forming a meaningful coherent construction (cf. A. Assmann 1999:137). The Gospel according to Mark is the earliest remaining evidence for the fact that an early Christian author turned the memory of those who followed Jesus into a written narrative. It gives evidence of the communal memory about Jesus of an important group of early Christians during the third quarter of the first century, but can we classify this as the evidence of the impact Jesus made on the memory of his followers (Dunn) or as an historical Jesus narrative (Schröter)? Even if we would discard the reconstructive nature of remembering and the social and cultural context of the act of remembering, we still have to account for the constraints writing imposes on ongoing oral performance. But let's take the Wrede road and travel through the episodical narrative Mark left us.

3.1   Taking the Wrede Road through the Text of Mark

In order to answer the question, whether Mark's narrative can be called a "historical Jesus narrative" or merely mediates second degree communal memories from the past, a few examples will have to do. It is impossible to give a full account of what can be inferred from the story on Mark's Son of God about Jesus of Nazareth. I shall for the sake of the argument concentrate on those parts of the Gospel which most probably belong to the redactional frame of the Galilean part of the narrative (chapters 1–10). The exploration of the plot, figures, space, intertextuality etc. in Mark left the questions as to where the text comes from and its communal function behind it.

3.1.1   The Road Plotted through Mark

Broadly seen, Mark's narrative is theo-logical. In the narrative which became entitled κατὰ Μᾶρκον during the second century C.E., the "good news" coming from God is told (1:14). This news is about his Son, Jesus Christ (1:1) and the beginning of the good news is in accordance with what has been written in the prophet Isaiah. During his baptism Jesus is introduced to the readers (1:11) and the inner circle of the disciples (9:7) by God's voice from the ripped heavens as the beloved Son of God. Jesus starts his proclamation of good news about the advent of God's royal rule after God has delivered John the Baptist and the time set by God has been fulfilled (1:14–15). The main character Jesus himself links his ministry to his death by declaring that it is a divine must that he will suffer very much, be rejected, killed and will rise after three days (8:31). The rule of God, which he proclaims, will come at the end, only the Father knows when, when Jesus will return as Son of Man, punishing those who rejected him and his words, saving those who withstood the deceiver and have not been led astray (13:30–32). The setting, main participants and their actions and intention of the macro-narrative of Mark draw heavily on the mental construct that the course of events are determined by God as it has been written (cf. 14:21).

But is this "memory", for memory is about the past? Is the emplotment of the events and teaching of Jesus in the Gospel according to Mark done in such a way that it recollects the individual memories of those who shared time and space with Jesus? The broader frame of the narrative between Isaiah and the return of the Son of Man does not have the "benefit of recognition". Can we distinguish it from imagination, fantasy, fiction? I doubt it, it is rather—to put it in Wrede's terms—"supernatural". It is the implied author's explanation why things transpired and his theological understanding why people acted in a specific way.

Let us turn to a second example. Since Lohmeyer's (1936) study it is clear that Jerusalem is no sacred place in the Gospel according to Mark. The author moulded communal memory into a narrative which is situated in Galilee, mainly in the town of Capernaum, the action located in and around the house of Simon and Andrew and around or on the Sea of Galilee. Why are these the places and spaces in which memory about the life, the powerful deeds and teaching of Jesus, the Son of God, and about the reactions of his followers, the crowds and his opponents come to us? Could Capernaum and surroundings have been the place where the first two generations of Galilean Christians remembered Jesus, locating his actions and words in familiar spaces and places? Given the role of visual images in the reconstruction of memory, this is highly probable. But it does not mean that the overall Markan construct Galilee–Jerusalem is a true refiguration of the course of Jesus' life. The passion narrative (14:13–14) and later the Gospel according to John help us to see that before Mark was written, there was a communal memory that he visited Jerusalem more than once and resided there longer.

Is it really appropriate to call the Gospel according to Mark a "historical Jesus narrative", as Schröter does? As far as the overarching plot is concerned, the implied author did not refigure the events in Jesus' life and his teaching in such a way that it is based on memory, not even second degree memory. The image it creates of the secret Son of God within an end-time drama, proclaiming the Gospel in Galilee and going to Jerusalem, directly into the temple (11:11), could hardly be recognised as being in accordance with the person or events being remembered. It rather explains the past by drawing on a construction of reality in which God is the main actor and what happens is according to what has been written. Mark's narrative is an episodical narrative and the coherence of the action narrated finally lies in the divine action.

Nevertheless, there are major aspects of the plot of this highly theological episodical narrative that can be utilised for historical construction. As I have already mentioned, in Mark's narrative nobody really understands who Jesus is. The closest followers fail to understand his mission,

Judas delivers him, Peter denies him, in the end they all flee and even the women seek his dead body although he repeatedly announced his resurrection (cf. du Toit 2006). Why have the disciples been refigured into this role? Isn't it likely that here the past is "presentified"? Similar questions can be asked with reference to other narrative roles. Why is the literary figure of Jesus' family depicted in a negative way? Why are the Herodians involved in the Galilean decision to kill Jesus (3:6), why does the Markan Jesus warn against the influence of Herod (8:15)? Why are there episodes in which Mark seems to draw on Peter's autobiographical memory (e.g. 14:54, 66–72)? I do not claim that such questions, which rise from the development of the plot, can all be answered with reference to the time of Jesus, some of them have to do with circumstances in which the Gospel according to Mark was written. But some, like the disbelief of the disciples and Peter's denial, are best explained with reference to the narrated time. Does the narrator here claim to represent true knowledge about the past of Jesus? Another example: In the light of Mark 12:35–37 it is clear that the implied author wants his audience to dismiss the scribal opinion that the Christ should be from the family in Davidic lineage because in the common memory behind Mark this was disputed (cf. Breytenbach 1997). The mere fact that both, Matthew and Luke, refigure the story of Jesus in order to establish his Davidic lineage should warn us not to neglect old-fashioned historical critical analysis. Drawing on narration does not relieve the historian of a critical role toward sources, and even the narrations of eye-witnesses are no exception!

3.1.2 *The Road along the Markan Frame*

What is the Markan "frame"? In most narrative texts we encounter intradiegetic frames (e.g. Mark 4:1–3, 33–34) that embed one or more hypodiegetic narratives (Mark 4:3–8, 26–32) into the main narrative (cf. Wolf 2006: 181–183). "These embedded texts are usually also narratives and constitute the centre or dominant part of the frame story as a whole, while the framing only forms its boarder" (Wolf 2006:181). The narrative road through the text of Mark rests heavily upon such frames which often form the scenic introduction to the episodes and upon the so-called "Sammelberichte" (cf. Onuki 1997). In the transition from oral to written story telling, frames partly substitute the immediate context, which is evident in the case of oral performance (setting, participants and communal knowledge) by embedding the story into the macro-narrative through framing. In such frames the model author furnishes his model recipients with a context for the embedded episodes (cf. Wolf 2006:188–189). From

FROM MARK'S SON OF GOD TO JESUS OF NAZARETH—*UN CUL-DE-SAC?*   41

the "frame" of Mark's narrative, which Schmidt rejected as insignificant, we learn that after John has been handed over, Jesus proclaims the good news about the advent of God's rule in towns[39] like Capernaum, Bethsaida, Gennesaret (1:21; 2:1; 9:33; 6:45, 53; 8:22) and recruits his followers from these towns and Magdala (15:40, 47; 16 :1). He seems to have stayed in the house of Simon (= Peter) and Andrew (1:29; 2:1; 7:17; 9:33; 10:10) in Capernaum and to have travelled to the nearby villages (6:6, 56; 8:27) and marketplaces (6:56) to proclaim his message. As Alt noted long ago, with the exception of Jerusalem, Jesus never enters a city (Alt 1949:438, 450–451). He merely visits the towns of Caesarea Philippi (8:27) and the territories of Tyre, Sidon and the towns of the Decapolis (7:31—cf. Alt 1949; Breytenbach 1999). The fact that the narrator sets the scenes for the individual episodes in such a way most probably implies that he refigures communal memory about the locations and addressees of Jesus' teaching.

3.2   Exploring Specific Locations in Mark's Narrative

When we now turn to individual episodes, it is important to note that cognitive psychological research into the remembering of narratives has illustrated the importance of constructive episodic memory. Without going into any detail here (cf. van Dijk 1987; van den Broek 1994:551–552) we underline that, when storing narrated action in the long-term memory, the events are organised in episodes with distinct settings fixing the location and time in which the events took place.

3.2.1   A Walk in Capernaum

Memory does not need to follow the temporal course of events. The temporal sequence of events could, in the process of being stored, be restructured as visual image (cf. A. Assmann 1999:27). In the Gospel according to Mark the narrator often uses this technique. The action of Jesus is narrated as coming into Capernaum and going into the synagogue on the Sabbath (1:21), leaving the synagogue and going into the house of Simon and Andrew (1:29). When Jesus leaves the house, he goes to a desolate place (1:32) or to the lake (2:13; 4:1). The sequence of the events narrated simply bases upon the visual memory of the narrator that Capernaum is on the shore of the lake of Galilee and the house of Simon and Andrew is

---

[39] Mark uses the word πόλις to refer to Capernaum (1:33), other towns (1:45; 6:33, 56) and cities like Gerasa (5:14) and Jerusalem (11:19; 14:13, 16), whilst κώμη denotes a small agricultural village (cf. 6:6, 36, 56; 8:23, 26–27; 11:2).

located not far from the synagogue. Here memory runs visually and not audibly (A. Assmann 1999:27).

It is well known that the house, which is the focal point of Jesus' teaching in Mark, with its one entrance (1:33) into the courtyard (2:2), where the children are around (10:10, 13), and with its flat roof (2:4) is depicted in such a way that it can easily be compared to archaeological reconstructions of houses in Capernaum in Roman times (cf. Breytenbach 1999). The graphic description might recollect visual memory of the location.

3.2.2 Out to the Countryside
The images the Markan Jesus uses in his teaching are drawn from agricultural life on the fertile plain of Gennesar: Some of his followers have left their arable land (10:30) and Jesus uses sowing (4:2–8), sprouting, ripening and plucking of grain (4:26–29), the mustard plant and seed (4:30–32) as metaphors in his parables. Some of his images reflect first-century Jewish family life: a wedding feast (2:19) and single room where both, a bed and a measuring vessel, were available and which could be lit with one oil lamp (4:21–22). It is probable that the author here refigured stories from the communal memory from the Markan tradition. The community remembered in such a way because they were familiar with the locations in which the events were placed. Nevertheless, the relation of such communal memory to the memory of those who followed Jesus has to be clarified in each individual case.[40] Some metaphors remind one that in Jesus' hometown evidence of wine growing were found (cf. Reed 2000:131–132). He speaks of wine-skins (2:22) and a vineyard, a wine-press and a tower (12:1–9). As a test case, let us go there.

3.2.3 Visiting Nazareth
When we utilise what is implied in the text (cf. Grice 1989) it is clear from the outset, the model author presupposes that his listeners will know who John who baptises and Jesus were (1:4, 9), where Judea, Jerusalem and the Jordan are (1:5) and that the river is near the desert (1:12). The implication

---

[40] The discussions and controversy on ethos circle around topics which were common to first century Judaic *halakhah*: how is the Sabbath to be kept (1:21–28, 29–31; 2:23–3:6), who is allowed to eat with whom (2:14–17), does one have to fast (2:18), which ritual washings are necessary before meals and what defiles the body (7:1–23), who is ritually pure and who is not (1:40–45)?

FROM MARK'S SON OF GOD TO JESUS OF NAZARETH—*UN CUL-DE-SAC?* 43

is that Jesus came from his hometown to John at the Jordan. Nazareth, though, needs to be identified as belonging to Galilee (1:10).[41]

In Mark's narrative, Jesus is a villager. Had it not been for Mark's episode (6:1–6a) on the rejection of Jesus in his father's town (πατρίς), we would not have known that Jesus was a craftsman from the village of Nazareth (6:1–3). We would not have known that his mother's name was Mary, and that he had brothers and sisters. We would not be able to place his childhood in a non-monetary economy based on the exchange of agrarian products in a village where one produced wheat, olive oil and wine. Thanks to archaeological surface surveys we can assume that under the reign of the Maccabees Jesus' family originally resettled from Judea to lower Galilee, most probably fairly early. For strategic and health reasons settlers were located in Nazareth on the hills overlooking the Jezreel plain. From this evidence we can also infer that his family, like the rest of the population which originated from Judea, used *miqva'ot* and stone vessels for purity reasons. Taking into account the economic structure and the geographic isolation of Nazareth (cf. Reed 2000:115–117, 131–132) and the level of literacy of the population (cf. Hezser 2001), it is highly unlikely that Jesus could read, write or speak any significant Greek. In order to claim this one would have to argue that early Christian memory deliberately suppressed any reference to that "pearl of all Galilee", Sepphoris, the city which Herod Antipas built north of Nazareth, where the levels of literacy and Hellenisation were higher. Unless deliberately suppressed, the name of Jesus' father was so unknown that it did not enter the communal memory initiated by the first followers.

3.3 *Summary*

When we, by reading Mark as a narrative, take the Wrede road and analyse the text properly as narrative, it is clear that it furnished the implied audience with valuable information on the person of Jesus. By reading Mark's narrative against the backdrop of the historical geography and archaeology of Galilee, taking every bit of information Josephus gives us into account, it might be possible to infer important aspects about how the community behind the Gospel according to Mark remembered Jesus of Nazareth and how this memory shaped their identity.

---

[41] The narrative seems to imply that after the baptism Jesus remained in the desert and only came back into Galilee after John had been handed over (1:14).

This does not mean, however, that this communal memory can be regarded as an effect of the "impact" Jesus made, without the required historical critical scrutiny. Neither does this make the Gospel according to Mark an historical narrative (*pace* Schröter), nor does it imply that we hear what the disciples heard and see what they saw (*pace* Dunn). In my view the loose way in which Schröter uses "Erinnerung" and Dunn draws on "remembering" has to be refined by reflecting what memory is and how the latter relates to historiography. At the same time the transition from the individual memory of the followers of Jesus and the communal memory of those behind the Gospel of Mark has to be clarified.

Because communal memory has been archived through writing, we—as uninvited, late readers—can read the narrative frame of the Gospel according to Mark and utilise the implied information for historical construction. But we could also dig up the tarmac of the Wrede road to see what is underneath it or look next to the road for signs where the old tracks went, knowing that this will be tedious.

3.4 *Looking under and next to the Wrede Road*

3.4.1 *The Mark/Q Substratum*
The narrator introduces John as the Baptiser and depicts him as the one who comes before Jesus (Mark 1:8–9). The parallel depiction in Q (Luke 3:16b–17/Matt 3:11–12) shows us that in the earliest traceable tradition common to Mark and Q, early Christians remembered that Jesus' ministry followed on that of John and interpreted it in the light of Exod 23:20 and Mal 3:1. The conflation in Mark 1:2b–c is a traditional quotation, since the very same conflation between Exod 23:20 and Mal 3:1 forms the basis of the independent tradition from Q (cf. Breytenbach 2009).

From Mark we learn that Jesus must have been attracted by John the Baptist and his message of conversion and was baptised by John as a sign of the forgiveness of his sins (Luke 3:21–22/Matt 3:16–17 hardly give independent evidence for the baptism of Jesus by John). There is no need to question the probability of Jesus' baptism. The specific Markan way of relating Elijah, John the Baptist and Jesus is disputed (cf. Pellegrini 2000). Nevertheless the sequence he created—John's call to be baptised; Jesus' baptism by John; Jesus' independent proclamation of the royal rule of God—has to be explained. It requires any construction of the mission and message of Jesus to clarify the relationship between the messages of John, who called for repentance in the light of the looming threat of God's

FROM MARK'S SON OF GOD TO JESUS OF NAZARETH—*UN CUL-DE-SAC?*   45

wrath, and Jesus who called for trust in the good news that God's reign is imminent (cf. Schröter 2001:71–78).

3.4.2   *Scriptural Milestones*

The textual form of the combined citation from Exodus and Malachi in Mark 1:2 betrays its origin from a community which utilised the Hebrew text. The fact that the author extends this conflated traditional citation in Mark 1:3 which still reflects the Hebrew by a second citation, is on par with his normal procedure in the case of combined citations (cf. Breytenbach 2006). In accordance with his usual procedure when citing or alluding to the Scriptures, the evangelist cites from the Septuagint. In using the Greek translation of what Moses said, the author expands several debates which reach back into the pre-Markan Jesus tradition. The citations from Gen 1:17 and Deuteronomy in Mark 19:5+6 were both taken from the Septuagint and combined by the author expanding an original dispute on divorce which formed the basis of Mark 10:2+9 (NRSV): "Some Pharisees came and asked Jesus, 'Is it lawful for a man to divorce his wife?' He answered them, 'What God has joined together, let no one separate'" (cf. Breytenbach 2006 on this text and Mark 7:11–12; 12:23+27) The author's use of the Septuagint as intertext in the expansion of basic questions on the Torah in the Jesus tradition illustrates that the impact of Jesus resounded in a context of transmission moulded by the Greek Bible. Merely the basis of the argument enables us to imagine which impulse came from Jesus. From Mark's text there is no road back into the Jesus tradition, but merely a trail. That there is a trail can be seen from the overlapping χωρίζω-motif in 1Cor 7:10b–11.

3.4.3   *The Trail of Genre*

As we argued, memory needs a medium. Leaving the parables aside (cf. Zimmermann 2008), we look at genres in Mark's episodical narrative. The lists of the names of the twelve confirm that Peter and Andrew, as well as John and James, were amongst those following Jesus (3:16–18). The narrative on their calling in Mark 1:16–20 interprets the occasion during which they started to follow Jesus in a sequence of events moulded upon the story of the calling of Elijah by Elisha (cf. 1Kgs 19:19–21).[42] The repetition

---

[42] The influence of the biblical narrative clearly excels in Josephus' retelling of the story in *Ant.* 8.353–354.

of key vocabulary of the Greek text of 3Kgdms 19:20 (ἀκολουθήσω ὀπίσω σου) further proves the point that Mark is depicting Jesus in a way that he surpasses Elijah, who for Mark returned as John the Baptist. But nevertheless, in this episode the calling of the first disciples is emplotted by utilising a narrative taken from the life of the famous prophet of the Northern Kingdom of Israel.

It is highly significant, that it is relatively easy to recognise the influence of Jewish text types and Semitic poetic forms on the parables and aphorisms the Markan Jesus tells. The aphorisms that show clear parallels in the Pauline epistles are all formulated in poetic parallelisms (Mark 7:15/Rom 14:14; Mark 11:23/1Cor 13:2; Mark 12:17/Rom 13:7). That Mark does not always tell his story utilising biblical pretexts becomes clear from his extensive use of original Greek genres like *chreiai*. A considerable part of the aphorisms and proverbs we find in Mark are narrated embedded in the form of *chreiai*. This illustrates that the stories were told and retold in a context where they have moved from the memory of an original Aramaic to a Hellenised community[43] without losing the common lower Galilean rural and village setting of the town of Capernaum and the "Sea of Galilee" and the plain of Gennesar setting of the macrostory. Of course Mark, writing Greek, mastered Greek literary forms. But is it historically plausible that the Galilean fishermen and small farmers from the villages around lake Gennesar, who saw and heard Jesus, cast their remembrance of Jesus' teaching and actions in the form of *chreiai* and narratives about the mighty deeds (δυνάμεις) of Jesus utilising predominantly Greek text forms? The literary forms in which Mark did cast his episodes do give us an indication as to the cultural context in which these stories were re-told and archived as written communal memory. Observations like these have to be taken into account when one classifies Mark as "historical Jesus narrative" or postulates that the impact Jesus made on the disciples shaped the tradition up to its narrativity. One has to give more attention to that what lies off and under the paving of the comfortable narrative road of Wrede.

---

[43] That Mark uses the Greek genre *chreia* is admitted even by those who argue that he drew on Peter's use of this form in his preaching (cf. Byrskog 2007). On the Greek roots of the *chreiai* in the Markan narrative cf. Moeser 2002.

4. From Mark's Son of God to Jesus of Nazareth—*Un Cul-de-Sac*?

My résumé can be brief. To my mind it can be fruitful to utilise the communal memory of the Galilean followers of Jesus which formed the basis of the Markan narrative about the Son of God in order to write a historical narrative about Jesus of Nazareth. But to get to that we have to take the reformulation and the growth of the synoptic tradition into account. We will have to look in and behind the text of Mark. Of course such a narrative will have to incorporate the memory encapsulated in Q and added unto Mark and Q by the Gospels of Luke, Matthew and John to claim to represent Jesus' past. But our imaginary road to Jesus of Nazareth leads through the Galilean countryside evoked by the Markan narrative. I have now dared to get off the Wredian road, to journey from Mark's Son of God to Jesus of Nazareth. If this is *un cul-de-sac*, future digs under the Wrede road will have to show.

5. How Many Real Jesuses along the Road?[44]

Adding to my journey on Markan roads, I respond to Michael Wolter's essay in this volume. I have difficulty in disagreeing with the main argument of his essay, but there are some questions begging for more clarification. Turning to the first section, one might agree that a historian does not have to believe that Jesus was raised from the death and inaugurated as God's Son to write a book about Jesus of Nazareth. From Wilhelm Dilthey (1983) however, a historian could learn, *inter alia*, two very important lessons.

First, all human knowledge is embedded in a specific context. It is knowledge by a person or persons embedded in their historical circumstances. A walk through more recent history could illustrate the point. Before February 1990 it was prohibited to publish anything about Nelson Mandela. He was still a political prisoner of the Apartheid regime. It is possible to write even today a book about him until 1989, thus excluding the announcement of his release, that extraordinary day itself and his subsequent career as the first president of a democratic South Africa. But even then any historian would have difficulty in excluding his own knowledge about the later life of Mandela from this selective perspective. He or

---

[44] This section was read at the New Testament research seminar at the University of Stellenbosch, April 15, 2011.

she would however, concede that the book covers only part of Mandela's long walk, freedom still at large. The example clearly illustrates not only the dependency of the outcome of historiography on the historiographer's temporal relationship to the events s/he is writing about. It also shows us that a sequence of events is best understood when taken as a whole.

This brings me to the second lesson from Dilthey. Any event or sequence of events can only be interpreted adequately from its end. Nelson Mandela's statesmanship as president, his zeal for reconciliation between the people of South Africa, throws a new light on his time on Robben Island. Every historian has to admit that Mandela's choice for reconciliation rather than retaliation forces one to assess the influence of his long imprisonment on his political career in another way as when he would have opted to punish his suppressors. In the late eighties a very few historians would have expected the release of Mandela and his key role in the transition of South Africa from a totalitarian to a democratic state. They simply would not believe that this could or would happen. But when it happened, it changed the perspective on the past.

The present has the power to change our construction of the past. I do not want to rehearse Wolfhart Pannenberg's Popperian argument about the meaning of Jesus' resurrection as anticipation of the future within the logic of falsification (cf. Pannenberg 1987). But it should be clear by now that should the Christian expectation about the *parousia* of the exalted Jesus transpire, Michael Wolter's statement (p. 7) holds its validity: "In terms of *methodology* there are no principles or requirements, even for theologically oriented historical investigations, other than those that are commonly applied by the guild of the historians in any other historical inquiry into any other figure of the past." But since one has to keep the future open, it becomes difficult to maintain as Wolter does, that it is possible to approach the quest for the historical Jesus "without regard to the Christian faith of Easter". This is often done by non-Christians as well as by Christians, but if historical questions about Jesus "do not differ in principle from depictions of the lives of other people in the past, such as Alexander the Great or Napoleon" then it is decisive for the historian's depiction of the life of Jesus to take account of Jesus' heritage in Christianity. Compared to the impact of the last stages of Mandela's long walk on his meaning in recent history, the 2,000 years of Christianity and its future must have a bearing on the historian's appraisal of Jesus' life and the belief that he was resurrected.

Isn't it only because Wolter detaches the impact Jesus made from his envisaged historical reconstruction that he maintains, that "anyone can write a book about the teaching and actions and fate of Jesus of Nazareth. To do this, one does not have to believe that Jesus was God's Son, that he is risen from the dead or that God's salvation is made available through him. One does not even have to believe in God. To write a good book about Jesus, one must merely be able to apply historical methods critically and honestly. One can surely write about Jesus in the same manner that one would write about Alexander or Luther or Churchill" (p. 1). A historian is accountable for the whole story and the major issue about Jesus of Nazareth is that his impact did not end at the cross. Jesus had a short walk, but his followers prolonged it into the future. This has corollaries for any quest for the historical Jesus, which itself will remain open until the end of time—if there is an end.

Drawing on Max Weber, Wolter constructs in section two of his paper seven images of Jesus. Basically I want to argue that even if seven be a perfect number, it is important to note these seven images are of different status. Let us start with the fundamental image, the image of the *earthly Jesus*. When I started teaching at Nelson Mandela's Alma Mater in Fort Hare in 1979, a clever text book written by the British historian of Christian Missions Stephen Neill was on the list of prescribed works. The book is titled *Jesus through Many Eyes* and introduces the reader to the way in which each evangelist depicted Jesus. We may call these Jesuses the earthly Jesus according to Mark, Matthew, Luke or John or even the narrated Jesus. The point is, such Jesus figures can be constructed from the text. Even if they are images by modern readers of these texts, their referent, the earthly Jesus, ought to be related to the discourse of one of the evangelists. In this sense, the images are "real", they emerge when the reader travels on the narrative roads through the Gospels. In this sense there are "real Jesuses" to meet on the road leading into Mark, Matthew, Luke, John and even Thomas. They are encoded in the texts and can be deciphered and constructed by competent readers.

In a related way, the images of a "historical Jesus" are also real. By reading those books that Albert Schweitzer and those who came after him have reviewed, one is able to draw oneself a picture of the images of the historical Jesus, which e.g. Renan, Strauss, Bultmann, Bornkamm, Crossan or van Aarde had in mind at the time they wrote their books. The recurring images of the historical Jesuses emerge from the pages of the books written by modern historians through the reading of contemporary readers. It is important to note however, that there is a fundamental difference between the images of the earthly Jesus, which are grounded in early Christian texts from the first century and those of the historical

Jesus, which emerge from the texts of modern historians. The latter are dependent on the former. It is the images of an earthly Jesus taken from the ancient sources, which are used for the construction of the images of a historical Jesus. Historical images of Jesus could never have come into being without those of the Gospels. Rephrasing Wolter (p. 8) we can agree that the historical Jesuses are creations by historians on basis of the Gospels. But nevertheless, the various images of Jesus that claim to be historical are "real" in relation to their authors and their books. They are imagined figures of Jesus created back at home by those who travelled the roads through the texts of the evangelists.

In a similar sense one can claim reality for the different images of the Christ of faith. They emerge when readers read through the pages of the works of Edward Schillebeeckx, Joachim Ringleben or Joseph Ratzinger. The fact that Benedict XVI claims that his Jesus of Nazareth is based on more than what historical method can offer, does not alter that the pages of these two volumes are filled with Joseph Ratzinger's images of Jesus as Wolter correctly pointed out. So both the historical Jesus and the Christ from faith are not encoded in the Gospels, they are to be found during reading journeys through monographs found in modern scholarly libraries.

The next three images of Jesus do exist, since there are researchers who have created them. I will argue however, that they can be re-classified either as images of historical Jesuses or of the Christ of faith or a combination of both und would suggest dropping these images from the typology Wolter designed. With reference to James D.G. Dunn's *Jesus Remembered* I recapitulate on section 3.3 above. Dunn's ill-reflected concept of remembering does not take into account, that we simply do not have the memories of those on whom Jesus made an impact in the Gospels. Those around Jesus had not revoked their experiences stored in their memory by an act of remembering and then wrote down what they have recognised from the past they carry in them. Given the results of Catherine Hezser's study on literacy in Roman Palestine it is moreover highly unlikely that any of the close followers of Jesus could write. Remembering is fundamentally the act by which a human subject recalls from his memory that what he has experienced and stored. As Paul Ricœur has argued, remembering recognises the past in the images that are made from memory. Before the relation between those who experienced the impact of Jesus and those who authored the Gospel and between individual remembering and communal memory are not clarified, the image that Dunn is claimed to have pointed out (p. 10), goes not beyond modern imagination. I am afraid that

FROM MARK'S SON OF GOD TO JESUS OF NAZARETH—*UN CUL-DE-SAC?*   51

there is *no real remembered* Jesus apart from the earthly Jesus in the Gospel narratives and they are not the documented memories of those who experienced Jesus. There is no need to claim a medial difference between the earthly Jesus as a literary figure and the remembered Jesus, since the latter is entailed in the former. Nobody has yet any way to access the undocumented memory of those around Jesus.

The same applies to the images named "Jesus from Nazareth". They too are secondary images based on the Jesus from the Gospels. Even if Wolter expects "just as many images of Jesus as there are people who had met Jesus", we have only those images that are derived from the literary images in the Gospels. Such images are not real for us because somebody from Nazareth cultivated them, but because they are part of the literary images.

Without any further ado: The images that Jesus is claimed to have had about himself also have no other basis as that scholars construct them on the basis of the literary images in the Gospels, including the utterance of the earthly Jesus of the Gospels. Even though the notion of Jesus' self-definition plays a crucial role in section three of Wolter's lecture, it should not be overlooked that this is of course not Jesus' self-interpretation, but the image scholars make of it on basis of the Jesus figures in the Gospels.

To wind it up, there are not that many different types of real Jesuses. There are the earthly Jesuses in the Gospels, and there are an array of images of the historical Jesus and of the Christ of faith which are really in the books about them. Memories about Jesus and the images that compatriots made of Jesus were real, as long as those people whose minds he entered through their experience lived. Since they are all gone now, we are left with the remains in the literary images in the Gospels. There is no need to operate with more types of imaginary images. Bound to the roads through the Gospels (first and foremost Mark's), one uses the literary images collected on the journey; either in historiography creating an image of a claimed to be historical Jesus or in theology producing an image of a Christ of faith. A merger between the two options normally blurs the image.

Wolter asks (p. 12), whether there is something like the figure which we may call the real Jesus. "Is there a 'real Jesus' as an ontic reality beyond the images that people have been making of him since the time he lived—and also beyond the image he had of himself?" What does "ontic reality" mean? Taking the lexical sense of the compound expression "ontic reality" seems to mean a reality having real being. There is a more specific meaning of "ontic", drawing on philosophical tradition, according to which the adjective "ontic" expresses that the "reality" is real, independent of the human mind and senses. If this is meant, Wolter implies that there is more than one reality, e.g. a social reality, a psychological reality or then an "ontic reality". So for instance, he regards the certitude that God has raised Jesus from the dead as "a certitude of fact within a Christian concept of reality" (p. 16). For him ontic reality is fundamental, "reality beyond the images that people have been making" (p. 12), inaccessible to human knowledge which "remains deprived of ontic reality" (p. 14).

The problem is, as a figure from the past, Jesus cannot have ontic reality. One of the basic things about the past is that it was (see 2.1 above). Now it is over. We have to take Ricœur's warning seriously that it is inappropriate to treat the past as an entity, as a place where forgotten memories are stored and whence they can be uncovered by memory. Since an object or event from the past has gone by, it is lost. The past has thus a dual character: It *is no* more, but it *was* (Ricœur 1998:23–28). Jesus of Nazareth thus cannot have ontic reality. He is not, he was, just as Nelson Mandela on Robben Island is no more. What remains of this past? *Inter alia*, the literary figures of the earthly Jesus in the Gospels. But does the Christ of the church have ontic reality? If by that a reality is meant that is real, independent of the human mind and senses, the answer must be no. The Christ of the church does not have reality independent of Christian faith. The ever changing images of the Christ of the church through the centuries (cf. Kuitert 1998) make it easy to grasp that they are images created faithfully and sincerely by Christians.

I thus want to conclude with the question if there is a "real Jesus" who "definitely exists in the sense of ontic reality" as Wolter (p. 13) maintains. This I think is a bridge too far. Christian images of the Christ of the church should be based on the Jesus figures in the Gospels, but have their origin in the minds of those who told the Gospel stories. They clearly presuppose the belief in Jesus' resurrection and vindication by God. As Wolter (p. 16) correctly states, "there can be no Christian faith, whose concept of reality does not contain certainty about the fact of the resurrection of Jesus".

Wolter's answer to the question on which the real Jesus is, is that the real Jesus is Jesus as he himself understood himself, since Jesus was vindicated by God. The problem is, no one can know how Jesus understood himself, but for the interpretation of the Gospels. We are thus still on the road through the Gospels again with the one real Jesus type, the literary figures in the Gospel narratives. They will have to suffice.

FROM MARK'S SON OF GOD TO JESUS OF NAZARETH—*UN CUL-DE-SAC?* 53

Bibliography

Alt, Albrecht. 1949. "Die Stätten des Wirkens Jesu in Galiläa territorialgeschichtlich betrachtet." Pages 436–455 in vol. 2 of idem, *Kleine Schriften zur Geschichte des Volkes Israels*. Munich: Beck, 1953.

Assmann, Aleida. 1999. *Erinnerungsräume: Formen und Wandlungen des kulturellen Gedächtnisses*. Munich: Beck.

———. 2002. "Wie wahr sind Erinnerungen?" Pages 103–122 in Harald Welzer, ed., *Das soziale Gedächtnis: Geschichte, Erinnerung, Tradierung*. Hamburg: Hamburger Edition.

Assmann, Jan. 1992. *Das kulturelle Gedächtnis: Schrift, Erinnerung und politische Identität in frühen Hochkulturen*. Munich: Beck.

Bailey, Kenneth E. 1991. "Informal Controlled Oral Tradition and the Synoptic Gospels." *AJT* 5:34–54.

Bauckham, Richard. 2006. *Jesus and the Eyewitnesses: The Gospels as Eyewitness Testimony*. Grand Rapids: Eerdmans.

Baum, Armin D. 2008. *Der mündliche Faktor und seine Bedeutung für die synoptische Frage*. TANZ 49. Tübingen: Francke.

Breytenbach, Cilliers. 1984. *Nachfolge und Zukunftserwartung nach Markus: Eine methoden-kritische Studie*. ATANT 71. Zurich: Theologischer Verlag.

———. 1985. "Das Markusevangelium als episodische Erzählung." Pages 138–169 in Ferdinand Hahn, ed., *Der Erzähler des Evangeliums*. SBS 118/119. Stuttgart: Katholisches Bibelwerk.

———. 1986. "Das Problem des Übergangs von mündlicher zu schriftlicher Überlieferung." *Neot.* 20:46–58.

———. 1992. "MNHMONEYEIN: Das 'Sich-Erinnern' in der urchristlichen Überlieferung." Pages 548–557 in Albert Denaux, ed., *John and the Synoptics*. BETL 99. Leuven: Peeters.

———. 1992a. "Vormarkinische Logientradition: Parallelen in der urchristlichen Brieflite-ratur." Pages 725–749 in Frans van Segbroeck et al., eds., *The Four Gospels*. BETL 100. Leuven: Peeters.

———. 1997. "Das Markusevangelium, Psalm 110,1 und 118,22f: Folgetext und Prätext." Pages 197–222 in Christopher Tuckett, ed., *The Old Testament in the Gospels*. BETL 131. Leuven: Peeters.

———. 1999. "Mark and Galilee: Text World and Historical World." Pages 75–85 in Eric M. Meyers, ed., *Galilee through the Centuries: Confluence of Cultures*. The Proceedings of the 2nd International Conference on Galilee. Winona Lake: Eisenbrauns.

———. 2006. "Die Vorschriften des Mose im Markusevangelium: Erwägungen zur Komposition von Mk 7,9–13; 10,2–9 und 12,18–27." *ZNW* 97:23–43.

———. 2009. "The Minor Prophets in Mark's Gospel." Pages 27–37 in Maarten J.J. Menken and Steve Moiyse, eds., *The Minor Prophets in the New Testament*. Edinburgh: T. & T. Clark.

Broek, Paul van den. 1994. "Comprehension and Memory of Narrative Texts: Inferences and Coherence." Pages 539–588 in Morton A. Gernsbacher, ed., *Handbook of Psycholin-guistics*. San Diego: Academic Press.

Bultmann, Rudolf. 1921. *Die Geschichte der synoptischen Tradition*. FRLANT Neue Folge 12. 2nd ed. 1931. Göttingen: Vandenhoeck & Ruprecht.

———. 1926. *Jesus*. Die Unsterblichen 1. Berlin: Deutsche Bibliothek.

———. 1967. "Das Verhältnis der urchristlichen Christusbotschaft zum historischen Jesus." Pages 445–469 in idem, *Exegetica: Aufsätze zur Erforschung des Neuen Testamentes*. Ausgewählt, eingeleitet und kommentiert von Erich Dinkler. Tübingen: J.C.B. Mohr (Paul Siebeck). Repr. from *Sitzungsberichte der Heidelberger Akademie der Wissenschaf-ten: Philosophisch-historische Klasse* 1960, no. 3, 5–27.

Byrskog, Samuel. 2007. "The Early Church as a Narrative Fellowship: An Exploratory Study of the Performance of the Chreia." *TTKi* 78:207–226.

54 CILLIERS BREYTENBACH

Casey, Edward S. 1987. *Remembering: A Phenomenological Study: Studies in continental Thought*. 2nd ed. 2000. Bloomington: Indiana University Press.

Dijk, Teun A. van. 1987. "Episodic Models in Discourse Processing." Pages 161–196 in Rosalind Horowitz and S. Jay Samuels, eds., *Comprehending Oral and Written Language*. San Diego: Academic Press.

Dijk, Teun A. van, and Walter Kintsch. 1983. *Strategies of Discourse Comprehension*. New York: Academic Press.

Dilthey, Wilhelm. 1983. *Texte zur Kritik der historischen Vernunft*. Edited by Hans-Ulrich Lessing. Göttingen: Vandenhoeck & Ruprecht.

Dodd, Charles H. 1932. "The Framework of the Gospel Narrative." *ExpTim* 43:396–400.

Dormeyer, Detlev. 2005. *Das Markusevangelium*. Darmstadt: Wissenschaftliche Buchgesellschaft.

Droysen, Johann Gustav. 1977. *Historik: Rekonstruktion der ersten vollständigen Fassung der Vorlesungen (1857), Grundriss der Historik in der ersten handschriftlichen (1857/1858) und in der letzten gedruckten Fassung (1882)*. Textausgabe von Peter Leyh. Stuttgart-Bad Cannstatt: Frommann-Holzboog.

Dunn, James D.G. 2003. *Jesus Remembered*. Vol. 1 of *Christianity in the Making*. Grand Rapids: Eerdmans.

Fried, Johannes. 2004. *Der Schleier der Erinnerung: Grundzüge einer historischen Memorik*. Munich: Beck.

Grice, Paul H. 1989. *Studies in the Way of Words*. Cambridge, Mass.: Harvard University Press.

Güttgemanns, Erhard. 1970. *Offene Fragen zur Formgeschichte des Evangeliums*. BEvT 54. Munich: Kaiser.

Halbwachs, Maurice. 1950/1992. *On Collective Memory*. Edited, translated, and with an Introduction by Lewis A. Coser. Chicago: University of Chicago Press.

Harnack, Adolf. 1907. *Sprüche und Reden Jesu: die zweite Quelle des Matthäus und Lukas*. Leipzig: Hinrichs.

Hezser, Catherine. 2001. *Jewish Literacy in Roman Palestine*. TSAJ 81. Tübingen: Mohr-Siebeck.

Joubert, Annekie. 2004. *The Power of Performance*. Berlin and New York: de Gruyter.

Kansteiner, Wulf. 2002. "Finding Meaning in Memory: A Methodological Critique of Collective Memory Studies." *History and Theory* 41:179–197.

Käsemann, Ernst. 1954. "Das Problem des historischen Jesus." *ZTK* 51:125–153 (= pages 187–214 in vol. 1 of idem, *Exegetische Versuche und Besinnungen*. Göttingen: Vandenhoeck & Ruprecht, 1960).

———. 1964. "Sackgassen im Streit um den historischen Jesus." Pages 31–68 in vol. 2 of idem, *Exegetische Versuche und Besinnungen*. Göttingen: Vandenhoeck & Ruprecht.

Kelber, Werner H. 2002. "The Case of the Gospels: Memory's Desire and the Limits of Historical Criticism." *Oral Tradition* 17:55–86.

———. 2005. "The Generative Force of Memory: Early Christian Traditions as Process of Remembering." *BTB* 36:15–22.

———. 2005a. "The Works of Memory: Christian Origins as MnemoHistory—A Response." Pages 221–248 in Alan Kirk and Tom Thatcher, eds., *Memory, Tradition and Text: Uses of the Past in Early Christianity*. SBL Semeia Studies 55. Atlanta: SBL.

Keppler, Angela. 2002. "Soziale Formen individuellen Erinnerns: Die kommunikative Tradierung von (Familien-)Geschichte." Pages 137–159 in Harald Welzer, ed., *Das soziale Gedächtnis: Geschichte, Erinnerung, Tradierung*. Hamburg: Hamburger Edition.

Kirk, Alan, and Tom Thatcher. 2005. "Jesus Tradition as Social Memory." Pages 25–42 in idem, eds., *Memory, Tradition and Text: Uses of the Past in Early Christianity*. SBL Semeia Studies 55. Atlanta: SBL.

Kuitert, Harry M. 1998. *Jezus: Nalatenschap van het christendom*. Baarn: Ten Have.

Lategan, Bernard C. 1979. "The Historian and the Believer." Pages 113–134 in Willem S. Vorster, ed., *Scripture and the Use of Scripture: Proceedings of the Second Symposium of the*

FROM MARK'S SON OF GOD TO JESUS OF NAZARETH—*UN CUL-DE-SAC?* 55

Institute for Theological Research (UNISA) Held at the University of South Africa in Pretoria on the 19th and 20th September 1978. Pretoria: University of South Africa.

———. 1984. "Reference: Reception, Redescription and Reality." Pages 67–93 in idem and Willem S. Vorster, *Text and Reality*. Philadelphia: Fortress.

———. 2004. "History and Reality in the Interpretation of Biblical Texts." Pages 135–152 in Jens Schröter and Antje Eddelbüttel, eds., *Konstruktion von Wirklichkeit: Beiträge aus geschichtstheoretischer, philosophischer und theologischer Perspektive*. Berlin and New York: de Gruyter.

Lightfoot, Robert Henry. 1934. *History and Interpretation in the Gospels*. New York and London: Harper & Brothers.

Lohmeyer, Ernst. 1936. *Galiläa und Jerusalem*. FRLANT 52. Göttingen: Vandenhoeck & Ruprecht.

Marxsen, Willi. 1956. *Der Evangelist Markus: Studien zur Redaktionsgeschichte des Evangeliums*. FRLANT Neue Folge 49. Göttingen: Vandenhoeck & Ruprecht.

Moeser, Marion C. 2002. *The Anecdote in Mark, the Classical World and the Rabbis*. JSNTSup 227. Sheffield: Sheffield Academic Press.

Onuki, Takashi. 1997. *Sammelbericht als Kommunikation: Studien zur Erzählkunst der Evangelien*. WMANT 73. Neukirchen-Vluyn: Neukirchener Verlag.

Pannenberg, Wolfhart. 1987. *Wissenschaftstheorie und Theologie*. stw 676. Frankfurt on Main: Suhrkamp.

Pellegrini, Silvia. 2000. *Elija—Wegbereiter des Gottessohnes: Eine textsemiotische Untersuchung im Markusevangelium*. Herders Biblische Studien 26. Freiburg: Herder.

Perrin, Norman. 1966. "The Wredestrasse Becomes the Hauptstrasse: Reflections on the Reprinting of the Dodd Festschrift." *JR* 46:296–300.

Reed, Jonathan L. 2000. *Archaeology and the Galilean Jesus: A Reexamination of the Evidence*. Harrisburg: Trinity.

Rhoads, David, and Kari Syreeni, eds. 1999. *Characterization in the Gospels: Reconceiving Narrative Criticism*. JSNTSup 184. Sheffield: Sheffield Academic Press.

Ricœur, Paul. 1998. *Das Rätsel der Vergangenheit: Erinnern—Vergessen—Verzeihen*. Essen: Wallstein.

———. 2002. *Geschichtsschreibung und die Repräsentation der Vergangenheit*. Münster: Lit (French original: "L'Écriture de l'Histoire et la Représentation du Passé." *Annales: Histoire, Sciences Sociales* 55 [2000]: 731–747).

———. 2004. *Memory, History, Forgetting*. Chicago: University of Chicago Press.

Schacter, Daniel L. 2001. *The Seven Sins of Memory*. Boston: Houghton & Mifflin.

Schmidt, Karl Ludwig. 1919. *Der Rahmen der Geschichte Jesu: Literarkritische Untersuchungen zur ältesten Jesusüberlieferung*. Berlin: Trowitzsch.

Schmithals, Walter. 1985. *Einleitung in die drei ersten Evangelien*. DeGruyter Lehrbuch. Berlin and New York: de Gruyter.

Schniewind, Julius. 1930. "Zur Synoptiker-Exegese." *TRu* Neue Folge 2:129–189.

———. 1933. *Das Evangelium nach Markus*. NTD 1. Göttingen: Vandenhoeck & Ruprecht.

Scholtissek, Klaus. 2005. "Grunderzählung des Heils: Zum aktuellen Stand der Markusforschung." *TLZ* 130:858–880.

Schröter, Jens. 1997. *Erinnerung an Jesu Worte: Studien zur Rezeption der Logienüberlieferung in Markus, Q und Thomas*. WMANT 76. Neukirchen-Vluyn: Neukirchener Verlag.

———. 2001. *Jesus und die Anfänge der Christologie: Methodologische und exegetische Studien zu den Ursprüngen des christlichen Glaubens*. Biblisch-theologische Studien 47. Neukirchen-Vluyn: Neukirchener Verlag.

———. 2006. *Jesus von Nazareth: Jude aus Galiläa—Retter der Welt*. Biblische Gestalten 15. Leipzig: Evangelische Verlagsanstalt.

———. 2007. *Von Jesus zum Neuen Testament: Studien zur urchristlichen Theologiegeschichte und zur Entstehung des neutestamentlichen Kanons*. WUNT I 204. Tübingen: Mohr-Siebeck.

56 CILLIERS BREYTENBACH

——. 2007a. "Der erinnerte Jesus als Begründer des Christentums? Bemerkungen zu James D.G. Dunns Ansatz in der Jesusforschung." *ZNT* 10:47–53.

Schweitzer, Albert. 1906. *Von Reimarus zu Wrede: Eine Geschichte der Leben-Jesu-Forschung.* Tübingen: J.C.B. Mohr (Paul Siebeck).

——. 1913. *Geschichte der Leben-Jesu-Forschung.* 2nd ed. Tübingen: J.C.B. Mohr (Paul Siebeck).

Theißen, Gerd, and Annette Merz. 1996. *Der historische Jesus: Ein Lehrbuch.* Göttingen: Vandenhoeck & Ruprecht.

Theißen, Gerd, and Dagmar Winter. 1997. *Die Kriterienfrage in der Jesusforschung: Vom Differenzkriterium zum Plausibilitätskriterium.* NTOA 34. Göttingen: Vandenhoeck & Ruprecht.

Toit, David S. du. 2006. *Der abwesende Herr: Narrative und geschichtstheologische Strategien im Markusevangelium zur Bewältigung der Abwesenheit des Auferstandenen.* WMANT 111. Neukirchen-Vluyn: Neukirchener Verlag.

Vorster, Willem S. 1977. *'n Ou Boek in 'n nuwe wêreld—gedagtes rondom die interpretasie van die Nuwe Testament: Intreerede W.S. Vorster.* Pretoria: Universiteit van Suid-Afrika.

——. 1980. "Die tekssoort evangelie en verwysing." *Theologia Evangelica* 13:27–48.

——. 1983. "Kerygma/History and the Gospel Genre." *NTS* 29:87–95.

——. 1998 *Speaking of Jesus: Essays on Biblical Language, Gospel Narrative and the Historical Jesus.* NovTSup 92. Leiden: Brill.

Wolf, Werner. 2006. "Framing Borders in Frame Stories." Pages 179–206 in idem and Walter Bernhart, eds., *Framing Borders in Literature and other Media.* New York: Rodopi.

Wrede, William. 1901. *Das Messiasgeheimnis in den Evangelien: Zugleich ein Beitrag zum Verständnis des Markus-Evangeliums.* Göttingen: Vandenhoeck & Ruprecht.

Zimmermann, Ruben. 2008. "Gleichnisse als Medien der Jesuserinnerung: Die Historizität der Jesusparabeln im Horizont der Gedächtnisforschung." Pages 87–121 in idem and Gabi Kern, eds., *Hermeneutik der Gleichnisse Jesu: Methodische Neuansätze zum Verstehen urchristlicher Parabeltexte.* WUNT I 231. Tübingen: Mohr-Siebeck.

THE REMEMBERED JESUS

James D.G. Dunn

Michael Wolter addresses an issue which is bound to be of first concern for many Christians and which will inevitably catch the interest of any historian concerned to appreciate the beginnings of Christianity and the Jesus from whom in one way or another Christianity sprang. Of course anyone with an historically inquiring mind will be interested in Jesus, who, on almost any account, has been one of the archetypal or pivotal figures in human history. Christians will be especially interested, since the doctrine of incarnation affirms that in a man who lived and moved around Galilee, probably in the late 20s C.E., God revealed himself more fully and more definitively than at any other time or through any other person. If such definitive revelation took place in Palestine over a number of years, then how can Christians not be concerned to know what the historical reality of that definitive revelation was. But Christian faith is hardly a *sine qua non* to provoke interest in the first century Galilean, at the very least one of the most intriguing figures of human history.

So the questions remain and can hardly be dismissed as irrelevant or meaningless. Who was this Jesus? What do we know, what can we know about him that may be of importance for our better understanding of the origins of Christianity?—and of Christianity today? Alternatively, despite the self-evident fascination and potential importance of such questions, are we bound to conclude that it is not possible, or necessary (even for Christians), to gain such knowledge? Wolter's analysis of what he refers to as the seven different images of Jesus, which have been the result of such inquiry regarding Jesus, poses such issues sharply and provocatively.

I find myself at once in disagreement with Wolter on the possibility of historical knowledge of Jesus. Here we are at once caught up in the problem of what or to whom the term, "the historical Jesus", refers. It is true, of course, that "the historical Jesus" in its technical usage refers to the historian's Jesus, that is, to Jesus as reconstructed by historical method. But almost unavoidably, the phrase is used also to describe the actual historical person who engaged in mission round the Sea of Galilee. This confusion, between the actual historical personage, and historians' reconstruction of that person, muddies the discussion and too easily leads to a

58   JAMES D.G. DUNN

sharp differentiation between the two "historical Jesuses", and to a denial
that historical method can attain any worthwhile historical information.
On this view, we only have and can only have the reconstruction, and not
the historical reality, not in any worthwhile degree.

Such an approach, however, fails to do justice to the possibility of fruitful historical inquiry. In *Jesus Remembered* I drew attention to the important distinction, important for historical research, between "event", "data"
and "fact".[1] No historian thinks it possible to access the historical *event*
in any direct way; that belongs to the irretrievable past. All that is available are the *data*—eye-witness accounts, reports, archaeological artefacts,
broader knowledge of the circumstances of the time, etc. The event is irre-
coverably past; but the data are *present* to the historian. From these data
the historian reconstructs the *fact*; the historical fact is the *interpretation*
of the data. To speak of "facts" as though they are the same as events is
once again to confuse the issue. There may be *bruta data*, but never *bruta
facta*. This is true of all historical inquiry. Of course, the interpretation
of the data will differ from historian to historian. But there will be many
cases where the interpretations of the data are sufficiently close for us to
be able to conclude that there is broad agreement on the history, on the
sequence of events and the persons involved. They will still be reconstructions, but they cannot be dismissed simply for that reason. Where the
data is plentiful, and where there is a broad measure of agreement on
the interpretation of that data, there can also be a strong conclusion that
the fact is a good or even a close approximation to the event. To deny this
is to deny the possibility and usefulness of all historical research—as it is
to deny the possibility of a jury reaching a legitimate verdict in a trial. So
I regard Wolter's dismissal of the "historical Jesus" as a "fiction" and a "fallacy" as much too negative a conclusion and unjust to a whole discipline
of historical inquiry.

A second quarrel I have with Wolter comes to the surface especially
when he writes:

> Yes, the "real Jesus" definitely exists in the sense of ontic reality, but we
> cannot really say anything about him, because every linguistic description
> and even every perception of such a reality is always contaminated with
> particular *interpretations*.

---

[1] J.D.G. Dunn, *Jesus Remembered* (vol. 1 of *Christianity in the Making*; Grand Rapids:
Eerdmans, 2003), § 6.3.

THE REMEMBERED JESUS 59

It is the word "contaminated" which raises my hackles. The implication is that any "interpretation" contaminates. But contaminates what? Contaminates the data? The implication presumably is that there is an ideal perception which might actually be possible, a perception uncontaminated by interpretation. But is that realistic? All perceptions, whether those of Jesus' contemporaries, or those of modern historians, or those of Christians generally, are interpretations. An interpretation is not to be dismissed simply because it is an interpretation. Some interpretations, indeed, will be part of the data. A historical interpretation, that is, an interpretation of someone closely involved in the event, may be a decisive clue to the event (what happened) and to the way the event was perceived. Since we cannot access the event in itself, the access we have to an interpretation of the event by someone involved in or near to the event may be the best access we can achieve to the event.

Here I introduce my own protest against the assumption, so characteristic of "the quest of the historical Jesus" over the decades, the assumption that *faith* is something which obscures our perception of the one who walked the hills of Galilee.[2] That the first questers were justified in trying to strip away the layers of Christian dogma which did indeed obscure the man Jesus, I in no way deny. The trouble is that this negative evaluation of faith was read back to the beginnings of Christianity. The faith that God had raised up Jesus from the dead was regarded as equally problematic for the quest, equally a layer which had to be removed if we were to see the Jesus of Galilee. And it followed that such faith had so influenced all the portrayals of Jesus in the Gospels, and indeed all the data, that it had "contaminated" any perception of Jesus which relied in any degree on the Gospels.

My protest is that, on the contrary, it can be assuredly assumed, as a starting point, that Jesus made an "impact" during his mission in Galilee (as Wolter has noted). It runs counter to all common sense to assume otherwise—that is, to assume that Jesus was an insignificant figure, who made no impact, and to whom fortuitously, a virtually unknown Jew, the great claims made in the Gospels and after Easter were somehow and for some unknown reason attached. The implausibility of such a scenario has

---

[2] More fully see my "Remembering Jesus: How the Quest of the Historical Jesus Lost its Way", in T. Holmen and S.E. Porter, eds., *Handbook for the Study of the Historical Jesus* (4 vols.; Leiden: Brill, 2011), 1:183–205, here 183–190.

always been the death-blow to all attempts to portray Jesus as an entirely mythical figure.

To acknowledge the inescapable probability that Jesus made an impact during his mission in Galilee and Judea, is already to speak in effect of "faith"; "impact" can be translated into "faith" without too much problem. Jesus gathered disciples around him; it would seem, and there is no reason to think otherwise, that the disciples gave up their way of life, their occupations and professions, even their families, in order to follow him. That was the impact he had. And since we can also say that these disciples trusted him, committed themselves to be his followers, a completely life-changing decision, we can speak of their faith in this Jesus and regarding this Jesus. It would not (yet) have been Easter faith, the faith that God had raised the crucified Jesus from the dead and exalted him to heaven. But it was still faith. And the relation of that faith to Easter faith is one which Wolter passes over too casually. For faith in Jesus did not begin with Easter; and though Easter faith is properly distinguished as Christian faith, the fact that the pre-Easter mission of Jesus forms the main body of the canonical Gospels assuredly indicates that the first disciples saw their post-Easter faith as in continuity with and of a piece with their pre-Easter faith. The alternative of denying that such pre-Easter faith is inaccessible, or irrelevant, or confusing to Christian faith (and therefore to be set aside), is simply unacceptable for any serious historical inquiry. After all, such an inquiry, particularly by Christians, will want to know what was the impact which Jesus made, what was the faith which he inspired. Apparently his calling transformed fishermen and tax-collectors into disciples and apostles. Who would not want to know more about this man?

Thirdly, I have to affirm strongly my conviction that we can discern much of that initial (pre-Easter) impact that Jesus made. By putting the historical task in these terms I agree with Wolter that Jesus in himself is inaccessible; he belongs to the category "event" as outlined above, irretrievable in his pastness. But I also assert that the impact which Jesus made on his disciples *is* accessible in that it belongs to the "data" which has come down to us. My focus here is on the synoptic Gospel tradition, the tradition shared by Matthew, Mark and Luke. This I claim represents and embodies the impact which Jesus made—the faith-creating impact which Jesus had on his disciples. So our access to Jesus is only possible through the impact he made on his disciples. Hence the title of my own study—*Jesus Remembered*. No direct access to the Galilean Jesus is possible; but through the impact he made, the impression he left on the disciples as evidenced in the synoptic tradition, we can discern the character of the

THE REMEMBERED JESUS 61

mission of the person who made that impact. Ironically (in the light of the quest's assumption that faith conceals the historical figure from our view) it is precisely through the faith impact on the first disciples that we can discern the forceful character who made that impact. If our goal is Jesus in himself, we will not get far. The goal of Jesus remembered may seem a lesser goal, but it is much more realistic and capable of success.

I am somewhat puzzled as to why so little has been made of the *character* of the synoptic tradition in the quest of the historical Jesus.[3] After an encouraging start, form-criticism moved on from analysing the way the Jesus tradition functioned in the decades before it was transcribed, and became more preoccupied with finding criteria by which to recognize sayings which began with Jesus or with discerning the theology (and sociology) of the communities which used the forms. And redaction criticism focused principally on how the individual Evangelists reworked the tradition which had come down to them. But the character of the synoptic tradition as a whole, as indicating the way Jesus was remembered, was paid too little attention. For me three features of the synoptic tradition stand out and deserve attention as indicating the possibility of discerning the impact which Jesus made and the character of the mission which made that impact.

First, the synoptic tradition has a distinctive character of its own. It confronts us with traditions which again and again are diverse versions of the same account or teaching. Sometimes we have only two versions, sometimes three; occasionally more! The distinctive character is summed up in the phrase, "the same, yet different"—the same event, but told differently, the same teaching but recorded in different groupings and words. This, of course, has been the heart of "the synoptic problem", which, since the nineteenth century has so fascinated Gospel scholars. The "problem", however, was seen in terms almost exclusively of sources: which source were the differing versions drawing on? The synoptic problem was seen almost solely in terms of sources, and written sources at that, with the well-known conclusions agreed by the majority of scholars that Mark was the earliest of the three synoptic Gospels and that Matthew and Luke were able to draw on another source, designated as Q.

The weakness of these approaches has been the too ready assumption that the synoptic problem is the problem of how to explain literary

---

[3] I develop the case which follows in various places—e.g. "Reappreciating the Oral Jesus Tradition", *SEÅ* 74 (2009): 1–17.

interdependence between the synoptic Gospels. The discussion is in terms of copying and redacting earlier written material. But the basic point seems to be easily missed: that the synoptic tradition demonstrates how the Jesus tradition was transmitted and used—by retelling and reusing material which was substantially the same, the same story, the same teaching, but adapted and varied, presumably by the circumstances in which it was reused. I see the process in oral terms: the synoptic tradition demonstrating how the Jesus tradition was transmitted and used prior to its being written down; the characteristic same yet different feature of the synoptic tradition is a characteristic familiar in oral tradition. Too much of the discussion of the synoptic problem has focused on the parallel passages which obviously demonstrate literary interdependence. But there are at least an equal number of passages where the story/teaching is the same, but the detail is quite diverse and gives no support to the thesis that one copied from the other or from a common literary source. The passages where the parallels are not close deserve as much attention as those where the parallels are close. The former, I believe, attest a tradition which was transmitted and used in oral forms.

However, whether we see the process in terms of oral or literary transmission, the synoptic tradition shows how the transmission and use of the tradition took place. There was regular concern for the substance or gist of the story/teaching, but there was much les concern for the detail; the detail could vary quite significantly. The *Sache* of the episode or teaching could focus in certain words or an exchange of dialogue; but otherwise the *Sache* was not dependent on the *Sprache*. There was evidently little or no concern for inconsistencies or contradictions between versions, so long as the main point of the story/teaching was conveyed. The agonizings over such tensions and inconsistencies, which have plagued all attempts at harmonizing from the second century onwards, were simply unnecessary and attested a failure to recognize the character of the Jesus tradition, as the same yet different.

Second, a striking feature of the synoptic tradition, again often overlooked, is the fact that so much of the tradition demonstrates what we might call simply a pre-Easter character. Of course, all the Jesus tradition in the canonical Gospels is held within a Gospel framework. So, as it now comes to us, it speaks to and expresses Easter faith. But individually the items which make up the tradition do *not* reflect a post-Easter perspective or Easter faith. A good example is the bulk of the Jesus tradition which makes up the "Sermon on the Mount" (Matthew) and the "Sermon on the Plain" (Q/Luke). Both versions end with the parable of the house built

THE REMEMBERED JESUS

on the rock and the house built on the sand/ground without foundation (Matt 7:24–27/Luke 6:47–49). The contrast is between the one who hears the words of Jesus and does them, and the one who hears the words of Jesus but does not do them. Is that good post-Easter Gospel? Is the Gospel that one must do what Jesus says? Surely the obvious answer is that this is teaching of Jesus, pre-Easter teaching, and unmodified by an Easter call for faith in the risen and exalted Lord.

Other examples are easily found. Is the parable of the Prodigal Son an expression of the post-Easter Gospel? Jesus' preaching of the Kingdom of God as already an active presence through his mission is not taken up in any real measure in the documents which reflect earliest Christian theological reflection (including John's Gospel!). Did the jibe that Jesus was "a glutton and a drunkard" (Matt 11:19/Luke 7:34) first emerge after Easter? Did the tradition's regular reference and address to Jesus as a "teacher", and the evidently wide-spread view that Jesus was a "prophet" first emerge as an expression of Easter faith?[4] I simply disagree with Wolter that these are all properly described as "a post-Easter image of Jesus".

The essential point is that the Jesus tradition, even as it now stands, for the most part embodies what was remembered as the teaching and doings of Jesus during his mission in Galilee and Judea. This tradition could be used and transmitted without post-Easter elaboration, we may infer, because the teaching and life-style of Jesus during his mission was important for the first Christians. That is presumably why it was treasured, performed, taught, transmitted—because the life, teaching and mission of Jesus was regarded as important for the first Christians. This is why, no doubt, this tradition, in its pre-Easter form, was included within documents which became known as "Gospels"—because the life and teaching of Jesus was *not* divorced from his passion, resurrection and exaltation, but provided teaching and *paraenesis* for those who had believed the gospel of the crucified and risen Lord. The distinction between the Christ of faith and the Jesus of history, which has proved so fundamental in Jesus research, is in the end more misleading than helpful. The Jesus of faith, that is the Jesus who inspired faith, is not to be set at odds with the Jesus of history, but is the key to the Jesus of history. The Jesus of the synoptic tradition is the remembered Jesus, and shows how Jesus was remembered.

My *Jesus Remembered* thesis has been criticized because I do not enunciate or work from a theory of memory. That is true. For me the starting

---

[4] *Jesus Remembered* (n. 1), 657–660, ch. 8, nn. 22–23, and ch. 14, n. 62.

64   JAMES D.G. DUNN

point was the synoptic tradition, with its same yet different character. In broad terms, the synoptic tradition is composed of the memories of Jesus. The same yet different character shows how Jesus was remembered. That includes the variations, as Jesus' teaching and deeds were remembered somewhat differently by different disciples and performers of the Jesus tradition. That includes a degree of elaboration and interpretation as part of that process; redaction did not begin with the later Gospel writers, though variation is a more accurate description of the process of oral performance and transmission. In fact such varied performances and adaptations of the tradition seem to have been a feature of the Jesus tradition from the first. And if Jesus had given the same teaching in different ways, using different parables to make the same point—and which teacher ever taught anything important only once?—then which version would be the "authentic" one?

Third, a very striking feature of the synoptic tradition is its coherence and consistency. For all the differences and variety between the three-fold versions of the synoptic tradition, a clear picture emerges of the Jesus who is the main theme of the tradition. Again I disagree with Wolter that there will be "just as many images of Jesus as there are people who had met Jesus", the implication being that all that can emerge from such an approach as I advocate is a kaleidoscope of irreconcilable images. On the contrary, even with the diversity which is characteristic of the synoptic tradition, a coherent and consistent picture of the main character of the tradition emerges. C.H. Dodd put the point well:

> [T]he first three gospels offer a body of sayings on the whole so consistent, so coherent, and withal so distinctive in manner, style and content, that no reasonable critic should doubt, whatever reservations he may have about individual sayings, that we find here reflected the thought of a single, unique teacher.[5]

When we link this feature to the assumption that Jesus made an impact on his first disciples, and the hypothesis that the synoptic tradition shows both that and how Jesus was remembered by his first disciples, then an obvious corollary also emerges. From the impression left in the synoptic tradition, we can gain a fairly clear idea of the one who made the impression. The metaphor is that of a seal: from the impression made by the seal and left in the wax, we can gain a clear idea of the shape and contours and details of the seal itself. The logic, then, is straightforward:

---

[5] C.H. Dodd, *The Founder of Christianity* (London: Collins, 1971), 21–22.

THE REMEMBERED JESUS

- Jesus made an impact;
- that impact is embodied in the way Jesus was remembered in the synoptic tradition;
- from the clear outlines of the character of the synoptic tradition a clear picture of the character of the one or of the mission which made that impact is readily discernible.

I am confident, then, that the modern historian can have access, not to Jesus *per se*, but to the remembered Jesus, Jesus as he was remembered by his first disciples. Of course, Jesus impacted more than the disciples whom we can assume stand behind the Jesus tradition and were primarily responsible for putting it into its enduring forms, for grouping and ordering the various items in the Jesus tradition as occasion allowed or demanded. But of these others, of these other impacts, we have little or nothing—at best a few possible echoes of Pharisaic-type critique of Jesus in the rabbinic traditions. Otherwise we are dependent on the Gospel tradition for accounts of other, hostile or otherwise responses to Jesus— negative impacts, as we may call them. It would certainly be more than interesting to have a first hand account from Caiaphas or Pilate of how they reacted to Jesus. But we don't. The channels of memory flow almost exclusively through the Christian documents. That is, of course, a more limited memory tradition than the historian would like to have. But at least it does focus our and the historian's attention on the impact Jesus had on his immediate disciples, those who became disciples in response to Jesus. For the historian that at least gives access to those most positively influenced by Jesus. And for the Christians, that is the impact made by Jesus in which they are most interested.

A final thought on the question whether there is an unbridgeable gulf between a secular historian's approach to the Jesus quest and that of a Christian historian.[6] I would say No. Historical method can be entirely shared between them. If the Christian will always have in the back of the mind the faith in and about Jesus which developed after Easter, it is not unimportant to note that such faith is itself part of the data which all historians must take into account. And if so much of the Jesus tradition in the synoptic Gospels embodies pre-Easter memories of Jesus, then the issue of Easter faith becomes less of a barrier. Notwithstanding

---

[6] This was the main subject of a review of *Jesus Remembered* by Robert Morgan, and my response, *ExpTim* 116 (2004–2005): 1–6, 13–16.

the fact that the pre-Easter memories are now contained within the context of Gospels, which as Gospels proclaim Easter faith, the pre-Easter character of so much of that tradition is clearly discernible. Only if a sharp distinction and discontinuity is maintained between the pre-Easter faith-creating impact of Jesus and post-Easter faith can the pre-Easter impact and faith be set aside as irrelevant or even a threat to post-Easter/Christian faith. Whereas the fact that the synoptic Gospels retain the impact/faith created by the pre-Easter Jesus in its pre-Easter character is, once again, a reminder that the first disciples saw a direct continuity and sameness in the pre-Easter faith and their post-Easter faith.

Here, perhaps above all, I wish to avoid the situation where the only language suitable for talk about Jesus is the language of Christian faith. I want to avoid the possibility that one can speak meaningfully and responsibly about Jesus only in the church, and not in the market place or secular academy. I do believe that the truth-seeking historian of whatever stripe, by taking the synoptic Jesus tradition in the ways I have suggested, can sense and possibly even experience something of the impact that Jesus made. The Gospels, after all, are good news to the seeker and to the so-far unpersuaded. Let us not lock them into the language of religious devotion and deprive them of all but a role in liturgy!

CONTOURS OF THE HISTORICAL JESUS

R. Alan Culpepper

The invitation to contribute an essay to this volume has called me out. After years of fascination with the Gospels and rare forays into Jesus' sayings, this is the first essay I have written on the historical Jesus. Interpretations of the historical Jesus are invariably subjective; they represent the era in which they are written and the particular values and biases of the interpreter, so what follows is inescapably a personal construction. Nevertheless, even granting the limitations of our evidence and the gyrations of historical Jesus research, I believe we can say some things about Jesus with a degree of confidence. If what is offered here is not entirely original, it is because others have done far more work on the historical Jesus than I have. Areas of consensus are beginning to emerge, and these may serve as our most secure foundation for further thought about Jesus. "Contours" suggests an outline, shape, or sketch. Its use in the title of this essay also acknowledges a healthy dose of historical humility—a contour is not a portrait.

As an initial response to Michael Wolter's helpful review of the ways New Testament scholars have handled the relationship between the historical Jesus, the Jesus reconstructed by historians, and the Jesus of the Christian *kerygma*—three conceptual entities—I should indicate at the outset that I find great value in the "path" of Reimarus and the "Third Quest." This "path" complements and adds a historical dimension that is missing in the church's creeds and confessions that emphasize Jesus' birth and his death and resurrection but say little or nothing about his life and ministry, his teachings, or the nature of the Kingdom of God that he proclaimed. Moreover, the life of Jesus is also theologically important. Would it not make a difference to the claim that Jesus was the agent of the Kingdom of God and that God raised him from the dead, if the historical evidence showed that Jesus was a violent revolutionary, or one who taught hatred? Or to put the question another way, how would Christianity be different if it derived from another historical figure of the time (Judas Maccabaeus, Caiaphas, Hillel, or the Teacher of Righteousness)? Without the Gospel accounts of Jesus' ministry, the claim of his resurrection and Lordship would be empty and essentially meaningless.

68 R. ALAN CULPEPPER

In the brief scope of this essay I propose to approach the historical Jesus from three angles of vision: the context of Jesus' life in Galilee early in the first century, the activities that characterized his ministry, and the teachings that give us a glimpse into his self-understanding. Where these three converge—that is the significance of Jesus' activities in his social, political, and religious context, and the relationship between his activities and his teachings—they shed light on the "contours" of his life.

1. First-Century Galilee: The Context of Jesus' Life

The context of Jesus' life has become a significant factor in the study of the historical Jesus. Whereas the "New Quest" started with the sayings and parables and employed "the criterion of dissimilarity," namely that what is most dissimilar from Judaism and early Christianity is most securely attributed to Jesus, starting with what we know of first-century Galilee invokes what we may call "the criterion of contextual affinity,"[1] namely that Jesus' activities and teachings must be understood in his social, economic, religious, and political context. This context gives us clues to influences on his life and ways his activities would have been understood. Of course, Jesus stood out dramatically in this context. Otherwise he would not have been remembered—and would not have been crucified. Still, this distinctiveness can be understood, and has meaning, only within the context and setting of his life.

As a focal text for the setting of Jesus' ministry we may take Matt 4:23–25. This passage is obviously Matthean and redactional. The argument, therefore, is not that this summary statement comes from an early source but that the Gospel tradition itself preserves, indeed is based on, this general understanding of Jesus' ministry.

> [23]And he went throughout all Galilee teaching in their synagogues and preaching the Gospel of the Kingdom and curing every disease and every sickness among the people. [24]And the report about him went out into all Syria, and they brought to him all who had various diseases: those tormented by pain, the demon possessed, epileptics, and the paralyzed, and Jesus cured them. [25]And great crowds followed him, from Galilee and the Decapolis and Jerusalem and Judea and across the Jordan. (Author's translation)

---

[1] G. Vermès, *Jesus the Jew* (New York: Macmillan, 1973), 42, took this approach in 1973: "...the present approach will attempt the contrary, namely to fit Jesus and his movement into the greater context of first-century AD Palestine." Cf. G. Theissen and A. Merz, *The Historical Jesus: A Comprehensive Guide* (Minneapolis: Fortress, 1998), 117–118.

CONTOURS OF THE HISTORICAL JESUS

Matthew famously quotes the characterization of Galilee in Isa 9:1, "Galilee of the Gentiles" (Matt 4:15), but is this an apt description of Galilee in the first century? Recent archaeology has demonstrated that it is not; Galilee was predominantly Jewish. Mark Chancey concluded that "The belief that pagans made up a large part, perhaps even the majority, of Galilee's population in the first century C.E.—a view that has influenced generations of New Testament scholars—exists despite the evidence, not because of it."[2] The archaeological evidence supports the view that the Hasmoneans extended Judaism into Galilee from the south.[3] 1Macc 5:15 refers to "Galilee of the Gentiles," in reference to the people of Ptolemais, Tyre, and Sidon. There was no cultic center in Galilee to sustain Jewish worship through the centuries. Beginning in the second century B.C., however, there is evidence of ritual baths (*miqvaoth*), stone jars that were necessary for ritual purity, ossuaries for Jewish burial practices, and an absence of pig bones.[4] Pre-70 synagogues have been found in Galilee at Magdala and at Gamla (in the Golan), where a synagogue dating to the first century B.C. has been excavated.[5] The Gospels represent Jesus going into synagogues throughout Galilee (Matt 4:23; 9:35), but these may have been gathering places that were not yet architecturally distinct. The picture that emerges is one of religiously observant Jews living in towns and villages. The population was not monolithic, but Galilee was thoroughly Jewish in the early first century, and after the destruction of Jerusalem in 70 C.E. Galilee became the center of Jewish life.[6]

The Gospel references to the groups Jesus encountered in Galilee confirm this general picture, while adding some interesting demographic data.

---

[2] M.A. Chancey, *The Myth of a Gentile Galilee: The Population of Galilee and New Testament Studies* (Cambridge: Cambridge University Press, 2002), 167.

[3] J.D.G. Dunn, *Jesus Remembered* (vol. 1 of *Christianity in the Making*; Grand Rapids: Eerdmans, 2003), 295.

[4] Ibid.; S. Freyne, "Galilee," in J.J. Collins and D.C. Harlow, eds., *The Eerdmans Dictionary of Early Judaism* (Grand Rapids: Eerdmans, 2010), 655; J.D. Crossan and J.L. Reed, *Excavating Jesus* (rev. ed.; New York: HarperCollins, 2001), 51–52; M.A. Chancey, "How Jewish Was Jesus' Galilee?" *BAR* 33, no. 4 (2007): 42–50, 76.

[5] S. Freyne, *Galilee, Jesus and the Gospels* (Philadelphia: Fortress, 1988), 203–204; C.A. Evans, *Jesus and His World: The Archaeological Evidence* (Louisville: Westminster John Knox, 2012), 49–51, 53–54.

[6] This paragraph is taken from the author's forthcoming commentary on the Gospel of Matthew (NTL; Louisville: Westminster John Knox Press). For further detail, see P. Richardson, *Building Jewish in the Roman East* (Waco: Baylor University Press, 2004).

Table 1. Representations of groups in Jesus' Galilean Ministry.

	Matthew	Mark	Luke	John
Sadducees	16:1			
Chief priests				
Priests and Levites				1:19
Pharisees	9:11, 34; 12:2, 14, 24, 38; 15:12; 16:1; 19:3	2:16, 18, 24; 3:6; 7:1, 5; 8:11; 10:2	5:17, 21, 30, 33; 6:2, 7; 7:30, 36, 37, 39; 11:37, 38, 39, 42–43, 53; 13:31; 14:3; 15:2; 16:14; 17:20	(1:24)
Leaders of the Pharisees			14:1	
Leaders of the Synagogue	9:18, 23		8:41; 18:18	
Elders			7:3	
Scribes	7:29; 8:19; 9:3; 12:38; 15:1	2:6, 16; 3:22; 7:1, 5; 9:11, 14	5:21, 30; 6:7; 11:53; 15:2	
Teachers of the Law			5:17	
Lawyers			7:30: 10:25; 11:45, 53; 14:3	
Herodians		3:6		
Royal officials				4:46, 49
Tax collectors	9:10, 11; 10:3; 11:19	2:15, 16	5:27, 29, 30; 7:29, 34	

The Gospel of John never mentions the *Sadducees*. The synoptics record an encounter with the Sadducees in Jerusalem (Matt 22:23, 34; Mark 12:18; and Luke 20:27). Matthew reports "many Pharisees and Sadducees" coming to John for baptism in the wilderness of Judea (Matt 3:1). Matthew also records one encounter with "the Pharisees and Sadducees" in Galilee (16:1), followed by references to the "yeast [= teaching] of the Pharisees and Sadducees" (16:6, 11, 12). In other words, the Gospels report only one

CONTOURS OF THE HISTORICAL JESUS

meeting with Sadducees in Galilee and that report uses the stock phrase (in Matthew), "the Pharisees and Sadducees." From this we may surmise that the Sadducees were centered in Jerusalem, or at least Judea, and were rarely found in Galilee (except in Sepphoris, the pro-Roman Herodian capital).

The *chief priests*, similarly, were confined to Jerusalem, and references to the chief priests in the passion predictions (Matt 16:21; 20:18; and 21 times in Matthew 21–28; Mark 8:31; 10:33 and 18 times in Mark 11–15; Luke 3:2; 9:22 and 13 times in Luke 19:47–24:20). The pattern follows in John also. Jesus never meets chief priests in Galilee.

Likewise, Jesus speaks of *priests* while he is in Galilee, but meets priests only when he is in Jerusalem (Matt 8:4; 12:4–5; Mark 1:44; 2:26; Luke 1:5; 5:14; 6:4; 10:31; 17:14; 20:1). The single exception is John 1:19, where "the Jews sent priests and Levites from Jerusalem." The Levites appear only at one other place in the Gospel record, the parable of "the Good Samaritan" (Luke 10:32).

By contrast, Jesus meets *Pharisees* in Galilee on various occasions. Pharisees and scribes are also sent from Jerusalem (Matt 15:1). In John, however, Jesus never encounters Pharisees in the few scenes in which he is in Galilee (1:43–2:12; 4:45–54; 6:1–7:9), except in John 1:24, where they are sent from Jerusalem.[7]

Matthew and Luke name other groups more often than Mark or John. The *leaders of the Pharisees* appear in Luke 14:1, leaders (of the synagogue) in Matt 9:18, 23; Luke 8:41; 18:18, and elders in Luke 7:3. *Scribes* appear more often in the synoptics: Matt 7:29; 8:19; 9:3; 12:38; 15:1 (sent from Jerusalem); Mark (see 1:22) 2:6, 16; 3:22 (sent from Jerusalem); 7:1, 5; 9:11, 14; Luke 5:21, 30; 6:7; 11:53; 15:2.[8] Luke takes particular note of the educated elite: *teachers of the law* (νομοδιδάσκαλοι, 5:17) and *lawyers* (νομικοί, 7:30; 10:25; 11:45, 53; 14:3).

Herodians are named only once (Mark 3:6), and a *royal official* (βασιλικός) only in John 4:46, 49. *Tax collectors* appear in all three synoptic Gospels but not in John: Matt 9:10, 11; 10:3; 11:19; Mark 2:15, 16; Luke 5:27, 29, 30; 7:29, 34.

This review, while inadequate apart from a broader survey which would include a careful survey of Josephus in particular, suggests that Pharisees

---

[7] See C.S. Keener, *The Historical Jesus of the Gospels* (Grand Rapids: Eerdmans, 2009), 223–224.

[8] On the role of the scribes in Galilee see Freyne, *Galilee, Jesus and the Gospels* (n. 5), 201–202.

were the only Jewish religious group commonly found in Galilee in the early first century. Groups related to the temple (chief priests, priests, and Levites) typically lived in Judea. Joachim Jeremias cited *m. Ned.* 2:4, "the Galileans know naught of things devoted to (the use of) the priests" and adds "since few priests lived there."[9] Sadducees were probably rarely found outside of Judea, but Pharisees, scribes, lawyers, and teachers of the law resided in Galilee as well as Judea. Herodians or "royal officials" (courtiers, officers, and leaders of Galilee, Mark 6:21) were clients of Herod Antipas in Jesus' day, and of course tax collectors were ubiquitous. Most of the inhabitants, however, were laborers, farmers (grain, fruit, grapes, olives, nuts), craftsmen and builders (cloth, wood, stone, pottery), fishermen and fish processors, and shepherds (sheep and goats)—the πολλοί and ὄχλοι, the 'am ha-aretz.

Alexander Jannaeus (r. 103–76 B.C.) attacked the Galilean city of Asochis on a Sabbath, which suggests that it had a sizeable Jewish population even then (Josephus, *Ant.* 13.337). Herod the Great subdued Galilee (Josephus, *Ant.* 14.413, 417), but did not build cities or fortresses there, as he did in Judea and Samaria. The development of urban life in Galilee was left to Herod's son, Herod Antipas, who built Sepphoris (beginning in 3 B.C.) and Tiberias (19 C.E.). Herod Philip later transformed Bethsaida into Julia in 30 C.E. James F. Strange suggests that the reconstruction of Sepphoris by Herod Antipas marked its transition from a Greek city to "a loyalist Roman city of Jewish and gentile population," moreover "a priestly or Sadducean city" (e.g., Jose ben Illem of Sepphoris, *m. Yoma* 6:3).[10] Sean Freyne comments on the significance of these developments for understanding Jesus:

> ... the refurbishment of Sepphoris and the building of Tiberias must have marked a turning point in the Galilean economy. Their construction coincided with Jesus' public ministry and provides the most immediate backdrop to his particular emphasis on the blessedness of the destitute and the call for trust in God's provident care for all. The new Herodian class had to be accommodated with adequate allotments in order to maintain a luxurious lifestyle (cf. Matt. 11:19), and inevitably this meant pressure on the peasants.[11]

---

[9] J. Jeremias, *Jerusalem in the Time of Jesus* (trans. F.H. and C.H. Cave; Philadelphia: Fortress, 1969), 72.

[10] J.F. Strange, "Sepphoris," *ABD* 5:1091. See also J. Murphy-O'Connor, *The Holy Land: An Oxford Archaeological Guide* (Oxford and New York: Oxford University Press, 2008), 468.

[11] Freyne, "Galilee" (n. 4), 656.

CONTOURS OF THE HISTORICAL JESUS 73

Both Sepphoris and Tiberias were attacked by the Galileans during the revolt of 66–70, dramatically confirming the exploitation of the peasants that was centered in these cities (Josephus, *Life* 66–67, 301–302, 373–384).[12] In this connection, it is significant that the Gospels never record that Jesus visited Sepphoris or Tiberias, which Sean Freyne suggests was "principled, based on Jesus' views of the values represented by these cities and his own call to minister to those who had become the victims of their elitist lifestyle."[13] His ministry was among the peasants in the towns and villages (Luke 8:1; Mark 1:38): Nazareth, Capernaum, Cana, Bethsaida, Chorazin, and Nain.

Every interpretation of Jesus is conditioned largely by three issues: his relationship to Roman authority, his relationship to Judaism, and his relationship to apocalypticism. *Roman domination*, the global reality of the time, was maintained locally during Jesus' ministry by the tetrarch, Herod Antipas, in Galilee and the prefect, Pontius Pilate, in Judea. Anti-Roman sentiment had erupted in 6 C.E. in the uprising of Judas the Galilean, and continued to simmer under the surface in Galilee thereafter. Until Jesus' confrontations with the chief priests, the merchants in the temple, and Pontius Pilate in Jerusalem, he probably had little direct contact with Roman power, but he could not escape it. His mentor, John the Baptist, was arrested and killed by Herod and Herodias (Mark 6:14–29; Matt 11:2–6). When some of the Pharisees warned Jesus that Herod was seeking to kill him, Jesus called Herod "that fox" (Luke 13:32). Later, when Herod questioned Jesus (recorded only in Luke 23:6–12), Herod "was very glad," but Jesus would not answer the charges brought against him. Jesus also said that the Galileans killed by Pilate (Josephus, *Ant.* 18.85–89; *War* 2.169–177) did not deserve to die any more than any other Galilean (Luke 13:1–5). Famously, Jesus avoided the trap set for him by the Pharisees and Herodians in Jerusalem by responding that taxes should indeed be paid to Caesar: "Give to the emperor the things that are the emperor's, and to God the things that are God's" (Mark 12:17).

Jesus' response to Roman domination was not revolt (Judas the Galilean and the later zealot groups), nor complicity (the Herodians, chief priests, and to some degree probably the Sadducees), nor withdrawal (the Essenes

---

[12] For assessments of the impact of Sepphoris and Tiberias on the Galilean economy see Reed and Crossan, *Excavating Jesus* (n. 4), 151–153, 204–206; and P. Fredriksen, *Jesus of Nazareth, King of the Jews: A Jewish Life and the Emergence of Christianity* (New York: Alfred A. Knopf, 2000), 182.

[13] S. Freyne, *Jesus, a Jewish Galilean* (London: T. & T. Clark, 2004), 144.

74 R. ALAN CULPEPPER

at Qumran). Instead, Jesus called the people to a radical renewal of their identity as the people of Israel in covenant with the God of their ancestors. In this respect, Jesus echoed the call of the Maccabees to their ancestral faith, while rejecting the call to arms (cf. 1Macc 2:19–22). He called the Galileans back to the higher claim on their lives: not Rome but God's dominion.

As a Galilean Jew, Jesus was steeped in the Scripture and lore of Judaism. His sympathies lay with the peasants, the '*am ha-aretz*, however, so he broke with the Pharisees over issues that had become important, in no small measure probably as a result of Hillel's influence, especially purity, ritual washings, and restricted table fellowship.[14] Jesus looked neither to a new Davidic kingdom (as had the Maccabees, the Hasmoneans, and the *Psalms of Solomon*) nor to a people living in priestly purity (the Pharisees and the Essenes). As a pious wonder worker, Jesus stood more nearly in the tradition of the charismatic Hasidim in Galilee (Ḥanina ben Dosa and Ḥoni the Circle-drawer) and his mentor, John the Baptist.[15] Contrary to what we know of the Hasidim, however, Jesus preached the Kingdom of God as the central rubric of his message and ministry, and contrary to John the Baptist he adopted open fellowship rather than an ascetic lifestyle as a hallmark of his message (Matt 11:18–20; Luke 5:33).

According to Luke, Jesus was raised in a family that traveled to Jerusalem for the festivals (Luke 2:41). He continued to do so as an adult (John 2:13, 23; 5:1; 7:10; 10:22–23; 12:1, 12), but opposed the commercialization and politicization of the temple (Mark 11:15–17; 14:58; 15:29; John 2:13–22). He even predicted the destruction of the temple (Mark 13:2), but his opposition to the temple was not based on an alternative calendar and priestly lineage, issues that lay at the base of the anti-temple ideology of the Essenes. On the other hand, the intent of Jesus' action in the temple is debated and open to various interpretations. David Fiensy argues that Jesus was a zealot for the temple, but that is hard to square with the saying, "I will destroy this house" (Mark 14:57–58; 15:39; John 2:19–20).[16]

---

[14] For different perspectives on Jesus and purity see M.J. Borg, *Meeting Jesus Again for the First Time* (New York: HarperSanFrancisco, 1994), 50–58; and Fredriksen, *Jesus of Nazareth* (n. 12), 197–207; D.A. Fiensy, *Jesus the Galilean: Soundings in a First Century Life* (Piscataway, N.J.: Gorgias, 2007), 163–186; Dunn, *Jesus Remembered* (n. 3), 573–577; and Keener, *The Historical Jesus of the Gospels* (n. 7), 221–222.

[15] Vermès, *Jesus the Jew* (n. 1), 68–80, esp. 79; J.D. Crossan, *The Historical Jesus: The Life of a Mediterranean Jewish Peasant* (New York: HarperSanFrancisco, 1991), 142–156; Keener, *The Historical Jesus of the Gospels* (n. 7), 40–41, 242–243.

[16] Fiensy, *Jesus the Galilean* (n. 14), 227.

CONTOURS OF THE HISTORICAL JESUS

E.P. Sanders contended that Jesus carried out a symbolic action to indicate "that the end was at hand and that the temple would be destroyed, so that the new and perfect temple might arise."[17] Sean Freyne, it seems to me, moves in the right direction when he seeks to understand Jesus' temple demonstration in the context of his Galilean ministry, "not least through his deeds of power"; "the temple-cleansing episode in Jerusalem spelled out in symbolic action their real significance."[18] As Crossan put it, "his symbolic destruction simply actualized what he had already said in his teachings, effected in his healings, and realized in his mission of open commensality."[19] Jesus preached a kingdom that lifted up the oppressed and included the marginalized. The temple cult, on the other hand, was identified with the aristocracy in Jerusalem and promoted religious practices based on purity, sacrifices, and social boundaries.

The popular hope for a new Davidic Messiah who would overthrow Roman domination was closely aligned with apocalypticism—the hope for a cataclysmic end to ordinary history, the coming of the Messiah, and the inauguration of the blessings of the age to come, all according to God's predetermined plan (see esp. *1Enoch* 37–71; *4Ezra* 7:28–44; *2Bar* 39:7–40:2; and the *War Scroll* [1QM]). Jesus announced the imminent coming of the Kingdom and called for the people to prepare themselves for it. Jesus was steeped in the prophets. His teaching drew on Deutero-Isaiah, Daniel, and Zechariah in particular and was framed in the expectation of the coming Kingdom, but the elements one finds in apocalyptic literature (animal symbolism, cosmic signs, deterministic view of history) are muted in the Gospels. Jesus' works often recalled those of Elijah.[20] Within this context of eschatological expectation, Jesus emphasized instead the call to prepare for the coming Kingdom by helping the poor, healing the sick, feeding the hungry, caring for widows and children, and breaking down social barriers. Even the law could be re-interpreted when it impeded the fulfillment of this prophetic vision of the covenant community. This new ethic, which called for the end of the status quo and the establishment of a new community order, directly challenged the delicate alliance forged

---

[17] E.P. Sanders, *Jesus and Judaism* (Philadelphia: Fortress, 1985), 75; cf. Keener, *The Historical Jesus of the Gospels* (n. 7), 291–294.

[18] Freyne, *Galilee, Jesus and the Gospels* (n. 5), 236.

[19] Crossan, *The Historical Jesus* (n. 15), 360; cf. N.T. Wright, *Jesus and the Victory of God* (Minneapolis: Fortress, 1996), 417.

[20] S. Freyne, *Galilee and Gospel* (Boston and Leiden: Brill, 2002), 267: "the role of Elijah as miracle worker on behalf of the marginalised in the environs of Galilee seems quite apposite also in terms of the understanding of Jesus' ministry."

76 R. ALAN CULPEPPER

between the priestly elite and Roman authority, and therefore led quickly to Jesus' crucifixion.

2. Jesus' Activities

Returning to the summary in Matt 4:23–25, we notice that Matthew identifies three characteristic activities (teaching, preaching, and healing) to which we may add a fourth (eating, which appears regularly in all four Gospels, and especially in Luke). These activities recur so frequently in the Gospels and are presented as so typical of his ministry that if Jesus did not engage in them, then we know nothing of his activities. A brief survey of these four recurring activities extends the "contours" of the historical Jesus.[21]

2.1 *Teaching*

Before rabbis were recognized as having an official status, Jesus was called "rabbi" (Matthew 4 times; Mark 4 times; John 8 times), "rabbouni" (Mark 10:51; John 20:16), and "teacher" (Matthew 8 times; Mark 12 times; Luke 13 times; John 6 times) by virtually all who addressed him. He taught in both formal and informal settings, on the road, by the sea, when crowds gathered around him, and in private settings with the disciples. He also taught in the synagogues on a regular basis. Luke says that Jesus read from Isaiah in the synagogue in Nazareth before offering a homily on the text that incensed the crowd. Mark says that in Capernaum "they were astounded at his teaching, for he taught them as one having authority, and not as the scribes" (1:22).

Jesus was an itinerant teacher who traveled around the towns and villages. Although Jesus seems to have made Capernaum the home base for his excursions, Mark pointedly records that he would not remain there (1:38). "He went throughout Galilee" (Matt 4:23), he "went about all the cities and villages" (Matt 9:35; cf. 10:11; Mark 6:6, 56; 8:27; Luke 5:17; 8:1; 9:6, 12; 13:22).

Like other teachers, Jesus gathered disciples and passed on his teachings by word and example. Unlike other teachers, however, he called his

---

[21] See C.A. Evans, "Authenticating the Activities of Jesus," in B. Chilton and C.A. Evans, eds., *Authenticating the Activities of Jesus* (Leiden: Brill, 2002), 3–29, who builds on the work of E.P. Sanders and N.T. Wright.

CONTOURS OF THE HISTORICAL JESUS

disciples to a personal relationship rather than to his teachings: "Follow me." As Jesus moved among the Galilean peasants, he taught them using parables that drew on ordinary activities (sowing, reaping, threshing, grinding, fishing, baking) and the everyday realia (seeds and soil, paths, rocks, thorns, fish, nets, plants, trees, birds) in rural Galilee. His teaching engaged his hearers where they lived, gave significance to the ordinary, invited connections between the earthly and the divine, and typically challenged those who heard him to respond decisively in ways they would determine. At other times he was explicit about the response: sell all you have, give to the poor, remove the beam from your own eye, be servant of all. He also taught in memorable, pithy sayings, proverbs, aphorisms, and riddles, many of which employ irony, hyperbole, and antitheses. He used heuristic questions effectively.[22] All of these didactic forms are found among other Jewish and Greco-Roman teachers and philosophers, but in the recorded tradition of Jesus' teachings they reach a high level of rhetorical force and polish, and characterize Jesus' teachings in an unparalleled way.

2.2 *Preaching*

Jesus' preaching can hardly be separated from his teaching. The facile answer is that he preached the Kingdom of God. Matthew uses teaching and preaching in close conjunction (see Matt 4:23; 9:35; 11:1). The Gospel of John, which refers to the Kingdom only twice (3:3, 5), never uses the verb κηρύσσω. Matthew characterizes the message Jesus preaches as "the good news of the Kingdom" (4:23; 9:35; 10:7; 24:14). Mark speaks of simply "the good news" (13:10; 14:9) or "the good news of God" (1:14). Luke uses the more definitive formula, "the Gospel of the Kingdom of God" (8:1; 9:2), and the risen Lord commissions the disciples to preach "repentance and forgiveness of sins" (24:47).

James D.G. Dunn reminds interpreters that implicit in the term "the Kingdom of God" is a larger story that embraces the relationship of Israel as God's people to Yahweh as Israel's God, Israel's vindication, an age of prosperity, the coming of a Messiah, renewal of the covenant and building of a new temple, cosmic disturbances, the defeat of Satan, the final judgment, and the resurrection.[23] For Jesus, devotion to God's Kingdom

---

[22] R.A. Culpepper, *Mark* (Smyth & Helwys Bible Commentaries; Macon: Smyth & Helwys, 2007), 300.

[23] Dunn, *Jesus Remembered* (n. 3), 389–390, 393–396.

78 R. ALAN CULPEPPER

(rather than the political dominion of Rome or the sacerdotal dominion of the Jerusalem priesthood) required purity of heart rather than ritual purity, forgiveness of debts and offences (even seventy times seven times if necessary, Matt 18:22), responsiveness to the needs of others even if it required plucking grain on the Sabbath (Mark 2:23–28), healing on the Sabbath (Mark 3:1–6), contact with a hemorrhaging woman (Mark 5:24–34), receiving a child (Mark 9:36–37; 10:13–16), and protecting women from divorce (Matt 5:31–32). Indeed, Jesus set a standard for the place of women in the community that the early church, functioning in Greco-Roman and Jewish surroundings, found hard to maintain (see Paul's efforts at accommodation in 1Cor 7:1–16; 11:2–16, and the still later problems caused by widows in the church in 1Tim 5:3–16).

2.3 Healing

Josephus records that Jesus was a "wise man" who "wrought surprising feats and was a teacher" (*Ant.* 18.63).[24] In the Gospels Jesus is remembered as a traditional healer and an exorcist who had the power to cleanse lepers, drive away a fever, stop a hemorrhage, cast out unclean spirits, and even raise the dead.[25] Even if these reports have been exaggerated or embellished over time, Jesus' healings and exorcisms were integral to his announcement of the Kingdom of God. Marcus Borg agrees:

> Behind this picture of Jesus as a healer and exorcist, I affirm a historical core. In common with the majority of contemporary Jesus scholars, I see the claim that Jesus performed paranormal healings and exorcisms as history remembered. Indeed, more healing stories are told about Jesus than about any other figure in the Jewish tradition. He must have been a remarkable healer.[26]

John P. Meier agrees with the late Morton Smith that "without his miracles, Jesus would never have attracted both the enthusiasm and the opposition that marked and finally ended his public life."[27] Regardless of one's view of miracles, the Gospels present Jesus as one whose activities gained for him a reputation as a healer and a wonder worker. Jesus' healings restored the afflicted to their place in society, demonstrated the power of the Spirit

---

[24] On the authenticity of this source, see J.P. Meier, *A Marginal Jew*, vol. 1: *The Roots of the Problem and the Person* (New York: Doubleday, 1991), 56–69.

[25] On Jesus' work as a traditional healer, see B. Malina and R. Rohrbaugh, *Social-Science Commentary on the Synoptic Gospels* (Minneapolis: Fortress, 1992), 70–72.

[26] M.J. Borg and N.T. Wright, *The Meaning of Jesus: Two Visions* (New York: HarperSanFrancisco, 1999), 66.

[27] J.P. Meier, *A Marginal Jew*, vol. 2: *Mentor, Message, and Miracles* (New York: Doubleday, 1994), 3.

CONTOURS OF THE HISTORICAL JESUS

that was active in him, and constituted an attack on the dehumanizing power of evil (understood in the first century as Satan).

2.4 *Eating*

Meals were important occasions for defining relationship and status. The Pharisees added to these considerations the maintenance of purity. Jesus challenged both status and purity customs by eating with tax collectors, outcasts, and "sinners" (Mark 2:15–17). Especially in the Gospel of Luke, Jesus seems to be always on his way to or from a meal![28] Perhaps not coincidentally Luke also pays the most attention to the poor, women, and tax collectors. The meal scenes in the Gospels dramatically define the new social order of the Kingdom, and the contrast is striking when compared to Pliny the Younger's description of a banquet:

> Some very elegant dishes were served up to himself [the host] and a few more of the company; while those which were placed before the rest were cheap and paltry. He had apportioned in small flagons three different sorts of wine; but you are not to suppose it was that the guests might take their choice: on the contrary, that they might not choose at all. One was for himself and me; the next for his friends of lower status (for you must know that he measures out his friendship according to the degrees of quality); and the third for his own freed-men and mine. (Pliny the Younger, *Letters* 2.6)

In contrast, Jesus defends the "woman of the city" who anoints him at the Pharisee's home (Luke 7:36–50). A parable images the Kingdom of God as a great banquet to which "the poor, the crippled, the blind, and the lame" are all invited (Luke 14:15–24, esp. verse 21), and the risen Lord is recognized "in the breaking of bread" (Luke 24:35).

3. JESUS' KNOWLEDGE OF GOD: "OUR FATHER"

Jesus' teaching, preaching, healing, and eating were all means of conveying the nature of the Kingdom he announced. Not only were these means of his itinerant ministry distinctive, so was the essential vision of his ministry. Drawing deeply upon the Scriptures, Jesus' message of the Kingdom of God grew out of his understanding of God, which in turn was also rooted in biblical motifs, some of which were muted in the Judaism of his time: God's love (*'ahavah*, ἀγάπη), justice (*mishpat*, δικαιοσύνη), and grace (*hesed*, χάρις). Jesus prayed to God as a Father whose love exceeded

---

[28] R.J. Karris, *Luke: Artist and Theologian, Luke's Passion as Literature* (New York: Paulist, 1985), 47.

80   R. ALAN CULPEPPER

that of any earthly parent. If an earthly parent would not give his child
a snake or a scorpion rather than the food (fish, egg) for which the child
asked, how much more will the heavenly Father grant the petitions of
those who ask him (Luke 11:11–13; Matt 7:9–10)? It is now clear that while
Jesus was remembered for praying to God as ἀββᾶ (Rom 8:15; Gal 4:6), it
was not unusual to pray to God as "Father," contrary to Joachim Jeremias,
who tried to drive too deep a wedge between Jesus' prayer to God as ἀββᾶ
and contemporary Jewish references to God as Father.[29] Davies and Allison list the following:[30]

> For you are our Father;...you, O Lord, are our Father (Isa 63:16; cf. 64:8);
> he is our Father and he is God forever (Tob 13:4);
> On whom can we stay ourselves?—on our Father in heaven (*m. Sotah*
> 9:15);
> R. Akiba said: "...Your Father in heaven" (*m. Yoma* 8:9);
>
> When the world was in need of rain, the rabbis used to send school-
> children to him [Ḥanan, Ḥoni the Circle-drawer's grandson and cousin of
> Abba Ḥilkiah], who seized the train of his cloak and said to him, "Abba,
> Abba, give us rain!" He said to God: "Lord of the universe, render a service
> to those who cannot distinguish between the Abba who gives rain and
> the Abba who does not." (*b. Ta'an.* 23b)

Jesus built an understanding of God on the base of a term already present
in the Judaism of his day. That God was known as a loving God is also
clear from biblical and early Jewish references:

> If you heed these ordinances, by diligently observing them, the Lord your
> God will maintain with you the covenant loyalty that he swore to your
> ancestors; he will love you, bless you, and multiply you. (Deut 7:12–13)
>
> The beloved of the Lord rests in safety—
> the High God surrounds him all day long—
> the beloved rests between his shoulders. (Deut 33:12)
> ...for the Lord reproves the one he loves,
> as a father the son in whom he delights. (Prov 3:12)

---

[29] J. Jeremias, "Abba," in idem, *The Prayers of Jesus* (trans. J. Bowden; Philadelphia:
Fortress, 1967), 19, "In short, although the community prays to God as Father in the
words אבינו מלכנו, although the individual occasionally speaks of God as his heavenly
Father...there is as yet no evidence in the literature of ancient Palestinian Judaism that
'my Father' is used as a personal address to God."

[30] W.D. Davies and D.C. Allison, *The Gospel according to Saint Matthew* (ICC; London
and New York: T. & T. Clark, 2000), 600–602; cf. Vermès, *Jesus the Jew* (n. 1), 210–213.

CONTOURS OF THE HISTORICAL JESUS

In addition, Song of Solomon is widely regarded as an allegory of God's love for Israel, and Hosea lived out God's steadfast love for Israel. The "dynamic" of piety is love, a "divine gift" (*Letter of Aristeas* 229). And R. Akiba said, "Beloved is man for he was created in the image [of God]; still greater is the love in that it was made known to him that he was created in the image of God" (*m. 'Abot* 3:15).

Jesus announced God's love to those who lived on the margins of society: lepers, tax collectors, women, and children. His popularity with the crowds was based in no small measure on his message of God's unconditional love, even for those who were marginalized by Jewish society for their failure to keep the commandments prized by the Pharisees. The leper he cleansed, he commanded to show himself to the priests, "as a testimony to them" (Mark 1:44); to the tax collector he said, "Today salvation has come to this house" (Luke 19:9); he called the hemorrhaging woman "daughter" (Mark 5:34); to the bent woman he said, "Woman, you are free from your ailment" (Luke 13:12); and when his disciples prevented others from bringing their children to him, Jesus reprimanded them and said, "Let the little children come to me; do not stop them; for it is to such as these that the Kingdom of God belongs" (Mark 10:14).

To appreciate how radical such actions may have appeared in his context, one must unfortunately rehearse a series of references that show that some religious leaders during Jesus' time had failed to grasp the implications of God's love for their community ethic.

> And let no person smitten with any human impurity whatever enter the Assembly of God. And every person smitten with these impurities, unfit to occupy a place in the midst of the Congregation, and every (person) smitten in his flesh, paralysed in his feet or hands, lame or blind or deaf or dumb or smitten in his flesh with any blemish visible to the eye, or any aged person that totters and is unable to stand firm in the midst of the Congregation: let these persons not en[ter] to take their place in the midst of the Congregation of men of renown ... (1QSa 2:3–8)[31]

> R. Dosa ben Harkinas: "Morning sleep, mid-day wine, chattering with children, and tarrying in places where men of the common people assemble destroy a man." (*m. 'Abot* 3:11)

> Jose b. Johanan of Jerusalem: "Talk not much with womankind." (*m. 'Abot* 1:5)

---

[31] A. Dupont-Sommer, *The Writings from Qumran* (trans. G. Vermès; Cleveland: World, 1961), 107–108.

82   R. ALAN CULPEPPER

> He who loves his son will whip him often, so that he may rejoice at the way
> he turns out.... Pamper a child, and he will terrorize you; play with him and
> he will grieve you. (Sir 30:1, 9)

If such sentiments were at all typical, we can readily understand why
Jesus' attention to those who had no standing created such excitement
and met with a ready response from the Galilean peasants.[32]

Jesus announced the imminent coming of the Kingdom of God: "There
are some standing here who will not taste death until they see that the
Kingdom of God has come with power" (Mark 9:1). He called for trust in
God to deliver Israel and fulfill the promises of the covenant. While Jesus
preached and taught the ethic of a new community based on justice for
the poor and oppressed; dignity and care for women, children, the sick
and disabled; piety oriented around love, inclusion, and community rather
than purity, privilege, or ritual; he also pointed ahead to God's future
deliverance of the faithful and judgment on the wicked. Jesus' eschatology
was rooted in the prophets of Israel, as was his ethic. While we may not
dismiss the future aspects of his teachings on the Kingdom, we may also
note that his eschatology was restrained and rejected the search for signs
and the calculation of times (Matt 12:38–39; 16:1–4; 24:3, 30; Acts 1:6–8).

The appeal of Jesus' proclamation of the Kingdom of God, therefore,
can probably be attributed to the hope that it gave Galilean peasants; its
roots in the writings of Israel's prophets; the consistency of Jesus' teachings and his challenge to societal conventions; its novelty in relation to
the alternatives offered by the Pharisees, Sadducees, priests, Essenes,
and zealot movements; and the healings and exorcisms he performed.
Devotion to the Kingdom demanded justice and confrontation of the
powers that exploited the people, so it is not surprising that Jesus eventually felt compelled to protest the corruption of the temple in Jerusalem,
which ultimately precipitated the plot to execute him as a dangerous
troublemaker (λῃστής).

4. JESUS' SELF-UNDERSTANDING

Since I first read James D.G. Dunn's *Jesus and the Spirit* in the mid-1970s,
Jesus' experience of sonship and the Spirit has seemed to me to be central

---

[32] See E. and F. Stagg, *Woman in the World of Jesus* (Philadelphia: Westminster, 1978).

CONTOURS OF THE HISTORICAL JESUS

to his self-understanding.[33] Dunn's conclusion is that *"Jesus thought of himself as God's son and as anointed by the eschatological Spirit, because in prayer he experienced God as Father and in ministry he experienced a power to heal which he could only understand as the power of the end-time and an inspiration to proclaim a message which he could only understand as the gospel of the end-time."*[34]

We may take Dunn's two points in reverse order. The assertion that Jesus was conscious of the Spirit of God working through him rests heavily on Matt 12:28/Luke 11:20, of which Dunn says, "if we cannot be sure that the Q saying preserved in Matt. 12.28/Luke 11.20 is a genuine saying of Jesus, we might as well give up all hope of rediscovering the historical Jesus, the man or his message."[35]

> But if it is
> by the finger of God (Luke 11:20; cf. Exod 8:19)
> by the Spirit of God (Matt 12:28)
> that I cast out demons, then the Kingdom of God has come upon you.

The basis assumed for this assertion is crucial: it was because of the experience of the exorcisms that Jesus was aware that the Kingdom of God had come, at least in the sense that it was at work through him.

Jesus' experience of sonship was the corollary of his knowledge of God as Father. Jesus' experience of sonship rests primarily on two points in the Gospels, his use of *abba* and the logion in Matt 11:27 and Luke 10:22. We have already discussed the significance of Jesus' use of *abba* briefly. It appears that Jesus' followers remembered his use of *abba* as distinctive, though not unique.[36] He taught his followers to pray "our Father." Dunn adds, "but even then he seems to have thought of their relationship as somehow *dependent* on his own, as somehow a *consequence* of his own."[37] This form of address recognized the character of God as that of a deity whose love and benevolence is best understood in human terms through our experience of the relationship of loving father and devoted child. Furthermore, through Jesus' example and teaching his followers came to a new appreciation for the possibility of their experience of God, not merely through their corporate identity as Israel, the people of God, but

---

[33] J.D.G. Dunn, *Jesus and the Spirit* (Philadelphia: Westminster, 1975), esp. chapters 2 and 3.

[34] Ibid., 67 (italics Dunn's).

[35] Ibid., 44.

[36] Ibid., 26.

[37] Ibid. (italics Dunn's).

84 R. ALAN CULPEPPER

individually in light of and as a consequence of Jesus' relationship to God. It was a short step, therefore, to the attribution of the Christological title, "Son of God," to Jesus, especially when one recognizes the use of this title in Jewish texts and in Roman political rhetoric.[38]

Jesus' parables generally reflect his self-understanding as agent of the Kingdom.[39] More specifically, the parable of the wicked tenants (Mark 12:1–9; Matt 21:33–41; Luke 20:9–19; and Gospel of *Thomas* 65) supplies further evidence of Jesus' self-understanding as the Son sent by God to complete the work of the prophets.[40] Efforts to identify an original, non-allegorical story are unconvincing. Neither Jesus nor the early church could have told such a story about a vineyard, its owner, the rejection of the owner's servants, and the sending of the owner's son without it being understood allegorically in light of the "Song of the Vineyard" in Isaiah 5. The alternatives are either that the parable is entirely a construction of the early church, or that it belongs to the authentic Jesus material, even given its allegorical sense. Unless one is predisposed, categorically, to disallow that Jesus used allegory or any self-reference in his teachings, a decision about the authenticity of the parable will rest heavily on whether the reference to "a son" reflects Jesus' own self-understanding or grows out of early Christian confessions.

James H. Charlesworth has collected fifteen uses of the term "son" in reference to an ideal figure in early Jewish literature, among them Sir 4:10; *1En.* 105:2; *T. Levi* 4:2; Wisd 2:18; *4Ezra* 7:28; 13:37, 52.[41] These references show that the designation "son" for an ideal or redeemer figure was current in first-century Judaism, so the reference to the "son" in the parable need not indicate that it originated in Gentile Christianity.

The parable of the wicked tenants belongs, therefore, to a small group of sayings in the synoptics in which Jesus speaks of "the son" in a self-referential sense:

Mark 13:32   But about that day or hour no one knows, neither the angels in heaven, nor the Son, but only the Father.

---

[38] See M. Hengel, *The Son of God* (trans. J. Bowden; Philadelphia: Fortress, 1976), 30, 41–56.

[39] See esp. G.R. Beasley-Murray, *Jesus and the Kingdom of God* (Grand Rapids: Eerdmans, 1986), 144–146.

[40] The following discussion is adapted from my article "Parable as Commentary: The Twice-Given Vineyard (Luke 20:9–16)," *PRSt* 26, no. 2 (1999): 147–168.

[41] J.H. Charlesworth, *Jesus within Judaism* (New York: Doubleday, 1988), 149–151.

CONTOURS OF THE HISTORICAL JESUS

Matt 11:27   All things have been handed over to me by my Father, and no one knows the Son except the Father, and no one knows the Father except the Son and anyone to whom the Son chooses to reveal him. (par. Luke 10:22)[42]

In the Gospel of John, the sayings in 3:35, 5:19, and 8:35–36 bear some resemblance to these synoptic sayings.[43] John 8:35–36, like the parable, contrasts the son and the slave. The other Johannine sayings deal with the relationship between the Father and the Son and the special knowledge it conveys to the Son. The parable of the wicked tenants stands alone in the synoptics, however, as a saying in which Jesus refers to his role as the Son (1) in a parable, (2) following in the line of the prophets, and (3) predicting that he would die a violent death. If authentic, therefore, the parable provides valuable evidence of Jesus' self-understanding and his awareness that his activities would ultimately lead to his death by violence. Like Wolter, therefore, I too end up at "the self-interpretation of Jesus," which while inaccessible to us is at least implicit in the parables and teachings edited and preserved by the evangelists.

Conclusion

The question of the historical Jesus is both endlessly fascinating and frustratingly elusive. Every analysis is in the end subjective, but the Gospels supply four early accounts of his life and teaching (five with Thomas). We also have a wealth of information about the time and region in which he lived. Neither can we escape the importance of the study of the historical Jesus for both historical and theological reasons. Recent research has given us a clearer understanding of the context of his ministry in Galilee that allows us to see what Jesus' proclamation of the Kingdom of God might have meant in his Jewish, Galilean context in the period of Roman domination. Whatever we think about the historical Jesus, therefore, our reconstructions will continue to be tested by study of the context of Jesus' ministry and study of the records produced by the early church.

---

[42] See Dunn's discussion of these verses in *Jesus and the Spirit* (n. 32), 26–37.

[43] Regarding John 5:19 esp. see my essay, "Jesus Sayings in the Johannine Discourses: A Proposal," in P.N. Anderson et al., eds., *John, Jesus, and History*, vol. 3 (Atlanta: SBL, forthcoming).

JESUS AS SAVIOR AND PROTECTOR—BEFORE EASTER AND AFTER

Craig A. Evans

Michael Wolter asks, "Which Jesus is the Real Jesus?" In light of the great diversity of answers that scholars have offered over the last two centuries it is a very appropriate and very pressing question. I am especially interested in the perceptive question that Wolter raises in the first section of his paper: "How important is this Jesus, reconstructed by means of historical analysis, for Christian faith?" The answer, it seems to me, is unavoidably ambiguous, for in one sense historical analysis is very important, but in another sense it really is not. Historical analysis is important, for at the heart of Christian faith is a story, a story about people who lived long ago and experienced events that changed how they understood God and life. Of course, historical analysis is always heuristic and tentative. It is always subject to revision and falsification. New hypotheses will be presented and new data will be uncovered, either confirming, modifying, or negating these hypotheses. Christian faith possesses a continuity that every provisional historical analysis does not. Historical analysis nevertheless plays an important role.

I want to take up what I think is important in historical analysis of Jesus, that is, important for what Christians believe about him. Is there meaningful overlap between historical analysis and faith? There may be. Much of Wolter's paper is given over to an exploration of a "third" possibility, which investigates "the story of Jesus in the light of the Easter faith."[1] This strikes me as a very promising approach. It may well uncover important areas where faith and history overlap. I shall explore one facet that almost everyone agrees was part of Jesus' pre-Easter activities and teachings. This is a facet that continued to come to expression in the life of the early Church and apparently played an important role in the early Church's apologetic. But in my opinion it is a facet whose relevance for Christian faith has not been adequately understood.

I refer to Jesus' reputation as exorcist and healer. Almost no serious historian or New Testament scholar doubts that the historical Jesus enjoyed

---

[1] Here Wolter has quoted R. Hoppe, *Von der Krippe an den Galgen* (Stuttgart: Katholisches Bibelwerk, 1996), 19.

88   CRAIG A. EVANS

the reputation of exorcist and healer. Indeed, almost in passing E.P. Sanders remarks that Jesus attracted large crowds *because he was able to heal*.[2] The evidence that Jesus was viewed by his contemporaries as a healer is substantial. First, Jesus is depicted as a healer in all four of the first-century Gospels. Specific healings and exorcisms are recounted, as well as a number of summaries (e.g., Mark 3:10; 6:53–56). Moreover, early Christian preaching presupposed Jesus' works of power as much as his resurrection (e.g., Acts 2:22, "Jesus of Nazareth, a man attested to you by God with mighty works and wonders and signs which God did through him in your midst, as you yourselves know...;" 10:38, "...how he went about doing good and healing all that were oppressed by the devil, for God was with him").

Secondly, some of the exorcisms and healings were controversial. Jesus is accused of violating the Sabbath (see Mark 1:21–28; 3:1–6; Luke 13:10–17; 14:1–6; John 5:1–18; 9:1–23) or even blasphemy (see Mark 2:1–12). He is also accused of being in league with Satan (Mark 3:20–30). If Jesus performed no healings or exorcisms, it is difficult to understand why early Christians would invent this sort of tradition. Many of the healings and exorcisms prompted amazed crowds to sing Jesus' praises (Mark 1:28, 37, 45; 2:12; 7:37; Luke 7:16–17). Why invent stories about Jesus being accused of sorcery or of breaking the Sabbath? After all, his crucifixion had nothing to do with these things. There was no need to create a series of healing stories, especially controversial ones, to deflect criticisms based on Jesus' execution.

Third, non-Christian writers knew of Jesus' reputation as healer and exorcist. The earliest and most important witness in this category is

---

[2] E.P. Sanders, *Jesus and Judaism* (London: SCM, 1985), 164. Sanders believes that it was the healing and exorcism more than the teaching that attracted crowds. Given the health and medical needs of people in the first century, it is not hard to imagine large crowds pressing Jesus for healing. Sanders is probably correct. The perspective of Sanders is fully in step with the prudent position articulated by Bruce Chilton. In an essay published only one year after the appearance of *Jesus and Judaism*, Chilton comments that "...historical enquiry must...rest content with a reasoned, exegetical account of how what is written came to be, and how that influences our appreciation of the received form of the text. The historical question centers fundamentally on what people perceived, and how they acted on their perception; the question of how ancient experience relates to modern experience is a distinct, interpretive matter." See B.D. Chilton, "Exorcism and History: Mark 1:21–28," in D. Wenham and C. Blomberg, eds., *The Miracles of Jesus* (Gospel Perspectives 6; Sheffield: JSOT Press, 1986), 253–271, here 265. The approach that Sanders and Chilton have taken to this subject is quite refreshing and reflects a different way of thinking in the so-called Third Quest. I offer an analysis of this change of thinking in my essay, "Life-of-Jesus Research and the Eclipse of Mythology," *TS* 54 (1993): 3–36.

JESUS AS SAVIOR AND PROTECTOR—BEFORE EASTER AND AFTER   89

Josephus (*ca.* 37–100 C.E.), who refers to Jesus as a "doer of wondrous deeds (παραδόξων ἔργων ποιητής)" (*Ant.* 18.63–64).[3] This description is at best ambiguous; it may even contain a hint of sarcasm.[4] In any event, it is an important early non-Christian witness to Jesus' reputation as healer and exorcist.

There is a fourth line of evidence that I find especially compelling. It is the observation that healers and exorcists were invoking the name of Jesus, *even during the pre-Easter period, before the proclamation of the resurrection.* In the Jewish setting, this is extraordinary. The passage that I have in mind is found in the Gospel of Mark:

> [38]John said to him, "Teacher, we saw a man casting out demons in your name, and we forbade him, because he was not following us." [39]But Jesus said, "Do not forbid him; for no one who does a mighty work in my name will be able soon after to speak evil of me. [40]For he that is not against us is for us. (Mark 9:38–40)

The probability that this is authentic pre-Easter tradition is seen in the remarkable response of Jesus, which stands in tension with early Christian teaching and practice, in which only *Christian* leaders, especially the apostles, have the authority to invoke the name of Jesus for purposes of healing and exorcism (or religious proclamation). Whereas Jesus seems to have no problem with an outsider making use of his name, the post-Easter community apparently could not accept such a degree of ecumenism. This point is dramatically illustrated in Acts, in the story of the young slave girl with the python spirit (Acts 16:16–18) and in the story of the seven sons of Sceva, the Jewish high priest, who "undertook to pronounce the name of the Lord Jesus over those who had evil spirits, saying, 'I adjure you by the

---

[3] Although there is little doubt that the passage has been tampered with, most scholars believe that most of it, including the small part that I have quoted, was composed by Josephus. For a careful, balanced discussion of the passage, see J.P. Meier, "Jesus in Josephus: A Modest Proposal," *CBQ* 52 (1990): 76–103.

[4] See G.N. Stanton, "Jesus of Nazareth: A Magician and a False Prophet who Deceived God's People?," in J.B. Green and M. Turner, eds., *Jesus of Nazareth: Lord and Christ. Essays on the Historical Jesus and New Testament Christology* (Grand Rapids: Eerdmans, 1994), 164–180, esp. 169–171. After careful study of the passage about Jesus in Josephus, Stanton says, "In short, in the *Testimonium* Jesus is said to have been a miracle worker/magician who impressed rather gullible people, and led many Jews (and many Greeks) astray" (171). Stanton interprets this language in the light of similar criticisms found in later Jewish sources. See also my discussion, "Historical Jesus Research: The Challenge of Sources and Methods," in A.B. McGowan and K.H. Richards, eds., *Method & Meaning: Essays on New Testament Interpretation in Honor of Harold W. Attridge* (SBLRBS 67; Atlanta: SBL, 2011), 5–20, esp. 10–12.

CRAIG A. EVANS

Jesus whom Paul preaches'" (Acts 19:13–20). In both cases the outsiders who proclaim Jesus meet with disaster. In the case of the slave girl, her familiar spirit is cast out and she loses her fortune-telling powers (and her owners lose all hope of profit). In the case of the sons of Sceva, the evil spirit turns on them and drives them into the street naked and wounded, utterly defeated and ashamed. The point in Acts is quite clear: Not just anyone can invoke the name of Jesus, certainly not professional soothsayers and exorcists.[5] Given the high probability that we have in the book of Acts the post-Easter Christian perspective, it is likewise quite probable that the story found in Mark 9 represents genuine pre-Easter tradition.[6]

The uniqueness of the story in Mark 9 is seen in that the exorcist outside of Jesus' following has invoked the name of Jesus rather than that of Solomon or some other Old Testament worthy. The example of Eleazar the exorcist, whose work is described by Josephus, is illustrative. Eleazar makes use of a ring and root, placed under the nose of the possessed person, and then invokes the name of Solomon and recites an incantation supposedly composed by Israel's famous monarch (*Ant.* 8.46–49). Solomon's legendary reputation is well attested in late antiquity, not

---

[5] See R.D. Kotansksy, "Greek Exorcistic Amulets," in M.W. Meyer and P. Mirecki, eds., *Ancient Magic and Ritual Power* (Religions in the Graeco-Roman World 129; Leiden: Brill, 2001), 243–277, esp. 243–245. Kotansky observes how true to magical practice, as seen in the magical papyri and lamellae, is the episode recounted in Acts 19. The defeat of Simon Magus in Acts 8 makes the same point: No outsider can "purchase" the Holy Spirit and then use its power for his own ends. See also H.-J. Klauck, *Magic and Paganism in Early Christianity: The World of the Acts of the Apostles* (Minneapolis: Fortress, 2003), 65–79 (slave girl with python spirit), 99–102 (sons of Sceva).

[6] See R. Pesch, *Das Markusevangelium*, vol. 2 (HTKNT 2/2; Freiburg et al.: Herder, 1977), 107; R.T. France, *The Gospel of Mark* (NIGTC; Grand Rapids: Eerdmans; Carlisle: Paternoster, 2002), 376. The options are judiciously weighed in J. Marcus, *Mark 8–16* (AB 27A; New Haven and London: Yale University Press, 2009), 685–686. Marcus seems to lean in favor of the authenticity of the tradition. For a notable exception, see A.Y. Collins, *Mark* (Hermeneia; Minneapolis: Fortress, 2007), 448. Collins observes that the disciple John complains of the exorcist because he is "not following *us*," instead of saying "not following *you*." In my view this language tilts only slightly in favor of a post-Easter origin. But should a disciple of Jesus in the pre-Easter setting not speak this way? Jesus had delegated to his disciples the authority to cast out evil spirits (Mark 3:14–15), so why should John not think of Jesus and his disciples as a group, a group of which the outside exorcist was not a member and therefore lacked authorization? Moreover, the saying in Mark 9:39–40 coheres with Matt 12:27//Luke 11:19 ("And if I cast out demons by Beelzebul, by whom do your sons cast them out?"), a saying that has good claim to authenticity. Why should not other Jewish exorcists invoke Jesus' name, once his reputation as a powerful healer and exorcist had become known?

least in the pseudepigraphon named after him, that is, the *Testament of Solomon*.[7]

In all probability the exorcist Eleazar was typical of Jewish exorcists of the first century. What is unusual is the exorcist who invoked the name of Jesus. Of course, this exorcist may well have invoked other names, such as Solomon. But the mere observation that he added the name of Jesus to his roster of sacred and powerful names is a remarkable testimony to the reputation that Jesus had acquired in so short a period of time. Indeed, one may wonder if the rumor that Jesus was "John the Baptist raised from the dead," which apparently had reached the ears of Antipas the tetrarch (Mark 6:14; 8:28), was yet another testimony to Jesus' remarkable powers, in the sense that they seemed well beyond what could be expected in "this world."

The uniqueness of the authority of Jesus is also seen in the apparent fact that he himself never invoked the name of Solomon or anyone else (including God), nor did he recite incantations or make use of paraphernalia. Jesus apparently invoked his own authority.[8] This is in part what occasions the amazement on the part of the crowds who witness Jesus' healings and exorcisms: "What is this? A new teaching! With authority he commands even the unclean spirits, and they obey him" (Mark 1:27); "We never saw anything like this!" (2:12). When comparison is made between Jesus and the scribes (e.g., Mark 1:22: "they were astonished at his teaching, for he taught them as one who had authority, and not as the scribes"), the mighty works of Jesus, as much as his words, are in view. Unlike the scribes, who consult their incantations and ponder the best remedy, Jesus merely speaks the word and the sufferer is made well.[9]

---

[7] See C.C. McCown, "The Christian Tradition as to the Magical Wisdom of Solomon," *JPOS* 2 (1922): 1–24; D.C. Duling, "The Eleazar Miracle and Solomon's Magical Wisdom in Flavius Josephus's *Antiquitates Judaicae* 8.42–49," *HTR* 78 (1985): 1–25. In an Aramaic incantation bowl we read: "Bound are the demons...with the bond of 'El Shaddai and with the sealing of King Solomon, son [of David]...Amen...." (C.H. Gordon, "Aramaic Incantation Bowls," *Orientalia* 10 [1991]: 116–141, 272–280, here 273–276 [no. 11, lines 17–18]). In another we read "with the seal-ring of King Solomon, son of David" (M.J. Geller, "Eight Incantation Bowls," *OLP* 17 [1986]: 101–117, here 109). See also *PGM* IV.850 ("a charm of Solomon").

[8] Perhaps on analogy with the well-known antitheses of Matthew 5: "You have heard it said, but I say to you."

[9] The immediacy of Jesus' healing and exorcism contrasts with that of Elijah and Elisha of Old Testament fame and with that of the charismatic rabbis, such as Ḥoni the Circle Drawer and Ḥanina ben Dosa. In all of these cases the holy man prays to God (sometimes at great length) and conducts some sort of ritual. For example, Ḥanina was remembered for tucking his head between his knees.

92 CRAIG A. EVANS

Jesus' success in healing and in exorcism and the apparent fact that he never invoked the name of Solomon or the name of some other Old Testament worthy probably encouraged the exorcist of Mark 9 to invoke the name of Jesus. Had Jesus invoked the name of Solomon and enjoyed success doing so, there is no reason to think that the outside exorcist would have invoked the name of Jesus. The apparent fact that Jesus did not invoke the name of Solomon (as was probably the common practice in the case of other Jewish exorcists) is probably one more indication that Jesus understood himself and his mission as unique.

Notwithstanding the warnings of the book of Acts, outsiders continued to invoke the name of Jesus, as we see attested in a number of incantations and charms. Among these important artifacts we have a magician's cup, whose inscription, "the magician through Chrēstos," may have been incised in the first century. If this date is correct (the stratigraphy of the find suggests the first half of the first century) and if the inscription does indeed refer to Jesus,[10] the magician's cup, found in 2008 in Alexandria's harbor, provides us with the earliest archaeological evidence of pagans invoking the name of Jesus.[11] We of course have the well-known late third-century charm of Pibechas against demons. This heavily reworked incantation invokes "the god of the Hebrews, Jesus." Typical of these kinds of charms, it appeals to a variety of sacred names, including the name of Solomon, as well as a number of Jewish elements (*PGM* IV.3007–3086).[12] To a fourth century pagan charm the names "Jesus Chrēstos, the Holy Spirit, the Son of the Father" are added (*PGM* IV.1227–1264).[13] The name of Jesus has been added to a charm intended to induce insomnia in a woman who has refused her suitor's amorous overtures (*PGM* XII.376–396). In an eclectic pagan charm the name Jesus appears, either as "Jesus the Great

---

[10] The Greek reads Χρηστός, not Χριστός. However, Christ and Christian, either in Greek or in Latin, were sometimes spelled χρηστός and χρηστιανός, in both Christian and non-Christian writings.

[11] The find was made by marine archaeologist Franck Goddio and his team. I thank Dr Goddio for the information that he and his staff provided. Study of this remarkable cup is only in the beginning stages. At this point no firm conclusions should be drawn.

[12] For critical Greek text, with textual notes, see K. Preisendanz, ed., *Papyri Graecae Magicae: Die Griechischen Zauberpapyri* (ed. A. Henrichs; 2 vols.; Leipzig: Teubner, 1928–1931; repr. Munich and Leipzig: Saur, 2001), 1:170–172. Several scholars provide brief discussions of this important incantation. Among these studies, see esp. P.W. van der Horst, "The Great Magical Papyrus of Paris (*PGM* IV) and the Bible," in M. Labahn and B.J. Lietaert Peerbolte, eds., *A Kind of Magic: Understanding Magic in the New Testament and its Religious Environment* (LNTS 306; London and New York: T. & T. Clark, 2007), 173–183.

[13] The text is Greek, with portions in Coptic. For Greek and Coptic text, see Preisendanz, *Papyri Graecae Magicae* (n. 12), 1:114.

JESUS AS SAVIOR AND PROTECTOR—BEFORE EASTER AND AFTER   93

Lord" or "Jesus the Megadon" (P. Mich. 757, lines 1–4).[14] The name of Jesus is also invoked in Jewish magic bowls (e.g., M163: "in the name of Yahweh Sebaoth and in the name of Jesus;" M155: "in the name of...Christ").[15] There are Manichean texts that refer to Jesus as "the healer."[16]

What this remarkable *Wirkungsgeschichte* suggests is that Jesus was no ordinary exorcist, during the time of his public ministry and, after his ministry, in the activities of the early church. Indeed, Jesus himself apparently viewed his exorcisms and healings as very important, as indicative of the presence of God's rule (or kingdom) in an unprecedented manner. He linked exorcisms to his proclamation of God's rule (Mark 3:14–15; 6:12–13). He appealed to his exorcisms as proof that the Kingdom of God had indeed "come upon" the Jewish people (Luke 11:20).

Even more remarkable is that Jesus apparently believed that in his coming, proclamation, and healing activities Satan has been defeated. When the disciples return from their mission, rejoicing and saying, "Lord, even the demons are subject to us in your name!" (Luke 10:17), Jesus declares that he "saw Satan fall like lightning from heaven" (10:18). But Jesus does not simply believe that in the proclamation of the rule of God Satan has fallen, he actually implies that he is stronger than Satan. In rebutting the charge that he is in league with Beelzebul Jesus reasons: "But no one can enter a strong man's house and plunder his goods, unless he first binds the strong man; then indeed he may plunder his house" (Mark 3:27). The implication is that Jesus has bound Satan, "the strong man," and now has entered his house, or domain, and has begun to "plunder his goods," that is, defeat his evil allies and rescue the people whom he had held captive. Luke's version should also be cited: "When a strong man, fully armed, guards his own palace, his goods are in peace; but when one stronger than he assails him and overcomes him, he takes away his armor in which he trusted, and divides his spoil" (Luke 11:21–22). In this version Jesus alludes to himself as the one "stronger" than Satan.

---

[14] The apparent mixing of Greek and Hebrew makes deciphering the components of the name difficult and ambiguous. For text and critical study, see D. García Martínez, ed., *P. Michigan XVI: A Greek Love Charm from Egypt (P. Mich. 757)* (American Studies in Papyrology 30; Atlanta: Scholars Press, 1991).

[15] For text, translation, and notes, see D. Levene, *A Corpus of Magic Bowls: Incantation Texts in Jewish Aramaic from Late Antiquity* (London and New York: Kegan Paul, 2003), 120–138 (on M163), 110–115 (on M155).

[16] See W.B. Henning, "Two Manichaean Magical Texts with an Excursus on the Parthian Ending—*endehi*," *BSOAS* 12 (1947): 39–66.

94 CRAIG A. EVANS

It is no wonder that his critics, unable to deny the reports and what in some cases they may have witnessed themselves, accuse Jesus of being in league with the Devil. The exorcistic and healing powers of Jesus are unmatched. It is not surprising that at least one professional exorcist, during Jesus' public activities, began invoking the name of Jesus. Nothing like Jesus had ever been seen.

It is in this remarkable exorcistic and healing power of Jesus, conjoined with his proclamation of the Kingdom of God and the defeat of Satan, that we may have found something of major importance for Christology, both before and after Easter. Jesus' exorcistic prowess takes on added significance when interpreted against the backdrop of the eschatology we find in some of the Dead Sea Scrolls. Two traditions are of special interest here. One is the portrait of the anticipated Melchizedek figure and the other is the portrait of the warrior Messiah who will crush the Romans and even slay the Roman emperor.

The coming Melchizedek figure fulfills a number of prophecies (11Q13 2:2–4), including the jubilee (Lev 25:13), the promise of forgiveness of sins (Deut 15:2), and the promise of the release of those held captive (Isa 61:1). The mysterious Melchizedek "will proclaim to them the jubilee, thereby releasing them from the debt of all their sins" (11Q13 2:6). He will make atonement for his people; it will be "the year of Melchizedek's favor" (11Q13 2:9). The modification of Isa 61:2 is quite remarkable. Instead of the "year of Yahweh's favor," it is the "year of Melchizedek's favor." In some sense Melchizedek is God or at least assumes the role of God. 11Q13 then cites parts of Psalms 7 and 82 to underscore the divinity or at least heavenly identity of Melchizedek (11Q13 2:10–12). The remarkable vision goes on to foretell that "Melchizedek will thoroughly prosecute the vengeance required by God's statutes. In that day he will deliver them from the power of Belial, and from the power of all the spirits predestined to him" (11Q13 2:13, with restorations). Melchizedek will deliver God's people from Belial, that is, Satan, and from "all the spirits" allied with him, that is, evil spirits or demons. The ministry of Jesus seems to answer this expectation.

The Melchizedek text goes on to explain that this is the "visitation" foretold in Scripture, when the prophecy of Isa 52:7 will be fulfilled: "How beautiful upon the mountains are the feet of the messenger who announces peace, who brings good news, who announces salvation, who says to Zion, 'Your God reigns'" (11Q13 2:15–16, with restorations). What is translated "God" (*'elohim*) is somewhat ambiguous, in view of what has been said of Melchizedek earlier, where he is linked to Psalms 7 and 82. The author may not be thinking of God (as in the God of Abraham) but of

JESUS AS SAVIOR AND PROTECTOR—BEFORE EASTER AND AFTER   95

a "divine being,"[17] part of God's heavenly council. The author next identifies the messenger as the "anointed" of Dan 9:26, who will announce the year of the Lord's favor, even the day of vengeance (11Q13 2:18–19). This anointed one is probably a prophet, rather than the Messiah. The "divine being" (or "God"), we are told, is Melchizedek. It is he who shall deliver God's people from the power of Belial (11Q13 2:24–25).

This remarkable text seems to envision the appearance of a divine being, though not exactly God himself, who will defeat Satan and save God's people, atoning for them and forgiving their sins. Again, the coherence with the ministry of Jesus is striking.

The War Scroll envisions defeat of Israel's human enemies and their spiritual allies. The opening words are quite suggestive: "For the Instructor, the Rule of the War. The first attack of the Sons of Light shall be undertaken against the forces of the Sons of Darkness, the army of Belial: the troops of Edom, Moab…" (1QM 1:1, with restoration). The "Sons of Darkness" are defined as the "army of Belial," comprising the troops of Edom, Moab, Ammon, etc. One might infer that this unflattering sobriquet is purely symbolic or metaphorical, but other statements in the scroll suggest otherwise. A few lines later we are told that "the great hand of God shall overcome Belial and all the angels of his dominion, and all the men of his forces shall be destroyed forever" (1QM 1:14–15). Here we have unmistakable reference to spiritual beings (בליעל וכול מלאכי ממשלתו: "Belial and all the angels of his dominion") and human beings (אנשי גורלו: "the men of his forces").

What role does the Messiah play in the anticipated victory over Belial and his spiritual and mortal allies? The fragmentary condition of the final columns of the great War Scroll makes it difficult to answer this question. However, thanks to 4Q285, a text that is related to the War Scroll, we may be able to answer our question. According to fragment 7 (with restorations):

> …just as it is written in the book of Isaiah the prophet, "And the thickets of the forest shall be cut down ²with an ax, and Lebanon with its majestic trees will fall. A shoot shall come out from the stump of Jesse ³and a branch shall grow out of his roots" [Isa 10:34–11:1]. This is the Branch of David. Then all forces of Belial shall be judged, ⁴and the king of the Kittim shall stand for judgment and the Leader of the congregation—the Branch of David—will have him put to death. ⁵Then all Israel shall come out with timbrels and

---

[17] This is in fact how the word is translated in M.O. Wise, M.G. Abegg Jr., and E.M. Cook, *The Dead Sea Scrolls: A New Translation* (San Francisco: HarperCollins, 1996), 456–457.

96   CRAIG A. EVANS

dancers, and the high priest shall order [6]them to cleanse their bodies from
the guilty blood of the corpses of the Kittim. (4Q285 frag. 7, lines 1–6 = 11Q14
frag. 1, lines 5–16)

The parallel in 11Q14 allows us to conclude this graphic scene with what
appears to be a blessing (with restorations):

> ... And he shall bless them in the name of the God of [3]Israel and say in
> response before all the Israelites, "Blessed are you [4]in the name of God Most
> High ... and blessed is His holy name [5]for ever and ever and blessed ... and
> blessed are all [6]His holy angels." (11Q14 frag. 1, lines 2–6)

This remarkable text envisions the appearance of the Branch of David
(which we know elsewhere to be the Messiah)[18] who, in fulfillment of
the prophecy of Isaiah, will defeat the Roman army (the Kittim) and slay
the Roman emperor (the king of the Kittim). Not only that, the "forces of
Belial" will be judged. In view of the statements found in the great War
Scroll (1QM 1:1, 14–15), we should assume that these forces include evil
spirits. Yet most of the time the "forces" of Belial are humans (see 1QM
4:1–2; 17:15; 18:1–3). What we read in 4Q285 and 11Q14 almost certainly is
part of the battle envisioned in the great War Scroll. The latter anticipates
that "All those pr[epared] for battle shall set out and camp opposite the
king of the Kittim and all the forces [3]of Belial that are assembled with him
for a day [of vengeance] by the sword of God" (1QM 15:2–3).

With the battle won, the high priest assumes the responsibility of cleans-
ing the land by having the unclean corpses of the slain Kittim removed
and properly buried, as the law commands (Deut 21:22–23). Meanwhile
the women of Israel celebrate with timbrels and dancing, as in days of
old when God triumphed over the enemies of Israel in dramatic ways (see
Exod 15:20; Judg 11:34; 1Sam 18:6).

It is in this context that I think the Messiah fragment of 4Q521 should
be placed. Fragment 2, column ii, describes the appearance of God's
Messiah, whom heaven and earth shall obey. With the appearance of this
figure God will restore Israel:

> For He will honor the pious upon the throne of His eternal Kingdom, [8]set-
> ting prisoners free, opening the eyes of the blind, raising up those who are
> bowed down [Ps 146:7–8; Isa 35:5–6; 61:1]. [9]And forever I shall hold fast
> to those who hope and in His faithfulness shall ... [10]and the fruit of good
> deeds shall not be delayed for anyone [11]and the Lord shall do glorious things

---

[18] See 4Q522 5:3: "and the thousands of Israel are 'the feet,' until the Righteous Messiah,
the Branch of David, has come."

JESUS AS SAVIOR AND PROTECTOR—BEFORE EASTER AND AFTER   97

which have not been done, just as He said. [12]For He shall heal the critically wounded, He shall make alive the dead, He shall send good news to the afflicted [Isa 61:1], [13]He shall satisfy the poor, He shall guide the uprooted, He shall make the hungry rich.... (4Q521 frag. 2, col. ii, lines 7–13, with restorations)[19]

What I find intriguing in this passage is the promise to set prisoners free (מתיר אסורים), to heal the wounded (ירפא חללים), and to make alive the dead (מתים יחיה). All three of these remarkable deeds cohere with the aftermath of the battle described in 4Q285 and 11Q14. When the battle ends, the high priest takes charge of the disposal of the enemy dead, the women celebrate, and God, through his Messiah, whom heaven and earth obey, will raise the dead (slain in battle?), heal the wounded (presumably wounded in battle), and release prisoners. The metaphorical imagery of Psalm 146 and the passages from the prophet Isaiah may have been understood in a very literalistic fashion by the composer of 4Q521, in a fashion not too different from the great battle envisioned by the author(s) of the War Scroll and related documents.

The men of the Qumran Scrolls anticipated an eschatological figure who can defeat Satan himself, a figure who in some sense represents the Lord or at least is thought of as divine, and will bring about the restoration and healing of Israel in the great eschatological jubilee, when Israel's sins and debts are forgiven and evil will be finally banished. Without claiming exact correspondence, I think the lofty portrait of Jesus as exorcist extraordinaire, who possesses the power and authority to defeat Satan, may hint at his divinity or at least a very close association with God. His exorcistic prowess, well attested in reliable pre-Easter tradition, may have been seen by his followers before and after Easter as an important element of Jesus' identity, or—to speak in post-Easter language—Christology.

It may well be that Jesus' reputation as an exorcist of great power—such that his name is invoked by others before and after Easter—was one of the factors that led his followers to confess him in divine terms and to see in him the very presence of God. In light of the many parallels with some of the Scrolls from Qumran it is not hard to see why Paul would declare in his second letter to the Corinthian church: "God was in Christ reconciling the world to himself" (2Cor 5:19). The principal difference is that Paul spoke of "reconciliation" between Israelite and Gentile, while

---

[19] Translation based on Wise, Abegg, and Cook, *The Dead Sea Scrolls* (n. 17), 421. The translators capitalize the third person singular pronoun ("He") because they think the reference is to the Lord (line 11). Even so, the Lord works through his Messiah.

98   CRAIG A. EVANS

the men of Qumran anticipated the complete destruction of their Gentile enemies.

In another publication Michael Wolter discerned a "distinctive implicit Christology" in some of the parables of Jesus. The parables of Jesus have long been viewed as the "bedrock" of the dominical tradition.[20] The presence in some of them of an implicit Christology goes a long way in addressing the problem with which this modest essay began. In my view, Jesus' success in exorcism and healing confirmed in his own thinking that he was indeed God's anointed. Without hesitation he can answer—admittedly implicitly—John's question in the affirmative: "Go and tell John what you hear and see: the blind receive their sight and the lame walk, lepers are cleansed and the deaf hear, and the dead are raised up, and the poor have good news preached to them" (Matt 11:4–5). It is no coincidence that Jesus has alluded to words and phrases from Isaiah, the very book of prophecy that contributed so richly to the anticipated Messiah of 4Q521. It is this self-understanding, this sense of mission, that expresses itself in some of the parables.

We find in Jesus' deeds and actions elements that will prove to be foundational in the development of the Christology of the early Christian movement. These may be little more than "traces,"[21] to be sure, but they are unmistakable and they are relevant to our concerns. At a very important point historical research and early (and continuing) Christian confession intersect. Christians place their faith in Jesus through whom God acted powerfully, defeating the very foes who would enslave humanity. This is a key component in Christology and at the same time it appears to be firmly rooted in the activities and teaching of the historical Jesus. These activities and teachings so strongly impacted followers and non-followers alike, that all appealed to his name, sensing in it a special power.

In my view, Wolter's "third way" provides a promising framework that should lead to positive results. It will be interesting to see how scholars work within it.

---

[20] See M. Wolter, "Jesus as a Teller of Parables: On Jesus' Self-Interpretation in His Parables," in J.H. Charlesworth and P. Pokorný, eds., *Jesus Research: An International Perspective* (Grand Rapids: Eerdmans, 2009), 123–139, here 139. The reference to the parables of Jesus as the "bedrock" of the tradition harks back to J. Jeremias, *The Parables of Jesus* (New York: Scribner's Sons, 1963), 11: "The parables are a fragment of the original rock of tradition."

[21] By "traces" I allude to the important introductory essay by R.L. Webb, "The Historical Enterprise and Historical Jesus Research," in D.L. Bock and R.L. Webb, eds., *Key Events in the Life of the Historical Jesus* (WUNT 247; Tübingen: Mohr Siebeck, 2009), 95–150.

A NEW STARTING POINT IN HISTORICAL JESUS RESEARCH: THE EASTER EVENT

Michael R. Licona

When I was a child, I had a book that had what appeared to be blank pages. Also included were plastic eye-glasses in which I could place lenses of different colors. If I looked at a certain page through the blue lenses, it remained blank. A few words appeared when the page was viewed through the green lenses. However, when viewed through the red lenses, I could read the entire page!

Something similar occurs in historical Jesus research. Rather than colored lenses, historians attempt to see Jesus through a paradigm. When Jesus is viewed as a Jewish cynic who was strongly influenced by Hellenistic culture, a portion of what the Gospels report comes into view. However, when he is viewed as an eschatological prophet within the culture of Second Temple Judaism, a whole lot more of the Gospel reports become decipherable. However, an uncomfortable amount of content in the Gospels remains elusive to historians of Jesus.[1]

Historians of Jesus continue to discuss what it is precisely that historians are supposed to be doing, whether there are historical "facts," what is the actual effectiveness of criteria of authenticity and so forth. And to complicate matters further, there is the factor of worldview. All of this has led to interpretive polarities to the point that some have questioned whether further progress in historical Jesus research is possible. Recently, Michael Wolter has offered a solution. In this essay, I will assess Wolter's proposal then offer my own.

---

[1] Graham Twelftree has proposed that the historical Jesus must be viewed in light of the profound historical evidence that suggests he was a miracle worker. See G.H. Twelftree, "The History of Miracles in the History of Jesus," in McKnight and G.R. Osborne, eds., *The Face of New Testament Studies: A Survey of Recent Research* (Grand Rapids: Baker, 2004), 191–208.

100

MICHAEL R. LICONA

1. Summary of Wolter's Proposal

Wolter describes the present stalemate in historical Jesus research and articulates two general approaches: (a) The "real Jesus" is inaccessible via historical research (*à la* Kähler and Bultmann). Thus, we can only know him via theology, and (b) using historical methods, one can peer through the theologically embellished clothing the early Church put on Jesus and see a fairly accurate portrait of him (*à la* Reimarus). Thus, we can know the "real Jesus" via historical investigation. Wolter proposes a solution he asserts is a path between the two: "the theological historian," that is, one who relies on historical and theological knowledge. The theological historian knows "the story of Jesus in the light of the Easter faith," which is knowable via historical investigation (p. 6) while also possessing the advantage of insight into God's view of reality. So, what is God's view of Jesus?

It is not asserted that random people have been raised from the dead by God, given a sovereign position in the heavenly realm and a title above all others. What was it, then, about Jesus that led the early Christians to do just that? Wolter contends that if one attempts to answer this question as a historian, the methodology must be the same as that employed by historians investigating any other figure of the past (p. 7). However, he then argues that this approach is bound to fail, because of the inherent challenges of historical knowledge in general.

> Is there a "real Jesus" as an ontic reality beyond the images that people have been making of him since the time he lived—and also beyond the image he had of himself? (p. 12) ... Yes ..., but we cannot really say anything about him, because every linguistic description and even every perception of such a reality is always contaminated with particular *interpretations*.... [Moreover], there is no knowledge without a simultaneous integration into the cultural encyclopedia that is available to the recognizing person. This skepticism derives from the epistemological insights of constructivism [because one has no knowledge independent of his horizon] (p. 13).... Any historian who asks about Jesus and wants to remain honest, must admit that "the real Jesus" is not accessible to him. He will not deny that there has been some kind of "real" Jesus, but he must be aware of the fact that he can neither know nor even describe him. It is also important that what is being said goes not only for Jesus and for knowledge of the past, but also for any kind of knowledge—also for "knowledge" of our own identity and the identities of our contemporaries. The Christian theologian will come to no other result if, concerning the "real Jesus", he posits this question as a historian: He (the real Jesus) existed, but no one can know him as such or even make statements about him (p. 14).

A NEW STARTING POINT IN HISTORICAL JESUS RESEARCH 101

In short, there was a "real Jesus." But we cannot know or describe him because all historical reports are contaminated with the interpretations of their authors as well as those of their sources. This challenge is not unique to historical Jesus research but also applies to all knowledge concerning our own identity and those of our contemporaries.

How then can an accurate knowledge of the "real Jesus" be obtained? If I understand Wolter correctly, he suggests that God's knowledge differs from human knowledge in that the latter can never have a one-on-one correspondence with reality, whereas the former does. The "real Jesus" is the Jesus as God knows him (p. 14). And that knowledge is available to us via the Christian Easter faith. This faith

> has its origin in the visionary experiences of Peter, James and Paul and the others named in 1Cor 15:5–8, who perceived Jesus as a figure appearing to them from heaven. These experiences were interpreted by them in a certain way. For all those who have not enjoyed such as experience, including ourselves—Christian Easter faith consists in accepting the interpretation these witnesses provided by their visionary experiences. (p. 15)

Wolter identifies two paramount interpretations in the Christian Easter faith: (1) That Jesus had appeared from heaven after having been crucified as a criminal suggests God raised him and exalted him in heavenly glory, and (2) by exalting Jesus, God vindicated him and legitimated his teachings and actions. A component of Jesus' teachings is his self-interpretation as God's authentic eschatological agent. Thus, Jesus' self-interpretation corresponds to God's knowledge of him. But the visionary experiences of Jesus by his disciples alone cannot account for the early Christians' extraordinary high view of Jesus. They could only have had such a view of Jesus if it had not also been how Jesus understood himself. Thus, by combining the visionary experiences with Jesus' self-interpretation (pp. 16–17), we are now prepared to make the following conclusion: Jesus had a very high Christological self-interpretation and God confirmed it to others in the visionary experiences.

In the end, Wolter suggests that the answer to the question "Who was the 'real' Jesus" cannot be answered by historians. Only the "theological historian," that is, the historian who includes theology in an explanation, can be prepared to provide an answer. And that answer will be based on Jesus' self-interpretation (p. 17). The theological historian cannot justify the Easter faith (p. 17). Thus, the "real Jesus" is known theologically rather than historically.

102   MICHAEL R. LICONA

2. Analysis

Wolter's thesis may be summarized in two-parts: (a) Historical knowledge is too limited to inform us about the "real Jesus" and (b) our only means of knowing the "real Jesus" is through the theology of Jesus' self-interpretation, which was approved by God via his resurrection/exaltation. My analysis will address both.

Wolter's articulation of the problems inherent in historical investigation is valuable, since it reminds scholars interested in learning about the "real Jesus" that a considerable amount of subjectivity is involved in historical research, requiring epistemological humility and restrained historical conclusions that will always be provisional.[2] Historical descriptions are limited and historians must now speak with a degree of diffidence.[3]

Notwithstanding, one need not adopt a view of history as pessimistic as the one painted by Wolter. Western minds long for firm and absolute certainty resulting from the methods of science. And when this degree of certainly eludes us, despair and Cartesian anxiety sometimes set in. However, as philosopher of history Chris Lorenz notes, this is often the product of an "all-or-nothing" fallacy, which states that if knowledge is not absolute and complete, it is relative.[4] Failure on the part of historians to know the whole truth does not prohibit them from having an idea of the past that is adequately relevant to a limited or more focused inquiry.[5]

---

[2] R.J. Evans, *In Defense of History* (New York: W.W. Norton, 1999), 216.

[3] See also D.C. Allison, "Explaining the Resurrection: Conflicting Convictions," *Journal for the Study of the Historical Jesus* 3, no. 2 (2005): 117–133, esp. 133. C. Behan McCullagh says that "Responsible historians will be careful not to exaggerate the certainty of their conclusions, but will point out how tentative they are when there is not strong evidence to support them" (C.B. McCullagh, *The Logic of History: Putting Postmodernism in Perspective* [New York: Routledge, 2004], 43). Hayden White says, "One of the marks of a good professional historian is the consistency with which he reminds his readers of the purely provisional nature of his characterizations of events, agents, and agencies found in the always incomplete historical record" (H. White, *Tropics of Discourse: Essays in Cultural Criticism* [Baltimore: Johns Hopkins University Press, 1978], 82). Admittedly, historical Jesus scholars rarely state their conclusions with reservation.

[4] C. Lorenz, "Can Histories Be True? Narrativism, Positivism, and the 'Metaphorical Turn,'" *History and Theory* 37, no. 3 (October 1998): 309–329, here 314.

[5] Sally Bachner says, "Few of us believe that language manages to communicate every aspect of the material world or of everyday sensation, yet we rarely contemplate their unspeakability" (S. Bachner, "When History Hurts," *History and Theory* 42, no. 3 [October 2003]: 398–411, here 411). John Zammito says, "In short, robust historicism need not be crippled by a hyperbolic skepticism: total incommensurability is preposterous, and local incommensurability is surmountable" (J. Zammito, "Koselleck's Philosophy of the Historical Time[s] and the Practice of History," *History and Theory* 43, no. 1 [February 2004]: 124–135, here 135).

A NEW STARTING POINT IN HISTORICAL JESUS RESEARCH   103

Historical tools are blunt and imperfect. However, they are effective to varying degrees. Inference often yields correct results. We know this because we can test it in the context of historical investigations involving modern people and events where many eye-witnesses, photographs, and video recordings of an event are available. On occasion, one can sometimes demonstrate that inference yields accurate results in historical investigations involving ancient persons and events. The classical historian A.N. Sherwin-White wrote, "From time to time external contemporary evidence of a sort less warped by the bias of personalities—e.g. the texts of laws and public accounts—confirms the conclusions drawn from the critical study of literary sources. Hence we are bold to trust our results in the larger fields where there is no such confirmation."[6]

Wolter correctly asserts that problems in historical knowledge are not unique to historical Jesus research, since they apply equally to one's self-identity and the identity of one's contemporaries (p. 12). However, this surely does not warrant his pessimism concerning the ability of historical method to provide us with statements about the "real Jesus" or ourselves that can be known with reasonable certainty. Does Wolter truly believe that the "real Michael Wolter," the "real Winston Churchill," and the "real Osama bin Ladin" are inaccessible to historians who cannot know or describe them? Biographers will paint portraits of their subjects that differ to varying degrees and one should never think of these portraits as exhaustive or perfectly accurate. However, there is much for biographers to get right and some will get it more right than others.

Wolter's degree of historiographical pessimism also leads to epistemological self-cannibalism. For it is likewise impossible for any of us to prove that we exist in the physical world rather than as a brain in a vat stimulated by an unknown entity in order to produce the false perceptions of reality we regularly experience. Since his perceptions of reality cannot be proven outside of his own interpretation of reality, would Wolter go so far to suggest that his inability to confirm the accuracy of his perceptions nullifies his confidence pertaining to his physical existence? Wolter correctly reminds us that historical knowledge is both incomplete and provisional. But, in my opinion, his pessimism goes too far.

The second part of our analysis concerns Wolter's proposed solution that our only means of knowing the "real Jesus" is through the theology of

---

[6] A.N. Sherwin-White, *Roman Society and Roman Law in the New Testament* (New York: Oxford University Press, 1963), 187.

104 MICHAEL R. LICONA

Jesus' self-interpretation, which was approved by God via his resurrection/ exaltation. This view of history has a double edge, creating an insurmountable problem. If Wolter is correct in (a) his assessment of historical knowledge and (b) that the only means for the theological historian to find the "real Jesus" is via Jesus' self-interpretation, we could never know Jesus' self-interpretation. For our knowledge of this would have to come from the New Testament literature, which Wolter contends is, like all other literature, encumbered with problems that prohibit historians from knowing or making any statements about their subject or, in this case, the "real Jesus!" On what grounds, then, does he think we can know that Jesus' disciples believed God had vindicated him? He is clear that historical method cannot do the job. That leaves him either presupposing the New Testament authors got it spot on or utilizing the historical method he has denied is legitimate.

Further problems plague Wolter's proposal. It requires a huge leap between God's knowledge of Jesus and the early Christian interpretation of the visionary experiences. How can we be assured there is an exact correspondence between the two? Wolter says the Christian Easter faith simply agrees to the interpretations provided by those who had the visionary experiences (p. 15). As a result, he does not defend the authenticity of the visionary experiences, which is a vital component of his historical case for Jesus' self-interpretation. Were the experiences ontic appearances of Jesus or natural psychological phenomena such as hallucinations? Did God vindicate Jesus' self-interpretation by resurrecting/exalting him or did Jesus' disciples experience grief hallucinations of the risen and exalted Jesus because he had expressed a high Christological view of himself? How could Wolter decide between the two hypotheses, since he admits that the theological historian cannot justify the Easter faith (p. 17)? If historians of Jesus were to employ Wolter's approach, those who are Christian believers will tend to believe the interpretation of Jesus' disciples were correct while non-believers will prefer a natural explanation. Hence, historians of Jesus who would employ Wolter's approach will find themselves in the same stalemate as before. In the end, Wolter's proposal is its own enemy.

3. Viewing the Historical Jesus in Light of the Easter Event

In what follows I will propose a more optimistic view of historical investigation. I will then propose a new starting point in historical Jesus research: the Easter event.

A NEW STARTING POINT IN HISTORICAL JESUS RESEARCH 105

We have already discussed some of the challenges to historical knowledge and here I am in agreement with Wolter. In any historical investigation, the data have been marinated in the horizons of the ancient historian and his sources before being further interpreted by modern historians who will likewise assess the surviving data in light of their own horizons. This calls for a great deal of caution when proceeding in any historical investigation.

In what is perhaps a simplified overview, we assert there are three approaches to understanding the past. The first is naïve realism, which holds that accurate historical judgments always result when a historian consistently employs strictly controlled method. This view can no longer be maintained and there are only a very few who embrace it, at least publicly, in the beginning of the twenty-first century. The second is a postmodernist approach, which holds that responsible method cannot lead us to accurate historical knowledge. Philosophers of history have thoroughly debated this view over the past few decades and the vast majority of historians practicing outside the community of biblical scholars have rejected it.[7] The third view is critical realism, which maintains that historians may hold their historical descriptions with varying degrees of certainty and possess a healthy dose of epistemological humility regarding their conclusions. This is by far how the overwhelming majority of historians view their practice and is the view embraced by this author.

Historians must learn to live with the knowledge that there will never be a consensus opinion pertaining to who Jesus actually was. This is because of the varying horizons and metaphysical commitments of historians. Dale Allison writes,

> Study of the historical Jesus belongs to the diversity and pluralism of modernity, or, if you prefer, postmodernity, and there can be no easy appeal to the consensus on much of anything. The biblical guild is not a group-mind thinking the same thoughts. Nor are the experts a single company producing a single product, "history." ... So if we are to do something with the historical

---

[7] See B. Fay, "Nothing but History?" (review of David Roberts, *Nothing but History: Reconstruction and Extremity after Metaphysics*), *History and Theory* 37, no. 1 (February 1998): 83–93, esp. 83; M.T. Gilderhus, *History and Historians: A Historiographical Introduction* (6th ed.; Upper Saddle River, N.J.: Prentice Hall, 2007), 124; D.D. Roberts, "Postmodernism and History: Missing the Missed Connections" (review of Ernst Breisach, *On the Future of History: The Postmodernist Challenge and Its Aftermath*), *History and Theory* 44, no. 2 (May 2005): 240–252, esp. 252; K. Jenkins, "Introduction: On Being Open about Our Closures," in K. Jenkins, ed., *The Postmodern History Reader* (New York: Routledge, 1997), 1–30, esp. 1, 9. See also M.R. Licona, *The Resurrection of Jesus: A New Historiographical Approach* (Downers Grove, Ill.: InterVarsity, 2010), 86–87.

106 MICHAEL R. LICONA

Jesus, it will have to be someone's particular historical Jesus—Wright's Jesus or Crossan's Jesus or Sanders's Jesus; it can no longer be the Jesus of the guild or the Jesus of the scholars, because they, in their writings and at their academic conferences, argue with each other over almost everything.[8]

What academic field of study is not driven by the obstinate disputations of the experts? And what religious opinion is without its countless dissenters?...If we are to believe anything, we must get used to disagreeing with lots of other people.[9]

This predicament is not unique to the guild of historical Jesus scholars. It is likewise present among historians outside of the community of biblical scholars. Philosopher of history Mark Gilderhus comments,

The body of literature on almost any historical subject takes the form of an ongoing debate.... By the very nature of the subject, history tends to divide scholars and set them at odds.... We no longer possess a past commonly agreed upon. Indeed, to the contrary, we have a multiplicity of versions competing for attention and emphasizing alternatively elites and nonelites, men and women, whites and persons of color, and no good way of reconciling all the differences. Though the disparities and incoherencies create terrible predicaments for historians who prize orderliness in their stories, such conditions also aptly express the confusions of the world and the experiences of different people in it.[10]

Lorenz contends that a proper philosophy of history

must elucidate the fact that historians present reconstructions of a past reality on the basis of factual research and discuss the adequacy of these reconstructions; at the same time it must elucidate the fact that these discussions seldom lead to a consensus and that therefore pluralism is a basic characteristic of history as a discipline.[11]

---

[8] D.C. Allison Jr., *The Historical Christ and the Theological Jesus* (Grand Rapids: Eerdmans, 2009), 11.

[9] Ibid., 12.

[10] Gilderhus, *History and Historians* (n. 7), 86, 113.

[11] C. Lorenz, "Historical Knowledge and Historical Reality: A Plea for 'Internal Realism,'" *History and Theory* 33, no. 3 (October 1994): 297–327, here 326. See also Gilderhus, *History and Historians* (n. 7), 85, 86, 93, 113. Thus, I think Pieter Craffert is mistaken when he asserts that "no one has the right to use the tag historical unless it can win the respect of fellow historians" (P.F. Craffert, "The Origins of Resurrection Faith: The Challenge of a Social Scientific Approach," *Neot.* 23 [1989], 331–348, here 341). Similar statements have been made by Bart Ehrman in W.L. Craig and B.D. Ehrman, "Is There Historical Evidence for the Resurrection of Jesus? A Debate between William Lane Craig and Bart D. Ehrman" (debate, College of the Holy Cross, Worcester, Mass., March 28, 2006), 25 (transcript available at http://www.4truth.net/WorkArea/linkit .aspx?LinkIdenti-fier=id&ItemID=8590118483); and A.F. Segal, "The Resurrection: Faith

A NEW STARTING POINT IN HISTORICAL JESUS RESEARCH   107

Scholars involved in historical Jesus studies should make their particular case for the logia and deeds of Jesus. They should articulate what methods they are using and why. In this way, others can critically assess each case and make judgments pertaining to its merits.

Some historical conclusions are more certain than others. In fact, some facts are so strongly evidenced that they may be said to be beyond doubt. Scholars often refer to these as *historical bedrock*, since any relevant historical reconstruction must be built upon the foundation of these facts. What are some of the historical bedrock pertaining to Jesus? That Jesus performed feats that both he and his followers interpreted as miracles and exorcisms is a fact strongly evidenced and supported by the majority of scholars.[12] Graham Twelftree, perhaps the leading authority on the miracles and exorcisms of Jesus, has argued in several works that the evidence that Jesus was a miracle worker is so strong that it is one of the best attested historical facts about Jesus.[13] Meier concludes, "The miracle

---

or History," in R.B. Stewart, ed., *The Resurrection of Jesus: John Dominic Crossan and N. T. Wright in Dialogue* (Minneapolis: Fortress, 2006), 121–138, here 136.

[12] Craig A. Evans says, "Scholarship has now moved past its preoccupation with demythologization. The miracle stories are now treated seriously and are widely accepted by Jesus scholars as deriving from Jesus' ministry" (C.A. Evans, "Authenticating the Activities of Jesus," in B. Chilton and C.A. Evans, eds., *Authenticating the Activities of Jesus* [Boston: Brill, 1999], 3–29, here 12). E.P. Sanders lists six "almost indisputable facts" about Jesus, the second of which is that he "was a Galilean preacher and healer" (E.P. Sanders, *Jesus and Judaism* [Philadelphia: Fortress, 1985], 11). Elsewhere he states that there is an agreement among scholars that "Jesus performed miracles" (E.P. Sanders, *The Historical Figure of Jesus* [London: Allen Lane–Penguin, 1993], 157). See also J.P. Meier, *A Marginal Jew: Rethinking the Historical Jesus*, vol. 2: *Mentor, Message, and Miracles* (ABRL; New York: Doubleday, 1994), 970; G. Theissen and A. Merz, *The Historical Jesus: A Comprehensive Guide* (Minneapolis: Fortress, 1998), 281. Even rather skeptical scholars agree that Jesus was an exorcist and miracle-worker. Rudolf Bultmann writes, "There can be no doubt that Jesus did the kinds of deeds which were miracles to his mind and to the minds of his contemporaries" (R. Bultmann, *Jesus and the Word* [London: Collins/Fontana, 1958], 124). Marcus Borg concedes that there are "very strong" reasons for concluding that Jesus performed healings of a sort and that a supernatural cause cannot be ruled out (M. Borg, *Jesus, A New Vision: Spirit, Culture, and the Life of Discipleship* [San Francisco: HarperCollins, 1987], 67–71; cf. idem, *Jesus: Uncovering the Life, Teachings, and Relevance of a Religious Revolutionary* [San Francisco: HarperCollins, 2006], 56). John Dominic Crossan concludes that "Jesus was both an exorcist and a healer" (J.D. Crossan, *The Historical Jesus: The Life of a Mediterranean Jewish Peasant* [New York: HarperCollins, 1991], 332; cf. 311). Robert W. Funk and the Jesus Seminar list among the "basic facts" about Jesus that he was a "charismatic healer and exorcist" (R.W. Funk and The Jesus Seminar, *The Acts of Jesus: What Did Jesus Really Do?* [San Francisco: HarperCollins, 1998], 527). See also B.D. Ehrman, *Jesus: Apocalyptic Prophet of the New Millennium* (New York: Oxford University Press, 1999), 198.

[13] Twelftree says, "There is now almost unanimous agreement among Jesus questers that the historical Jesus performed mighty works" (in *The Face of New Testament Studies* [n. 1], 206). Elsewhere he says, "If we can be certain of anything about the historical Jesus

108   MICHAEL R. LICONA

traditions about Jesus' public ministry are already so widely attested in various sources and literary forms by the end of the first Christian generation that total fabrication by the early church is, practically speaking, impossible."[14]

That Jesus viewed himself as God's eschatological agent—the figure through whom the Kingdom of God was coming—is also widely recognized by biblical scholars and amply attested in the sources.[15] That the Kingdom of God was at the core of Jesus' preaching is secure.[16]

Jesus' death by crucifixion is regarded as being beyond doubt by a nearly universal and heterogeneous consensus of modern scholars who have written on the topic. John McIntyre comments,

> Even those scholars and critics who have been moved to depart from almost everything else within the historical content of Christ's presence on earth have found it impossible to think away the factuality of the death of Christ.[17]

---

it is that his contemporaries considered him to have performed wonders or miracles.... [I]n answer to the question 'Did Jesus perform miracles?' we have to reply with an unequivocal and resounding 'Yes!' We have seen that it is not a matter of so-called blind faith that enables us to say this.... The necessary conclusion, in light of our inquiry, is that *there is hardly any aspect of the life of the historical Jesus which is so well and widely attested as that he conducted unparalleled wonders*" (G.H. Twelftree, *Jesus: The Miracle Worker* [Downers Grove, Ill.: InterVarsity, 1999]: 258, 345).

[14] Meier, *Marginal Jew*, vol. 2 (n. 12), 630.

[15] Theissen and Merz, *Historical Jesus* (n. 12), 512–513.

[16] Meier, *Marginal Jew*, vol. 2 (n. 12), 289–506. Theissen and Merz, *Historical Jesus* (n. 12), 246–274. James D.G. Dunn notes that "[a]t the very least we overhear in the words of the remembered Jesus a claim for the divine significance of his mission, as the (not just an) eschatological emissary of God" (J.D.G. Dunn, *Jesus Remembered* [vol. 1 of *Christianity in the Making*; Grand Rapids: Eerdmans, 2003], 707; cf. 762).

[17] J. McIntyre, "The Uses of History in Theology," *Studies in World Christianity* 7, no. 1 (January 2001): 1–20, here 8. For rather skeptical scholars, see G. Lüdemann, *The Resurrection of Christ: A Historical Inquiry* (Amherst, N.Y.: Prometheus, 2004), 50; Crossan, *Historical Jesus* (n. 12), 375, cf. 372; idem, *Jesus: A Revolutionary Biography* (San Francisco: HarperCollins, 1994), 145; Borg, *Jesus* (n. 12), 271–272; R.J. Miller, "Back to Basics: A Primer on Historical Method," in B.B. Scott, ed., *Finding the Historical Jesus: Rules of Evidence* (Jesus Seminar Guides 3; Santa Rosa, Calif.: Polebridge, 2008), 7–18, here 14; G. Vermès, *The Passion: The True Story of an Event That Changed Human History* (New York: Penguin, 2006), 9; P. Lapide, *The Resurrection of Jesus: A Jewish Perspective* (trans. W.C. Linss; Minneapolis: Augsburg, 1983; repr., Eugene, Or.: Wipf and Stock, 2002), 32; P. Fredriksen, *Jesus of Nazareth, King of the Jews: A Jewish Life and the Emergence of Christianity* (New York: Random House, 1999), 8; B.D. Ehrman, *The Historical Jesus: Lecture Transcript and Course Guidebook* (pt. 2 of 2; Chantilly, Va.: Teaching Company, 2000), 162; cf. idem, *The New Testament: A Historical Introduction to the Early Christian Writings* (4th ed.; New York: Oxford University Press, 2008), 235, 261–262. Moderate to somewhat conservative scholars likewise grant Jesus' death by crucifixion as historical. See R.E. Brown, *The Death of the Messiah:*

A NEW STARTING POINT IN HISTORICAL JESUS RESEARCH   109

A nearly unanimous consensus of modern scholars writing on the subject have concluded that subsequent to Jesus' execution, a number of his followers had experiences that convinced them Jesus had risen from the dead and had appeared to them in some manner. Paula Fredriksen asserts that "the disciples' conviction that they had seen the Risen Christ...[is part of] historical bedrock, facts known past doubting."[18] A.J.M. Wedderburn similarly comments, "It is an indubitable historical datum that sometime, somehow the disciples came to believe that they had seen the risen Jesus."[19] Gary Habermas has catalogued the opinions of hundreds of scholars writing on the subject of Jesus' resurrection in French, German, and English since 1975. His database divides the opinions into more than one hundred categories pertaining to questions related to the resurrection of Jesus. He comments, "As firmly as ever, most contemporary scholars agree that, after Jesus' death, his early followers had experiences that they

From Gethsemane to the Grave; A Commentary on the Passion Narratives in the Four Gospels, vol. 2 (New York: Doubleday, 1994), 1373; J.H. Charlesworth, *The Historical Jesus: An Essential Guide* (Nashville: Abingdon, 2008), 111; L.T. Johnson, *The Real Jesus: The Misguided Quest for the Historical Jesus and the Truth of the Traditional Gospels* (San Francisco: Harper Collins, 1996), 125; Sanders, *Jesus and Judaism* (n. 12), 11.

[18] Fredriksen, *Jesus of Nazareth* (n. 17), 264.

[19] A.J.M. Wedderburn, *Beyond Resurrection* (Peabody, Mass.: Hendrickson, 1999), 13. See also D. Baggett, "Resurrection Matters: Assessing the Habermas/Flew Discussion," in idem, ed., *Did the Resurrection Happen? A Conversation with Gary Habermas and Antony Flew* (Downers Grove, Ill.: InterVarsity, 2009), 122; Borg in M.J. Borg and N.T. Wright, *The Meaning of Jesus: Two Visions* (San Francisco: HarperCollins, 1998), 135; C.E. Braaten, "The Resurrection Debate Revisited," *Pro Ecclesia* 8 (February 1999): 147–158, here 148; P. Carnley, *The Structure of Resurrection Belief* (Oxford: Clarendon, 1987), 224; Charlesworth, *Historical Jesus* (n. 17), 113; P.F. Craffert, " 'Seeing' a Body into Being: Reflections on Scholarly Interpretations of the Nature and Reality of Jesus' Resurrected Body," *Religious Theology* 9 (January–February 2002): 89–107, here 99–100; J.D.G. Dunn, *Beginning from Jerusalem* (vol. 2 of *Christianity in the Making*; Grand Rapids: Eerdmans, 2009), 212–213; Ehrman, *Jesus* (n. 12), 230–232; cf. idem, *The Historical Jesus* (n. 17), pt. 2, 282–283; idem, *Jesus, Interrupted: Revealing the Hidden Contradictions in the Bible (and Why We Don't Know about Them)* (New York: HarperCollins, 2009), 177–178; Lapide, *Resurrection of Jesus* (n. 17), 126; Lüdemann, *Resurrection of Jesus* (n. 17), 80; H. Montefiore, *The Miracles of Jesus* (London: SPCK, 2005), 105; Sanders, *Historical Figure of Jesus* (n. 12), 280, cf. 11; G. Vermès, *The Resurrection* (New York: Doubleday, 2008), 149; D.W. Viney, "Grave Doubts about the Resurrection," *Encounter* 50 (February 1989): 125–140, here 126; N.T. Wright, *The Resurrection of the Son of God* (vol. 3 of *Christian Origins and the Question of God*; Minneapolis: Fortress, 2003), 710.

110   MICHAEL R. LICONA

at least believed were appearances of their risen Lord."[20] Scholars differ,
however, on the perceived nature of the experiences.[21]

The majority of modern scholars also grant that the Church persecutor
Paul had an experience he was convinced was the risen Jesus appearing to
him. Relating to studies on the resurrection Habermas writes,

> Perhaps no fact is more widely recognized than that early Christian believ-
> ers had real experiences that they thought were appearances of the risen
> Jesus. In particular, virtually all scholars recognize Paul's testimony that he
> had an experience that he believed was an appearance of the risen Jesus....
> Seldom is the historical authenticity of any of these testimonies or the genu-
> ine belief behind them challenged by respected critical scholars, no matter
> how skeptical.[22]

In summary, our relevant historical bedrock gives us Jesus, a man who
thought of himself as God's eschatological agent chosen to usher in his
Kingdom, a man who performed deeds that both he and his followers
regarded as divine miracles and exorcisms, and a man who was crucified by the Romans. Moreover, almost immediately following his death,
his disciples and at least one skeptic had experiences they interpreted as
appearances of the risen Jesus to them.

With this historical bedrock in mind, I wish to propose a new starting point for historical Jesus research. While giving consideration to the
relevant historical bedrock, from what perspective may we view Jesus that
will provide us with greater illumination of who he actually was? While

---

[20] G.R. Habermas, "Mapping the Recent Trend toward the Bodily Resurrection Appearances of Jesus in Light of Other Prominent Critical Positions," in Stewart, ed., *Resurrection
of Jesus* (n. 11), 78–92, here 79. Elsewhere Habermas provides a list of more than sixty
"recent critical scholars who believe that Jesus's disciples had real experiences that led
them to conclude that they saw appearances of the risen Jesus, whether or not the resurrection actually occurred" (G.R. Habermas, *The Risen Jesus and Future Hope* [Lanham, Md.:
Rowman and Littlefield, 2003], 46, n. 148). One scholar who doubts that the disciples had
such experiences is R.M. Price, "Brand X Easters," in B.B. Scott, ed., *The Resurrection of
Jesus: A Sourcebook* (Jesus Seminar Guides 4; Santa Rosa, Calif.: Polebridge, 2008), 49–59,
here 57.

[21] Craffert, "'Seeing' a Body into Being" (n. 19), 91; Fredriksen, *Jesus of Nazareth* (n. 17),
261–262; G.R. Habermas, "Resurrection Research from 1975 to the Present: What Are Critical Scholars Saying?," *Journal for the Study of the Historical Jesus* 3, no. 2 (2005): 135–153,
here 151; Sanders, *Historical Figure of Jesus* (n. 12), 280; Wedderburn, *Beyond Resurrection*
(n. 19), 143.

[22] G.R. Habermas and M.R. Licona, *The Case for the Resurrection of Jesus* (Grand Rapids:
Kregel, 2004), 74. See B.D. Ehrman, *Lost Christianities: The Battles for Scripture and the
Faiths We Never Knew* (New York: Oxford University Press, 2003), 96; H. Koester, *History
and Literature of Early Christianity* (2nd ed.; vol. 2 of *Introduction to the New Testament*;
New York: Walter de Gruyter, 2000), 108.

Wolter proposes the Christian Easter faith, I wish to propose the Easter event itself. I am fully aware that many scholars, including Wolter, have stated rather forcefully that historical investigation cannot produce a conclusion related to the Easter event. Instead, it can inform us that the early Christians had experiences they interpreted as appearances of the risen Jesus. However, I have answered these objections elsewhere and, due to space limitations, will not touch on that subject here.[23]

Elsewhere I have argued comprehensively, and will briefly argue below, that the "real Jesus" was raised from the dead in a physical and bodily sense.[24] I am fully aware that the majority of biblical scholars will not agree with me that the resurrection of Jesus' physical corpse can be historically confirmed. But I ask for the reader's temporary patience and an open mind for the remainder of this short essay.

If the physical resurrection of Jesus could be historically confirmed, how might this impact historical Jesus research? I will suggest three areas. First, it would render a greater historical plausibility to the reports of Jesus' miracles. This is certainly not to suggest that all of the miracle reports of Jesus would be confirmed as historical. It is to say that any hesitations based simply on the miraculous nature of the events reported might be ill-founded. After all, if Jesus' physical resurrection was a historical event, then walking on water and healing a man born blind are relatively easy feats. Second, if the physical resurrection of Jesus could be historically confirmed, it would render a higher probability that Jesus actually predicted his imminent death and resurrection. That Jesus predicted these is already, in my opinion, very certain.[25] However, the historicity of his resurrection only adds to the historical certainty of these predictions. Third, if Jesus' physical resurrection could be historically confirmed, it would shed illumination on the question of Jesus' self-interpretation. Larry Hurtado comments,

---

[23] See Licona, *Resurrection of Jesus* (n. 7), 160–191; idem and J.G. van der Watt, "Historians and Miracles: The Principle of Analogy and Antecedent Probability Reconsidered," *HTS Teologiese Studies/Theological Studies* 65, no. 1 (2009): 56–61, doi:10.4102/hts.v65i1.129; M.R. Licona and J.G. van der Watt, "The Adjudication of Miracles: Rethinking the Criteria of Historicity," *HTS Teologiese Studies/Theological Studies* 65, no. 1 (2009): 62–68, doi:10.4102/hts.v65i1.130.

[24] See Licona, *Resurrection of Jesus* (n. 7).

[25] See M.R. Licona, "Did Jesus Predict His Death and Vindication/Resurrection?," *Journal for the Study of the Historical Jesus* 8, no. 1 (2010): 47–66; idem, *Resurrection of Jesus* (n. 7), 284–300.

MICHAEL R. LICONA

> [A] number of scholars have argued over, especially in recent years, the most remarkable innovation in first-century Christian circles was the inclusion of the risen/exalted Jesus as recipient of cultic devotion. For historical analysis, this is perhaps the most puzzling and most notable feature of earliest Christian treatment of the figure of Jesus.[26]

How did this devotion come about, especially when it would certainly have seemed blasphemous to the early followers of Jesus, of whom most were Jews? There are no strong hints suggesting that Second Temple Jews believed the Messiah was divine. Moreover, since many Jews and Christians believed in the general resurrection of the righteous on the final day, Jesus' resurrection in itself would not have led his disciples to regard him as a divine being. What then was the catalyst of such devotion to Jesus?

I would like to suggest that, whether explicitly or implicitly, Jesus spoke of himself in divine terms during his earthly ministry and in a manner similar to what is reported in the canonical Gospels. After he rose from the dead and appeared to his disciples, any doubts or confusion they may have had concerning those claims dissolved. It is true that Jesus' claims to divinity in the canonical Gospels are typically regarded as inauthentic. But this conclusion is primarily reached by presupposing that the high Christology we find among the early Christians existed only in the post-Easter Church.[27] But the Gospels present Jesus making divine claims in so many ways and in such varied contexts that attributing all of them to the creativity of the Evangelists or their sources stretches credulity. Remove that presupposition and grant the unique event of Jesus' resurrection and the high Christology present among the earliest Christians loses its perplexity as the puzzle pieces come together quite nicely. This is something on which Wolter would agree, since he regards the visionary experiences of the early Christians to be the catalyst of the Christian Easter faith. He writes that the resurrection appearances alone could not have created the beliefs that

> Jesus has been placed by God in the heavenly, sovereign position of the Son of God (Rom 1:4), and did so with the *Kyrios* title of the "Name above all names" (Phil 2:9–11). This cannot be explained unless it had a corresponding basis in Jesus' own self-interpretation.[28]

---

[26] L.W. Hurtado, "Jesus' Resurrection in the Early Christian Texts: An Engagement with N.T. Wright," *Journal for the Study of the Historical Jesus* 3, no. 2 (2005): 197–208, here 205.

[27] We see this move clearly demonstrated by C.K. Barrett, *Jesus and the Gospel Tradition* (London: SPCK, 1967), 25–26, and Dunn, *Jesus Remembered* (n. 16), 723.

[28] See above, p. 14. Hurtado in "Jesus' Resurrection in the Early Christian Texts" (n. 26) also regards experiences of the risen Jesus as one of the major causes behind the high Christology of the earliest Christians (ibid., 206).

A NEW STARTING POINT IN HISTORICAL JESUS RESEARCH 113

Of course, all of the above is futile if it cannot be demonstrated that Jesus rose from the dead. In what follows, I will present a necessarily brief historical case for Jesus' physical resurrection from the dead.[29] As above mentioned, there is a virtually unanimous and heterogeneous consensus among modern scholars that shortly after Jesus' death, a number of his followers and at least one militant skeptic named Paul had experiences which they interpreted as the risen Jesus appearing to them. We may add that these same scholars would agree that Paul knew and had some contact with the Jerusalem apostles Peter, James, and John.[30] Scholars disagree, however, with the following claim: In the Gospel essentials, Paul was preaching the same message as the Jerusalem apostles. However, there are at least three reasons for believing he did.

First, Paul asserted he was teaching what they were teaching (Gal 2:1–10; 1Cor 15:9–11). Second, it is quite likely that Clement of Rome and Polycarp had been personally acquainted with Peter and John respectively, perhaps were even mentored by them.[31] Had the content of Paul's teachings been contradictory to that of Peter, John, or Jesus, we would have expected Clement and Polycarp to have chided and corrected Paul on the matter, especially since he was dead at the time they wrote. While it would be carelessly aggressive to think that Clement and Polycarp expressed all of their sentiments toward Paul in their two extant letters, it is what they say about him in those letters that is helpful. Clement places Paul on par with Peter (*1 Clement* 5) and Polycarp comments that the "glorious Paul … taught the word about the truth, accurately and reliably" (Pol. *Phil.* 3:2). Third, it is possible to demonstrate that Paul resisted the temptation to do what many scholars accuse the early Christians of doing: Inventing teachings of Jesus to import authority into an apostolic teaching meant to address a post-Easter situation in the Church. In 1Corinthians 7, Paul addresses three questions on marriage and divorce. His *opinion* concerning marriage is that it's preferable to remain single if one is able, since it allows one to be completely devoted to kingdom interests (7:1–9). When it comes to the matter of divorce, Paul appeals to the Jesus tradition ("not

---

[29] For a comprehensive case, see Licona, *Resurrection of Jesus* (n. 7). Also see D.C. Allison, *Resurrecting Jesus: The Earliest Christian Tradition and Its Interpreters* (New York: T&T Clark, 2005); W.L. Craig, *Assessing the New Testament Evidence for the Historicity of the Resurrection of Jesus* (New York: Edwin Mellen, 1989); Habermas, *Risen Jesus and Future Hope* (n. 20); Wright, *Resurrection of the Son of God* (n. 19).

[30] See Gal 1:18–19; 2:1–14; 1Cor 15:11; Acts 9:26–28; 15:1–30; 21:17–26; not to mention his time with Barnabas and Silas who were from among the Jerusalem Christians, the latter of which was a leader in the Jerusalem church (Acts 15:22).

[31] See Licona, *Resurrection of Jesus* (n. 7), 249–256.

114   MICHAEL R. LICONA

I but the Lord"): Except for spousal unfaithfulness, divorce is not allowed
(7:10–11). What may be said, however, when the believer is married to a
non-believer? Paul answers, "I say, not the Lord" (7:12) and proceeds to
render an apostolic ruling on the matter that must be followed (7:12–17).
In the pre-Easter Church, the distinction between a Christian believer and
non-believer had not been clearly defined. So, apparently, there was no
Jesus tradition pertaining to marriage and divorce between a believer and
non-believer. It is precisely here that Paul had an opportunity to fabricate
a logion of Jesus or simply fail to mention that what he was about to write
did not belong to the Jesus tradition, leaving an ambiguity for the reader
who might interpret it as belonging to the Jesus tradition. But Paul was
painfully careful not to comingle the Jesus tradition with his own binding
apostolic ruling. The Jesus tradition was to be kept pure. Accordingly, in
the few places where we can identify Jesus tradition in the Pauline literature, we can be very confident we are likewise hearing the voice of either
Jesus or the Jerusalem apostles. One of these places is the pre-Pauline
tradition embedded in 1Cor 15:3–7:

> For I delivered to you of primary importance what I also received: that
> Christ died for our sins according to the Scriptures 4and that he was buried
> and that he was raised on the third day according to the Scriptures 5and that
> he appeared to Cephas, then to the Twelve, 6then he appeared to more than
> five hundred brothers at one time, from whom most remain until now, but
> some have died, 7then he appeared to James, then to all the apostles.

Space limitations prohibit us from saying more here on this fascinating
text.[32] However, it is of interest that in 1Cor 15:1, Paul says he is about to
remind them of the "Gospel" (εὐαγγέλιον) he had preached to them and
says the other apostles were preaching (κηρύσσομεν) the same (15:11). In
Gal 2:2, Paul says he had reviewed the Gospel (εὐαγγέλιον) he had been
preaching (κηρύσσω) with the Jerusalem apostles to ensure his content
was similar to theirs. And it may be more than a coincidence that the
names of the two Jerusalem apostles with whom Paul had twice met are
listed in the oral formula in 1Cor 15:3–7. Thus, we possess further clues
suggesting the Jerusalem apostles were also teaching the content mentioned in this oral formula.

Virtually all scholars who have written on the subject, including rather
skeptical ones, maintain that in 1Cor 15:3–7, Paul has provided tradition(s)

---

[32] For more on this text, see Licona, *Resurrection of Jesus* (n. 7), 223–235, 318–343.

A NEW STARTING POINT IN HISTORICAL JESUS RESEARCH   115

about Jesus he did not form but rather received from others as he claims.[33] There is likewise wide-spread agreement that it was composed very early[34]

---

[33] Allison, *Resurrecting Jesus* (n. 29), 233–234; P. Barnett, *Jesus and the Rise of Early Christianity: A History of New Testament Times* (Downers Grove, Ill.: InterVarsity, 1999), 181; R.W. Funk, "The Resurrection of Jesus: Reports and Stories," in Scott, ed., *Resurrection of Jesus* (n. 20), 7–44, here 11; Funk and The Jesus Seminar, *Acts of Jesus* (n. 12), 454; Habermas, *Risen Jesus and Future Hope* (n. 20), 17; cf. idem, *The Historical Jesus: Ancient Evidence for the Life of Christ* (Joplin, Mo.: College Press, 1996), 153; R.W. Hoover, "Was Jesus' Resurrection an Historical Event? A Debate Statement with Commentary," in Scott, ed., *Resurrection of Jesus* (n. 20), 75–92, here 78; C.S. Keener, *1–2 Corinthians* (New Cambridge Bible Commentary; New York: Cambridge University Press, 2005), 123; Koester, *History and Literature of Early Christianity* (n. 22), 91; idem, *Ancient Christian Gospels: Their History and Development* (Harrisburg, Pa.: Trinity Press International, 1990), 6–7; S.J. Patterson, "Why Did Christians Say: 'God Raised Jesus from the Dead'? 1 Cor 15 and the Origins of the Resurrection Tradition," *Forum* 10 (March–April, 1994): 135–160, here 137, 138; Theissen and Merz, *Historical Jesus* (n. 12), 487; Wedderburn, *Beyond Resurrection* (n. 19), 113.

[34] John M.G. Barclay says this tradition about Jesus "may date from as early as the 30s" (J.M.G. Barclay, "The Resurrection in Contemporary New Testament Scholarship," in *Resurrection Reconsidered* [ed. G. D'Costa; Rockport, Mass.: OneWorld, 1996], 16). Paul Barnett says this Jesus tradition may date "within two or three years of the First Easter" (P. Barnett, "The Apostle Paul, the Bishop of Newark, and the Resurrection of Jesus," *Crux* 30 [March 1994]: 2–11, here 6). Richard A. Burridge and Graham Gould say that this tradition is "dating from only a few years after Jesus' death" (R.A. Burridge and G. Gould, *Jesus Now and Then* [Grand Rapids: Eerdmans, 2004], 46). Dunn says, "This tradition, we can be entirely confident, was *formulated as tradition within months of Jesus' death*" (Dunn, *Jesus Remembered* [n. 16], 855); J. Engelbrecht says this Jesus tradition is "probably reaching back to within the first five years after Jesus' death" (J. Engelbrecht, "The Empty Tomb [Lk 24:1–12] in Historical Perspective," *Neot.* 23 (February 1989): 235–249, here 244). Funk and the Jesus Seminar say this tradition dates within "two or three years at most" (Funk and The Jesus Seminar, *Acts of Jesus* [n. 12], 466). Funk also states that most of the fellows of the Jesus Seminar believe the tradition predates Paul's conversion around 33 C.E. (ibid., 454); see also The Jesus Seminar, "Voting Records: The Resurrection Appearances," *Forum* 10 (March–April 1994): 260, S6. Michael Goulder says, "Paul 'received' the tradition—that is, he was taught it at his conversion—perhaps two years after Jesus' death (1Cor 15:3–8)" (M. Goulder, "The Explanatory Power of Conversion Visions," in *Jesus' Resurrection: Fact or Figment? A Debate Between William Lane Craig and Gerd Lüdemann* [ed. Paul Copan and Ronald K. Tacelli; Downers Grove, Ill.: InterVarsity, 2000], 86–103, here 98). Michael Grant says this Jesus tradition was "very early" (M. Grant, *Jesus: An Historian's Review of the Gospels* [New York: Charles Scribner's Sons, 1977], 177). Richard B. Hays says the tradition about Jesus dates "within about three years after Jesus was crucified in Jerusalem" (R.B. Hays, *First Corinthians* [Interpretation; Louisville: John Knox Press, 1997], 255). Koester says that "the traditions extant in Paul's letters can be dated to the time before Paul's calling, that is, no later than within five years after Jesus' death" (Koester, *History and Literature of Early Christianity* [n. 22], 90). Lüdemann says the tradition about Jesus dates within "the first two years after the crucifixion of Jesus" (Lüdemann, *Resurrection of Christ* [n. 17], 31). Hershel Shanks and Ben Witherington III say, "This list dates to at least within twenty years of Jesus' death" (H. Shanks and B. Witherington III, *The Brother of Jesus: The Dramatic Story and Meaning of the First Archaeological Link to Jesus and His Family* [San Francisco: HarperCollins, 2003], 109, n. 3). Wedderburn says this Jesus tradition dates to the "first half of the 30s" (Wedderburn, *Beyond Resurrection* [n. 19], 113).

116   MICHAEL R. LICONA

and may be the oldest extant tradition pertaining to the resurrection of Jesus.[35]

I am going to contend that Paul taught a physical resurrection of Jesus' corpse in 1Corinthians 15. If I am correct, then there are no clear cases in the first century of a contrary view while the Gospels present a compatible view.[36] So does Clement of Rome who provides several parallels of resurrection, all of which coincide with a revivification of the corpse (*1Clement* 24–26; see also *2Baruch* 49–51). Accordingly, the burden of proof will rest on the shoulders of those who wish to contend that the early Christians thought of resurrection differently than a physical action to the corpse.

In 1Cor 15:20, Paul states that Jesus was the first to experience a resurrection.[37] He is the first fruits of the dead. *First fruits* is an agricultural term referring to the first of the crops to be ready for harvesting. Anyone who has had a vegetable garden knows that some vegetables are ready for harvesting prior to others. These will be harvested at a later date. Jesus was resurrected in the first century while those who belong to him will experience their resurrection at the *parousia* (15:23, 52; cf. 1Thess 4:13–17). It will be similar in nature to Jesus' resurrection (1Cor 6:14; 15:12–23; cf. Rom 6:5; 8:11; 2Cor 4:14; Phil 3:21). In the interim, believers who die prior to the *parousia* are with Christ in heaven (2Cor 5:8; Phil 1:23–24; 1Thess 4:14).

Now there are a number of scholars who contend that resurrection simply referred to Jesus' vindication by God in heaven and did not refer to an event that happened to his corpse.[38] But remember Paul's statements

---

[35] D. Kendall, "Why Disobedient Silence?," *Priests and People* 2 (March 1988): 91–96, here 91; Lapide, *Resurrection of Jesus* (n. 17), 98; B. Lindars, "Jesus Risen: Bodily Resurrection but No Empty Tomb," *Theology* 89 (1986): 90–96, here 91; Patterson, "Why Did Christians Say" (n. 33), 136. See also R. Bauckham, *Gospel Women: Studies of the Named Women in the Gospels* (Grand Rapids: Eerdmans, 2002), 259; L.W. Hurtado, *Lord Jesus Christ: Devotion to Jesus in Earliest Christianity* (Grand Rapids: Eerdmans, 2003), 71; Lüdemann, *Resurrection of Christ* (n. 17), 138.

[36] Even if one regards some of the traditions in the *Gospel of Thomas* as very early, the only two logia pertaining to resurrection (37, 51) are probably not authentic. See R.W. Funk, R.W. Hoover, and The Jesus Seminar, *The Five Gospels: What Did Jesus Really Say? The Search for the Authentic Words of Jesus* (San Francisco: HarperCollins, 1997), 494, 502–503.

[37] The widow's son who had been raised by Elijah (1Kgs 17:18–23) and perhaps others Paul may have known of (Mark 5:22–42/Luke 8:41–55; Luke 7:12–15; John 11; Acts 20:9–12) were raised in the same type of body, only later to die again. Jesus was raised in a resurrection body that Paul goes on to describe in 1Cor 15:35–55.

[38] It appears that Wolter may be one such scholar when he contends that the visionary experiences of Jesus' disciples included seeing him as a figure appearing to them from heaven (see above, p. 15). See also A. Baxter, "Historical Judgement, Transcendent Perspective and 'Resurrection Appearances,'" *HeyJ* 40 (January 1999): 19–40, here 27; Barclay, "Resurrection in Contemporary New Testament Scholarship" (n. 34), 17; Borg in Borg and

that we will be raised as was Jesus. Since believers go to be with Christ in heaven immediately upon death, what does Paul mean when he says that those who belong to Christ will be raised at the Parousia? It can refer to none other than the corpses of believers. 1Thess 4:14–16 erases any ambiguity:

> For if we believe that Jesus died and rose, so also *God will bring with him those who have fallen asleep in Jesus.* For this we say to you by a word of the Lord, that we who are alive and remain until the coming of the Lord will not precede those who have fallen asleep. For the Lord himself will come down from heaven with a shout, with the voice of the archangel and with the trumpet of God and *the dead in Christ will rise first.*

The Lord will bring the dead in Christ with him and then raise them. For Paul, when a believer dies, his spirit leaves his body and exists with Christ in heaven (2Cor 5:8; Phil 1:23–24). When Christ returns, he will bring the spirits with him and reunite them to what is left of their corpses. Their corpses will then be resurrected and transformed. And if the resurrection of believers refers to an event that revives and transforms their corpses and Jesus is the first fruits of the dead, Paul—and very likely the Jerusalem apostles—must have been teaching that Jesus had been raised in his transformed physical corpse.[39]

We are now prepared to create a list of five knowable facts relevant to our case for the historical resurrection of Jesus:

1. The Church persecutor Paul had an experience that he interpreted as the risen Jesus appearing to him.
2. Paul knew the Jerusalem apostles.
3. Paul was teaching the same essentials as they.

Wright, *Meaning of Jesus* (n. 19), 133; Funk, "Resurrection of Jesus" (n. 33), 13; S.H. Hooke, *The Resurrection of Christ as History and Experience* (London: Darton, Longman and Todd, 1967), 55; J. Murphy-O'Connor, *1 Corinthians* (Doubleday Bible Commentary; New York: Paulist, 1998), 171; Patterson, "Why Did Christians Say" (n. 33), 146; K. Quest, *Reading the Corinthian Correspondence: An Introduction* (New York: Paulist, 1994), 96, 122–123; J.D. Tabor, *The Jesus Dynasty: The Hidden History of Jesus, His Royal Family, and the Birth of Christianity* (New York: Simon & Schuster, 2006), 232; Wedderburn, *Beyond Resurrection* (n. 19), 66.

[39] Paul's statements in 1Cor 15:44 and 50 have often been misinterpreted to mean that he envisioned an immaterial resurrection body that did not involve the corpse. However, these interpretations are no longer sustainable. See Licona, *Resurrection of Jesus* (n. 7), 403–423. Moreover, if the apostles were proclaiming the physical resurrection of Jesus, Wolter's understanding of the early Christian claim pertaining to the resurrection appearances of Jesus as being exalted in heaven is mistaken.

118   MICHAEL R. LICONA

4. They were teaching that Jesus had been raised from the dead and had appeared to others.
5. They were teaching that Jesus had been raised in his transformed physical corpse.

4. Method

How are we to handle these five facts? Scholars involved in historical Jesus research often employ numerous criteria of authenticity in order to adjudicate on whether the "real Jesus" actually said or did something attributed to him in the Gospels. These criteria generally provide scholars a range of answers that may be held with varying degrees of certainty and are more fruitful when applied broadly. For example, as mentioned earlier, that Jesus had the reputation of a miracle-worker and exorcist is widely accepted by scholars for numerous reasons. It appears that his reputation was known among those sympathetic and in opposition to him. It is multiply-attested in every Gospel source (i.e., Mark, Q, M, L, John) and Josephus. It also appears in multiple literary forms, such as narrative, summaries of his activities, and references to his miracles in logia attributed to him. They are also quite early when compared with most other miracle claims in antiquity.

When applied to specific logia or acts, however, the criteria of authenticity do not yield results as certain. It is difficult to know the extent to which the evangelists exercised literary freedoms when reporting Jesus' teachings. It is certain that John took far more liberties than Matthew and Luke. But how much liberty did Mark take? Although Paul appears to have resisted any temptation he may have had to invent logia and attribute them to Jesus, can the same be said of Mark? It is difficult to test Mark—or his source(s)—on the matter as we can test Paul.

The criteria of authenticity also have limited use when weighing competing hypotheses. As one can pound a nail into a wall using a screwdriver rather than a hammer, the criteria of authenticity can be a helpful tool in weighing hypotheses but not be the best for the task. For this, historians outside the community of biblical scholars employ four general criteria in using inference to the best explanation.

a) *Explanatory Scope.* This criterion looks at the quantity of facts accounted for by a hypothesis. The hypothesis that includes the most relevant data has the greatest explanatory scope.

A NEW STARTING POINT IN HISTORICAL JESUS RESEARCH   119

b) *Explanatory Power.* This criterion looks at the quality of the explanation of the facts. The hypothesis that explains the data with the least amount of effort, vagueness, and ambiguity has greater explanatory power.[40] Said another way, the historian does not want to have to push the facts in order to make them fit his theory as though he were trying to push a round peg through a square hole.

These first two criteria may be understood using the analogy of completing a jigsaw puzzle. We may imagine two contestants with the same puzzle but who have presented different solutions (hypotheses). In the first puzzle, a number of pieces (historical facts) remain unused and one or more of the puzzle pieces appear forced. In the second puzzle all of the pieces have been used and fit perfectly. The first puzzle lacks the scope and power enjoyed by the second and, therefore, the second solution would be preferred. Most good historical hypotheses look like a puzzle with some missing pieces. As the number of missing pieces increases, so do the chances that puzzle pieces discovered in the future will change the current puzzle solution (or preferred hypothesis).

c) *Less* ad hoc. A hypothesis possesses an *ad hoc* component when it enlists non-evidenced assumptions.[41] When two or more hypotheses seem equal, usually due to a paucity of data, historians often employ a greater amount of imagination in order to account for the available data.[42] A hypothesis possessing an *ad hoc* component has the opposite problem of one lacking explanatory power. The former goes beyond what the data warrants whereas the latter may not go far enough. This criterion has also been referred to as *simplicity*.[43] It prefers the

---

[40] N.T. Wright combines criteria one and two. Listing the requirements of a good hypothesis, he writes, "First, it must include the data. The bits and pieces of evidence must be incorporated, without being squeezed out of shape any more than is inevitable" (N.T. Wright, *The New Testament and the People of God* [vol. 1 of *Christian Origins and the Question of God*; Minneapolis: Fortress, 1992], 99).

[41] Robert J. Miller says that *"a superior hypothesis explains the data with fewer presuppositions which beg relevant questions"* (R.J. Miller, "Historical Method and the Deeds of Jesus: The Test Case of the Temple Demonstration," *Foundations and Facets Forum* 8, no. 102 [March–June 1992]: 5–30, here 11).

[42] A. Tucker, *Our Knowledge of the Past: A Philosophy of Historiography* (New York: Cambridge University Press, 2004), 142–145, 240.

[43] Wright, *New Testament and the People of God* (n. 40), 100–101. Tor Egil Førland describes simplicity as the hypothesis having the fewest amount of *ad hoc* suppositions (T.E. Førland, "Acts of God? Miracles and Scientific Explanation," *History and Theory* 47, no. 4 [December 2008]: 483–494, here 491).

120   MICHAEL R. LICONA

hypothesis with fewer presuppositions rather than combined factors, since historical events often result from multiple causes.[44]

d) *Plausibility*. The hypothesis must be implied to a greater degree and by a greater variety of accepted truths (or background knowledge) than other hypotheses.[45] This criterion assesses whether other areas known with confidence suggest a certain hypothesis.[46] Therefore, it is appropriate to inquire whether certain components of a hypothesis are supported in the literature of other disciplines.[47]

Rather than providing a magic formula for discovering the past, these four criteria define how one may engage in a fair-minded critical examination of the data. Historians using arguments to the best explanation should weigh each hypothesis according to how well it meets these four criteria. The hypothesis fulfilling the most criteria is to be preferred, although its truth is not guaranteed. The more a hypothesis distances itself from competing hypotheses in fulfilling the criteria, the greater likelihood it has of representing what actually occurred. Hypotheses must likewise be judged by how well they answer disconfirming arguments.

With our five facts and method articulated, I will now subject two competing hypotheses to the method: hallucination and resurrection.

4.1   *Hallucination Hypothesis (HH)*

HH in one form or another is perhaps the most common natural explanation posited by scholars to account for the disciples' post-Easter experiences of Jesus. Generally stated, Jesus' disciples were grief-stricken and confused as a result of his sudden and brutal death. Knowing the Jewish Scriptures and literature, they knew that God vindicates his righteous ones. Grief and expectation provided a psychological condition that was

---

[44] C.B. McCullagh, *Justifying Historical Descriptions* (Cambridge: Cambridge University Press, 1984), 19–20. Miller in "Historical Method and the Deeds of Jesus" (n. 41) notes that hypotheses proposing multiple causes may often possess greater explanatory scope and explanatory power than hypotheses with a single cause (ibid., 10–11).

[45] McCullagh, *Justifying Historical Descriptions* (n. 44), 19; idem, *Logic of History* (n. 3), 51–52; Tucker, *Our Knowledge of the Past* (n. 42), 148–149. This appears to be what Wright in *New Testament and the People of God* (n. 40), 100–101, has in mind with his third criterion while hinting that illumination is also involved.

[46] Førland, "Acts of God?" (n. 43), 491–492.

[47] See McCullagh, in *Justifying Historical Descriptions* (n. 44), 27, where he distinguishes between a hypothesis that lacks plausibility from one that is implausible.

A NEW STARTING POINT IN HISTORICAL JESUS RESEARCH 121

fertile for hallucinations of an exalted Jesus and they experienced him in that sense.

Explanatory Scope. Of the five facts, HH easily accounts for facts 2–4, but leaves 1 and 5 stranded. Since Paul was persecuting Christians, he almost certainly was not experiencing grief over Jesus' death. It is also difficult to explain how the apostolic leadership came to believe Jesus had been raised in his revivified and transformed corpse if their visionary experiences were mere hallucinations of an exalted Jesus.

Explanatory Power. HH must work to include facts 1 and 5 in order to increase its explanatory scope. There is not enough data to know why Paul may have experienced a hallucination of the risen Jesus. Thus, one will need to speculate in order to explain why Paul may have experienced a hallucination of the risen Jesus. However, this will introduce an *ad hoc* element into the hypothesis.

If one is willing to grant the historicity of Jesus' passion/resurrection predictions, it could be posited without an appeal to a non-evidenced assumption that the disciples had them in mind. When combined with grief, very vivid hallucinations of a bodily raised Jesus resulted. However, while this may account for the appearance to individual disciples of Jesus, modern psychology has produced little in support of the occurrence of group hallucinations.[48]

Less ad hoc. In order to account for the first fact, one could posit that Paul had been experiencing private doubts pertaining to his crusade against the early Christians. Guilt had set in and Paul was seeking a reason for ceasing his hostilities. His dilemma led to a hallucination of the risen Jesus in which he received forgiveness. Although this explanation is possible, its drawback is that it is pure speculation without a scrap of supporting data. There is nothing in Paul's letters suggesting he experienced guilt during his hostilities toward the Christians. In fact, he appears to include these actions as a positive quality on his pre-conversion resume (Phil 3:6). Accordingly, the explanation is *ad hoc.* One can observe the dilemma historians often find themselves faced with: leaving a fact unaccounted for (lacking explanatory power) or improvising in order to account for it (*ad hoc*).

---

[48] See Licona, *Resurrection of Jesus* (n. 7), 483–486, 573–578.

122   MICHAEL R. LICONA

Plausibility. Do other widely known facts imply hallucinations? In other words, does our present knowledge in psychology predict that hallucinations of the risen Jesus were very likely to have been experienced by his closest followers? In order to answer this question, it will be helpful to summarize some of the current findings.[49] A hallucination is a false sensory perception of something that is not present. One may see (visual), hear (auditory), taste (gustatory), smell (olfactory), or feel (tactile) something not present or experience a sense of motion that is not actually occurring (kinesthetic). Hallucinations are most frequently experienced in a single mode (e.g., visual), although multiple-mode hallucinations (e.g., visual and auditory) are commonly experienced by schizophrenics and those on drugs. Multiple studies have revealed that senior adults bereaving the loss of a loved one are those most prone toward experiencing a hallucination at approximately 50 percent. Of the 50 percent, the most common hallucination (39%) is a sense that their deceased loved one is present, although not perceived through the natural senses. Thus, approximately 19.5 percent of all bereaving senior adults will sense that their deceased loved one is present with them without perceiving them via their natural senses. Only seven percent of all senior adults bereaving the loss of a loved one will experience a visual hallucination of that person.

Let us now consider how plausible it would have been for the disciples to experience hallucinations of the risen Jesus. We return to the oral tradition in 1Cor 15:3–7, which we previously showed is very likely what the Jerusalem apostles were proclaiming. In it, the risen Jesus is said to have *appeared* to the Twelve, which is very likely a reference to the group of twelve major disciples who would possess the main authority going forward. This explains why Matthias was chosen from a larger group of Jesus' followers to take the place of Judas. The tradition likewise states that Jesus *appeared* to more than five hundred and an *appearance* to all of the apostles. That the individual names of two apostles, Cephas and James, are mentioned suggests that the appearances to the Twelve and to *all* of the apostles occurred in group settings, since Cephas and James also belonged to these groups. Thus, "he appeared to Cephas, then to the Twelve" reports an appearance to Cephas and an appearance to the group of the Twelve.

While only seven percent of those most likely to experience a hallucination have a *visual* experience, the hallucination hypothesis requires

---

[49] See ibid., 483–486.

A NEW STARTING POINT IN HISTORICAL JESUS RESEARCH   123

an unthinkable 100 percent of the major disciples and all of the apostles to have experienced a visual hallucination of Jesus. Moreover, since their grief was almost certainly accompanied by intense fear of being arrested and experiencing a fate similar to their rabbi, it would be remarkable for all to have experienced a hallucination of Jesus rather than some imagining Jewish or Roman guards on their way to arrest them. Even more remarkable is that most of them experienced their hallucinations simultaneously.[50] Although group hallucinations are posited by some scholars as though they are quite common, supporting documentation is in fact very rare.[51] Thus, group hallucinations are at best very, very rare. But the hallucination hypothesis we are considering requires not one but three of these very, very rare events. In summary, the hallucination hypothesis requires (a) an unthinkable 100 percent of group members to have experienced (b) visual hallucinations (c) of Jesus (d) simultaneously (e) on three occasions.

Accordingly, the plausibility of the hallucination hypothesis is quite low. As my friend Lydia McGrew has said, if Jesus did not rise from the dead, the most likely thing to have occurred is ... nothing. No one hallucinates, Paul stays put in Judaism, and the Christian messianic movement falls apart in time just like every other failed messianic movement.[52]

In the end, HH will lack either explanatory power or possess an *ad hoc* component. It is also implausible. Accordingly, it fails two of the four criteria for the best explanation.

4.2   *Resurrection Hypothesis (RH)*

I define RH as follows: Following an event of an indeterminate cause, Jesus appeared in his revivified and transformed physical corpse to a number of his disciples and at least one hostile person named Paul.

Explanatory Scope. RH easily accounts for all five facts.

---

[50] The position that the appearances listed in 1Cor 15:3–7 were only for the purposes of legitimizing the apostolic authority fails for numerous reasons, two of which are (1) there is no evidence of an early authoritative group consisting of more than five hundred members and (2) there are no clear examples within the first one hundred years after Jesus where an appearance of the risen Jesus was invented and assigned to a person or group in order to confer authority on it. See Licona, *Resurrection of Jesus* (n. 7), 339–343.

[51] See the comment by Gary A. Sibcy in Licona, *Resurrection of Jesus* (n. 7), 484.

[52] Lydia McGrew, personal conversations with author, December 2009.

124   MICHAEL R. LICONA

Explanatory Power. RH easily accounts for all five facts without any forcing or ambiguity (i.e., Jesus was raised physically).

Less ad hoc. At most, one might claim that RH requires the existence of God. However, I have not appealed to divine causation in RH but have focused on whether the event itself occurred. This is a frequent practice in historical investigation. As Plutarch wrote, one need not know the cause of Scipio Africanus' death in order to conclude that Scipio is dead (*Romulus* 27:4–5). If Jesus was actually raised from the dead, God is probably the best candidate for the cause. But that would be the possible theological implications of a historical conclusion. Moreover, even if I were to suggest divine causation, it would not be a non-evidenced assumption, since there is rather good evidence for God's existence.[53]

Plausibility. Do other widely known facts imply a resurrection? This is difficult to answer without making any assumptions. It is certainly widely known that people do not return from the dead, at least by natural causes. Accordingly, the chances of one being revivified by natural causes is next to zero. However, if Jesus was raised, it was almost certainly by a supernatural cause and if God exists and wanted to raise Jesus the probability of his resurrection is nearly 100 percent. Of course, one could say that of anyone. But the context in which the evidence for Jesus' resurrection appears is quite different than for almost everyone else. As stated above, there is a virtual unanimous agreement among historians of Jesus that Jesus claimed to be God's eschatological agent who had been chosen to usher in his Kingdom and that he performed deeds both he and his followers interpreted as divine miracles and exorcisms.

In other words, without presupposing God's existence or his desire to vindicate Jesus, when the strong evidence for Jesus' resurrection is considered alongside of the historical context of his unique teachings and deeds, we have good reason to think we may be touching on an event that involved supernatural (perhaps divine) intervention.

Let us take a look at this from a final angle that may provide additional clarity.

---

[53] See W.A. Dembski and M.R. Licona, eds., *Evidence for God: 50 Arguments for Faith from the Bible, History, Philosophy, and Science* (Grand Rapids: Baker, 2010).

A NEW STARTING POINT IN HISTORICAL JESUS RESEARCH 125

A: person claims to be a prophet
B: person makes no claims of being a prophet
R: reports of a resurrection[54]
~R: no reports of a resurrection
E: resurrection is the best historical explanation of reports

A and B are almost always followed by ~R. This renders plausibility to any claim that A or B did not rise from the dead when ~R.

> There are few accounts of B followed by R.[55]
> There are no accounts of B followed by R and E.
> There is only one example of A followed by R and E: Jesus.

I am not claiming that this renders plausibility to RH. I am claiming that RH is not implausible. In the end, RH has great explanatory scope, explanatory power, and is not *ad hoc*. While it may not possess plausibility, it may not be said to be implausible. Accordingly, RH is far superior to HH and other naturalistic hypotheses fail when subjected to the same criteria.[56]

Accordingly, when the knowable data pertaining to Jesus' fate is subjected to strictly controlled historical method, the hypothesis that Jesus rose physically from the dead is, by far, the best historical explanation. It should, therefore, be regarded as an event that occurred in history.

Conclusion

What does this mean for historical Jesus research? I stated earlier that progress might be made in three areas if the resurrection of Jesus can be historically confirmed. First, historical confirmation of Jesus' resurrection renders greater plausibility to the reports of Jesus' miracles. For if Jesus was raised, one would be hard-pressed to regard healing a man born blind as too fantastic for belief. One might remain skeptical pertaining to the report of Jesus healing a blind man. However, any pause would have to be based on the lack of historical evidence in support and not on an aversion to the supernatural.

---

[54] By "resurrection," here I do not include any theological components of what a resurrection body might entail and could refer to a miraculous revivification.

[55] Herodotus' report concerning Aristeas of Proconnesus (*Hist.* 4.14) is one of only a handful of examples.

[56] See Licona, *Resurrection of Jesus* (n. 7), chap. 5.

Second, historical confirmation of Jesus' resurrection renders a higher probability that Jesus actually predicted his imminent death and resurrection, especially since there are already good reasons in place for holding that Jesus made such predictions. Stated differently, let us say there are multiple reports of a poor and humble man named Fritz who predicts he will win the lottery five times in a year. This is a remarkable claim. If it can be proven that Fritz won the lottery five times in a year (an even more remarkable chain of events), belief that Fritz predicted the outcome becomes more plausible, especially since there is already good evidence that Fritz made the prediction.

Third, and perhaps most important, historical confirmation of Jesus' resurrection sheds illumination on the question of Jesus' self-interpretation. Many scholars acknowledge that, at a very early stage in the history of the Church, Christians came to worship Jesus, the one act Jews reserved for God alone.[57]

Hurtado lists six cultic actions of the early Church toward Jesus that distinguishes him from other Jews revered: "hymns sung in the gathered worship setting both concerning Jesus and to him; prayer to Jesus and in his name; ritual use of Jesus' name in public cultic actions such as baptisms, exorcisms, excommunications, and so on; participation in the corporate sacred meal as 'the Lord's Supper'; ritual 'confession' (*homologein*) of Jesus in honorific terms; and prophecy uttered in Jesus' name and even as his spirit or voice."[58] Hurtado concludes that the early Christians involved in these actions "must have felt compelled by God to reverence Jesus in ways otherwise reserved for God alone."[59]

What may account for this remarkably high view of Jesus held by Jews who would have been extremely hesitant to make such a move? It seems to me that the only plausible explanation is that Jesus made claims to this effect and that his disciples came to understand them more fully in light of their being fully convinced that Jesus had been raised from the dead. That there are numerous texts in the New Testament that at least suggest Jesus made such claims strengthens this conclusion. Accordingly, historical confirmation of Jesus' resurrection suggests that Jesus made very high Christological claims about himself.

---

[57] See L.W. Hurtado, *How on Earth Did Jesus Become a God? Historical Questions about Earliest Devotion to Jesus* (Grand Rapids: Eerdmans, 2005), 129.

[58] Ibid., 198.

[59] Ibid.

A NEW STARTING POINT IN HISTORICAL JESUS RESEARCH 127

In summary, historical confirmation of Jesus' resurrection does not authenticate every logion and deed of Jesus reported in the Gospels. However, it grants a greater plausibility toward the conclusion that the deeds performed by Jesus regarded by himself and others to be divine miracles and exorcisms were in fact divine miracles and exorcisms, that he predicted his imminent death and resurrection, and that he actually claimed for himself a divine status. Thus, there is one major point on which Professor Wolter and I agree: The "real Jesus" may be best understood in light of his resurrection.

A scholarly consensus of the "real Jesus" is not forthcoming in the near future. Not surprisingly, many scholars who scorn the idea of miracles will similarly scorn the approach I have suggested. However, this is to reject an idea *a priori* because of worldview commitments. This move places those historians in a dangerous position where their worldviews guide them rather than the very evidence that could reveal those worldviews as mistaken. The danger is manifest: bad philosophy corrupts good history.

It is the responsibility of the historian to consider what the evidence would look like if he were not wearing his metaphysical bias like a pair of sunglasses that shades the world. It is not the responsibility of the evidence to shine so brightly that it renders such glasses ineffectual.

THEOLOGICAL HERMENEUTICS AND THE HISTORICAL JESUS: A CRITICAL EVALUATION OF GADAMERIAN APPROACHES AND A NEW METHODOLOGICAL PROPOSAL[1]

Christopher M. Hays

1. INTRODUCTION

As a practitioner of a discipline that combines both critical historical research and theological inquiry, the New Testament scholar walks, as it were, the line of a narrow mountain ridge, from which vantage point she can observe the rugged prominences of rigorous historical scholarship on her left and the verdure of ecclesio-theological reflection on her right. The scope of vision of the interpreter is widest when she remains atop this ridge, even if the trek requires sure-footedness and constant correction and adjustment.

In the touchstone essay of this volume, Michael Wolter offers his account of how to negotiate such challenging terrain when speaking about Jesus. Wolter endorses a route between the existential minimalism of Bultmann and the perpetual creation of new historical Jesuses by those whom Wolter construes as the academic heirs of Reimarus. Wolter argues that Jesus ought to be investigated in light of the Easter faith, explaining that the resurrection of Jesus vindicates his life and teachings (1Tim 3:16). In spite of the fact that the object of this scholarly research is irreducibly theological, Wolter urges that this investigation be conducted with atheological methodology.

To aid this study, Wolter elaborates a typology of seven Jesuses, delineating various images of Jesus, categories of ways that people have construed Jesus depending on their historical locations and ideological suppositions. In so doing, Wolter provides conceptual clarity where the lack of specific terminology has often times led to miscommunication and

---

[1] I am grateful for the constructive comments I received on this essay from the members of the *Neutestamentliche Sozietät* of the theological faculties of the University of Bonn, the Biblical Theology Group at the SBL International Meeting in London 2011, the Fundación Universitaria Seminario Bíblico de Colombia, and the New Testament Senior Seminar of the University of Oxford.

misrepresentation of diverse perspectives; Wolter's framework facilitates a more informed methodology for Jesus research.

With gratitude to an exceptional scholar from whom I have benefited greatly, in the present essay I aim alternately to endorse, supplement, and dispute features of Wolter's essay. First and briefly, I want to complement Wolter's criticism of those who have followed Reimarus' path in the construction of historical Jesuses; to this end, I will offer a summary account of recent discussion on the limitations of the scholarly methods by which "Questers" have attempted to uncover the historical Jesus. In this section I will, however, indicate why I think that methodologically atheological historical Jesus research, for all of its many advantages, remains seriously deficient for the study of Jesus.

For the bulk of the essay, I will comment further on the way that researchers have attempted to approach investigation of Jesus in light of the post-Easter faith. I will examine the recent scholarly appropriation of Hans-Georg Gadamer's hermeneutical theory as one expression of a (generally atheological) way to speak about Jesus, and I will point out what I consider to be both the benefits of this appropriation and its theological limitations.

Finally, I will sketch my own methodological proposal by which I hope confessional[2] historical Jesus scholars might be able to do theologically robust Jesus scholarship without excluding themselves from conversation with non-confessional scholars.

2. THE LIMITATIONS OF HISTORICAL JESUS SCHOLARSHIP

In order to underscore the poignant challenges of relating historical Jesus research to Christian theology, I will begin by echoing what is a growing consensus among historical Jesus scholars that the endeavours to cull the original sayings and deeds of Jesus have hardly borne uncontested results.

---

[2] In describing certain historical Jesus scholars as "confessional", I refer to those whose research is actively informed by their religious faith in Jesus. I prefer this to "Christian" or "religious" historical Jesus scholar because there are many Christian scholars of the historical Jesus who endeavour not to allow their religious beliefs to influence their scholarship.

THEOLOGICAL HERMENEUTICS AND THE HISTORICAL JESUS

2.1 *Criteriological Insufficiency*

Notwithstanding the much-publicized assurances of the Jesus Seminar that their efforts would uncover the Jesus who really was (as opposed to the Church's Jesus, ostensibly shrouded by dogmatic accretions), scholars both from within, e.g. Allison (1998:2–10; 2008:79–83; 2009:54–57) and without, e.g. Johnson (1996:126–133) the "Questers" have repeatedly decried the confidence placed on "criteria for historicity", e.g. coherence, dissimilarity, multiple-attestation, embarrassment) that so determine the shape of historical Jesus scholarship.

Consider two of the staple criteria of historical Jesus research: coherence and dissimilarity.

- The criterion of coherence (a saying or deed of Jesus is original if it coheres with what we already know about the life and teachings of Jesus) both assumes that everything Jesus said and did *was* coherent, and rests upon in irreducible circularity whereby we claim *a priori* to know what Jesus taught, according to which we can evaluate whether or not sayings attributed to him fit with the content of that preaching.
- The criterion of (double-)dissimilarity (a saying of Jesus is original if it does not reflect the assumptions of his Jewish contemporaries or his Christian followers) produces an unduly iconoclastic Jesus, one who only ever disagrees with his ancestral tradition and the views of those who called themselves his disciples.

Moreover, these criteria often are counter-indicative:[3] a text with multiple attestation might also fail the criterion of dissimilarity. Clearly, then, these criteria of historicity cannot be considered sufficient and reliable means by which to construct a full-orbed picture of the historical Jesus. This is by no means to deny the common-sensical value of many of these criteria as factors in evaluating how likely a given saying or event is to derive from the historical Jesus. I merely intend to point out that these criteria are not to be confused with scientific laws that can be applied with certainty to any given scenario.[4]

---

[3] As illustrated at length in Allison's critique of Crossan's *Historical Jesus* (see Allison 1998:20 and passim).

[4] For this reason, Allison helpfully suggests that the term "criteria" be done away with in favour of the term "indices" (Allison 1998:51–58), recognizing that ideas such as double dissimilarity, embarrassment, coherence, etc. may help us evaluate the relative likelihood

132 CHRISTOPHER M. HAYS

Anyone who doubts the subjectivity involved in culling information on the historical Jesus need only to examine the opinions of the premier scholars in the field. The 1990s witnessed the production of diametrically opposite Jesuses by academics of the highest calibre. There is no way to reconcile the egalitarian, iconoclastic sage of Crossan and Funk (a wisdom teacher devoid of eschatological or apocalyptic expectation; Crossan 1991; Funk 1997) with the primarily apocalyptic prophet of Allison (1998) or Ehrman (1999). Without being nihilistic in my assessment of what historical Jesus scholarship can produce (I am convinced that Allison and Ehrman are far closer to the mark than the fellows of the Jesus Seminar), we should recognize that at this point the "secured results" of historical Jesus scholarship are more modest than sometimes admitted.

2.2 Hermeneutical Insufficiency:
The Difference between Events and Significance

Nonetheless, a more fundamental problem has yet to be addressed: the difference between events and *meaning*. Even if we could agree on which events did occur and which things Jesus really did say, that would not amount to certainty about what events precipitated others, what the motivations of key characters might have been, or what theological inferences should be drawn from the happenings in question. Any given state of affairs or sequence of events could be accounted for in a number of ways (cf. Allison 2009:57); even when scholars agree that (a) Jesus did enter Jerusalem amidst a crowd of cheering Israelites and (b) cause a stir in the temple in the last week of his life, and (c) that he was crucified shortly thereafter, they still offer a variety of explanations for the causal links between these events. As such, the meaning of that sequence of events remains out of the reach of historical certainty (cf. Johnson 1996:83, 133; Bockmuehl 1994:154).

In short, even with unanimous agreement about which deeds and sayings really do derive from Jesus we would have no scientific way of establishing what Jesus' life and teachings *meant* in the first century, let alone what they *mean* for us today. Instead, scholars *a priori* adopt certain paradigms which they hope will make sense of the most data possible. Crossan appeals to the sociology of power relations (kinship, village dynamics, benefaction, patronage, etc.); Allison relies on comparative religious studies

---

that a given item is unhistorical, but will never provide us with anything akin to certainty on the matter.

THEOLOGICAL HERMENEUTICS AND THE HISTORICAL JESUS   133

of millenarian prophets; Wright develops a salvation-historical Jewish meta-narrative of exile and restoration (Wright 1996). The adoption of such paradigms is not problematic *per se* (in fact, it is inexorable, as we will see below), but it should disabuse us of any notion that scholars approach the historical Jesus without *determinative* prejudices.

2.3   *Theological Insufficiency*

Finally and most significantly, the hegemony of historical critical presuppositions (what Wolter refers to as atheological methodology) in Jesus scholarship, while accruing the highest degree of credibility *vis-à-vis* secular historiography, hamstrings the *theological* endeavour; conventional critical methods are fundamentally inadequate for discussing transcendent claims.[5] Historical critical research does not allow us, as a rule, to discuss whether transcendent/supernatural events (miracles, resurrection, virgin birth, the incarnation of God) happened, only whether or not people *believed* that such things happened (so Ehrman 1999:193–196). In their time-space occurrence-character (that is, their character as having occurred in time-space history), such events are either euhemerized (H.E.G. Paulus), disregarded as the mythopoeic conflagrations of the pre-rational mind (D.F. Strauss), or outright rejected as a matter of principle, as in the case of Lüdemann (1999:11, 14).[6] The problem is that the material with which historical critical methodology is least capable of dealing is also the material that is most determinative for who the Church has believed Jesus to be (cf. Watson 2001:165).

Consider Jesus' resurrection, the crucial event for the development of traditional christology: although the New Testament authors clearly consider Jesus' resurrection from the dead to have occurred in time-space history, the resurrection by definition breaks the rules of how history works. Even for the New Testament authors (who readily enough accepted miracles and resuscitation from the dead to be extraordinary but nonetheless precedented events) Jesus' resurrection, transfiguration, and ascension

---

[5] When I talk about "transcendent" claims, I follow William Placher in referring to claims that "reach beyond ordinary history, toward either an eschatological future or a realm different from that of events in this world" (Placher 2008:38).

[6] There are some exceptions. Allison, for example, draws on a variety of comparative religious, anecdotal, and personal evidence and ventures to discuss the possibility of people being visited by ghosts (Allison 1998:49). Gerd Theissen also endeavours to walk a more careful line in e.g. his form-critically driven discussion of Jesus' miracles (Theissen and Merz 1998:291–313).

134   CHRISTOPHER M. HAYS

were *sui generis* such that the disciples could only perceive therein the
dawning of a new era of existence (Bockmuehl 2001:109, 116; Johnson
1996:136). Accordingly, the Gospels provide the reader with an alternative
frame of historical reference, a notion of time and space in which future
time and divine-kingdom-space have invaded the mundane (Minear
2002:55). Small surprise that prosaic historical critical assumptions about
time and space do not lend themselves to dialogue with the theology of
the Gospels. Methodologically atheological scholarship is insuperably psi-
lanthropist. While eagerly and voluminously discussing the humanity of
Jesus, it cannot evaluate whether he truly did miracles, was truly born of a
virgin, was truly crucified for the salvation of humanity, or was truly resurrected from the dead (Morgan 2005:221), in short, whether or not in Jesus
we truly have to do with God. Such notions can only be engaged from the
perspective of belief. And yet without discussing precisely these issues,
our historical Jesus research will remain theologically deficient.

> What must not be missed here is that by deleting from Jesus' history all ref-
> erences to divine action, critics set aside precisely those parts of the gospels
> by which the Evangelists expressed most explicitly their understanding of
> the ongoing significance of Jesus. (Keck 2000:5)

So then, the largely neglected task of Christian historical Jesus scholarship
is to balance the empirically construed historical Jesus with attention also
to the theological assertions of Christianity about Jesus, since any engagement with the latter excludes the hegemony of the former. But how does
one bring such ideologically distinct approaches into conversation?

3. HANS-GEORG GADAMER

In recent years, some biblical scholars have come to think that the work
of Hans-Georg Gadamer might provide a way forward. Gadamer's mag-
num opus *Truth and Method* (*Wahrheit und Methode*, 1960) was one of the
seminal works in hermeneutical theory in the twentieth century. His work
has exerted influence on biblical scholarship both by way of the general
progress of hermeneutics, and more explicitly through the recent attention to effective history (*Wirkungsgeschichte*). In keeping with Wolter's
proposal, Gadamer might also be thought to provide us with an atheological method by which to investigate Jesus in light of the Christian agreement with the apostles' experiences of the resurrected Jesus. In order to
unpack the benefits and limitations of Gadamer's thought for historical
Jesus scholarship, it would be worthwhile to summarize some of the ideas

THEOLOGICAL HERMENEUTICS AND THE HISTORICAL JESUS

Gadamer presents in the fourth chapter of *Truth and Method*, entitled "Elements of a Theory of Hermeneutic Experience".

3.1 Gadamer's Historical Hermeneutics

Gadamer begins by highlighting Heidegger's observation that all human efforts at understanding are mediated by the "fore-meanings" or "pre-understandings" with which an individual approaches a text (Gadamer 2004:267–268). The finitude of the human consciousness cannot accommodate perfect knowledge, such that we invariably operate with simplifications, suppositions, and limitations; prejudices (*prae-iudicio*) are inevitable for historical beings. The existence of such fore-meanings tempers any naive optimism about pure objectivity in understanding and requires each interpreter to examine and evaluate the legitimacy of his or her fore-meanings.

Our various prejudices (fore-meanings) are handed on to us from our immediate surroundings, our family, friends, schools, and society, and thus can be justifiably referred to as "traditions", leaving open the question of whether or not a given tradition is valid or invalid (whereas the term "prejudices" tends to imply the latter).[7] Since our existence, our very way of knowing, is invariably bound up with traditional prejudices, we need to discard the dichotomy between tradition and historical research, and instead inquire into the manner in which tradition connects us to history, enables us to examine an historical object.[8]

Gadamer explains that it is by tradition that past events come to us. Most details of the past are lost forever. We know about past events only because they made an impact, had an effect (*Wirkung*) somehow on the physical world or human traditionary history. We never encounter events as they were, but through what they left behind, through their impact, what they meant, their historical significance. An event does not present itself to us directly, but its effects, its aftermath, stretch forward to us, allowing us to grasp the past not as it was (in a manner that requires an infinitude foreign to the human historical condition), but for what it became, what it meant.

---

[7] "We are always situated in traditions and . . . we do not conceive of what traditions say as something other, something alien. It is always part of us . . ." (Gadamer 2004:283).

[8] In this vein, Gadamer (2004:297) asserts that time is not a gulf to be bridged, "it is actually the supportive ground of the course of events in which the present is rooted. . . . It is not a yawning abyss but is filled with the continuity of custom and tradition, in the light of which everything handed down presents itself to us."

Gadamer characterizes the hermeneutical endeavour as akin to reading a difficult text in an ancient language. Since the meaning of a challenging ancient text is not immediately obvious to the translator, she works piecemeal in her translation, *anticipating* the text's meaning, attempting to construe little bits of a sentence at a time, and reworking her understanding of constituent words and phrases until the whole text comes together and makes sense. Her anticipation of the text's meaning, before she has understood its constituent parts, does not prevent her from reading the text; rather it guides her as she seeks to cobble together the smaller pieces, moving cyclically through lexical, syntactical, and contextual possibilities, constantly adjusting each, until the text's meanings become clear. So it is with hermeneutics. We approach a text with certain fore-meanings, given to us through tradition, and then when our fore-meanings prove inadequate for fully describing the meaning of a text, we are forced to adjust those fore-meanings. The idiosyncrasies of the text provoke an awareness of our pre-understandings, foregrounding (*aufheben*) them as a first step towards suspending, analysing, and evaluating them.

The same dynamics apply in the case of interpreting an historical event. We can only truly gain understanding of another historical era, text, or person after we recognize that our own existence is historically constituted, that our perspective on previous history is embroidered in the warp and woof of own historical moment. "A hermeneutic adequate to the subject matter would have to demonstrate the reality and efficacy of history within understanding itself. I shall refer to this as a 'history of effect' (*Wirkungsgeschichte*). *Understanding is, essentially, a historically effected event*" (Gadamer 2004:299).

Generally, when Gadamer talks about history, he refers not so much to establishing the facts of what happened as to articulating the significance of those facts. Gadamer assumes that the task of the historical discipline is not merely to describe what was, but to explain the impact of what was, how it, in one way or another, contributed to our current state of affairs. A World War II historian must of course trace troop movements, calculate climate conditions, describe domestic and international politics, and estimate food supplies and weapons production, but these statistical and archaeological considerations are only a part of the historian's task. The historian also has to assess the impact of this data on people's enduring morality, tendencies, hopes, and fears, and ultimately to describe the aftermath of the war for the entire world. At the same time, he has to come to terms with and articulate the way in which the transcript of history has been altered by the rhetoric and metanarrative of the victors,

THEOLOGICAL HERMENEUTICS AND THE HISTORICAL JESUS 137

shaping people's memory and understanding of the war, even influencing the historian's own understanding. In short, historical hermeneutics must explain what an historical event or series of events came to mean for us, how they have made us who we are.

When one apprehends that one's own consciousness "is itself situated in the web of historical effects" (Gadamer 2004:300), Gadamer says that one possesses *historically effected consciousness* (*wirkungsgeschichtliches Bewußtsein*), which entails that one is always aware of the limitations of one's own knowledge, limitations which obtain as a consequence of one's own historical finitude. This requires a perpetual caution "against overhastily assimilating the past to our own expectations of meaning. Only then can we listen to tradition in a way that permits it to make its own meaning heard" (Gadamer 2004:304). Thus, as we are provoked by the past as an Other, we foreground our prejudices and the prejudices of the Other which are readily apparent to us, seeking understanding by highlighting the differences in our respective historically effected consciousnesses. By foregrounding one's own prejudices and those of the text, one is able to begin truly understanding the Other, rather than just describing or mastering the Other.

If an interpreter apprehends that she is historically effected, that she only thinks from within her tradition, and that this does not limit her but is in fact the pre-condition of her understanding at all, then she can be truly *open* to understand and learn from an event mediated to her through tradition, in its difference from her. Just as human relationships require the acknowledgement of the Other's personhood, admitting that you have something to say to me, so also the historically effected consciousness "must allow the tradition's claim to validity, not in the sense of simply acknowledging the past in its otherness, but in such a way that it has something to say to me. This too calls for a fundamental sort of openness" (Gadamer 2004:355).

When attempting to interpret without imposing one's pre-understandings on the Other of the past, Gadamer advises that the interpreter proceed by asking questions. The questions that we ask should be among those suggested by the text itself, the questions to which the text itself attempts to offer an answer, and questions which the interpreter also shares. Then the interpreter attempts to hear the text's answer to that question, and brings forth his own answer to the question. In this process, the interpreter must make the effort to keep the dialogue open, to allow the traditionary word to provoke him, to call into question his own fore-meanings and prejudices. "The voice that speaks to us from the past . . . itself poses a question and places our meaning in openness" (Gadamer 2004:366–367). This applies particularly to the historical Jesus scholar as he or she reads the Gospels, not just to find the information they betray about Jesus, but also to hear the *meaning* they give to Jesus as his witnesses, his effects.

I should stress, lest Gadamer (or I) be dismissed as a solipsistic, postmodern relativist, that this is not tantamount to embracing the validity of every ancient perspective. We cannot but consider suspect some things which an ancient person accepted without hesitation (cf. Roberts and Rowland 2010:135). We can, however, suspend our dismissal of their supposition in order to engage genuinely with their perspective, to hear their questions and apply them to ourselves in such a way that we too can ask their question.[9] When we can both ask the same question, invariably reframed and further opened to accommodate our modern inquiry, then we can dialogue with the traditionary word about the question we now share, thereby connecting the past horizon to our own and expanding our field of vision.[10] (For the purpose of brevity, I will avoid delving into Gadamer's notion of the fusion of the horizons.)

3.2 The Benefits of Gadamerian Hermeneutics for Confessional Jesus Scholarship

One reason for which Gadamer has found a warm reception in biblical scholarship is because his account of the history of effects has permitted members of the guild to renew engagement with, e.g., Gospel and patristic materials *as historical witnesses to the events and meanings of Jesus' life* without tarnishing their historical credibility; in Wolter's terms, he offers us an atheological method by which we conduct our theological research in light of the Easter faith.

Gadamer has reminded us of the truism that effects tell us a great deal about their causes. This allows, indeed, requires us to bring new data to bear on old historical questions, reminding us that later "strata" of material

---

[9] "Historical scholarship first seeks to understand every text in its own terms and does not accept the content of what it says as true, but leaves it undecided" (Gadamer 2004:330). Assent and obedience depend upon the degree to which one finds the text's perspective credible *after* one has heard its perspective.

[10] "We cannot avoid thinking about what the author accepted unquestioningly and hence did not consider bringing it into the openness of the question. This is not to open the door to arbitrariness in interpretation but to reveal what always takes place.... [P]art of real understanding, however, is that we regain the concepts of a historical past in such a way that they also include our own comprehension of them" (Gadamer 2004:367).

THEOLOGICAL HERMENEUTICS AND THE HISTORICAL JESUS 139

are not only accretions (though they are often that) but are in many ways the "footprint"[11] of an historical event.[12] Conversely, in so far as the Gospels can be seen as expressions of the effect that Jesus had on his disciples, we should *hold in suspicion* any reconstructions of the historical Jesus that produce a man dramatically different from the Jesus of the Gospels (Morgan 2005:222).

Gadamer has also helped biblical scholars remember that the *meaning* of an event resides in large part in its effects. This idea of course predates Gadamer even in the biblical guild, having been forcefully argued by Martin Kähler in his 1892 essay *Der sogenannte historische Jesus und der geschichtliche, biblische Christus,*[13] but Gadamer provides the notion with a new philosophical lease on life. Jesus' significance cannot be separated from how his disciples understood him. A person's effects (how she is received by other people, what impression she makes on others) help constitute her meaning (cf. Keck 2000:7; Allison 2008:93–95). Identity is an object held by and determined by one's family, friends, enemies, and associates, at least in part during one's life and entirely after one's death. Jesus in particular was a man whose life reached beyond his death and transformed his disciples; "If we ignore them, don't we ignore him?" (Allison 2009:29, cf. 23–25; Johnson 1996:152). This construal of meaning partially in terms of "effects" should provide a corrective to the "archaeological" approaches that try to sweep away the scriptural accounts of Jesus' life (which are themselves among the most significant effects of Jesus' life) in order to recover "the bare, indisputable facts" (only to find that they are without means to explain indisputably what those facts *mean*).

Finally, Gadamer reminds us not only that our prejudices and presuppositions are inexorable, but that they are prerequisite to understanding;

---

[11] Here I use a favorite term of my *Doktorvater*, Markus Bockmuehl. Using a similar metaphor, Dunn notes, "From the impression in the wax we can discern the shape of the seal. From the impression left on the disciples we can discern the 'shape' of the one who made that impression" (Dunn 2004:15).

[12] The debts of Bockmuehl and Dunn to Gadamer are clear, as the former comments, "We will learn about Jesus best from the tradition he generated" (Bockmuehl 1994:8) and the latter claims that the tradition "*is itself part of the effect Jesus had on those he called to discipleship*" (Dunn 2003:329, italics original).

[13] "Schon rein geschichtlich gegriffen ist das wahrhaft Geschichtliche an einer bedeutenden Gestalt die persönliche Wirkung, die der Nachwelt auch spürbar von ihr zurückbleibt." "Der wirkliche, d. h. der wirksame Christus...."; "Sein Werk ist seine Person in ihrer geschichtlich-übergeschichtlichen Wirkung" (Kähler 1953:38, 44, 78; cf. Watson 1997:52; Bockmuehl 2006:167; 2010a:19).

prejudices provide us with a starting point, and direct us towards the traditions by which they were generated so that we can traverse those traditions back towards an historical event. Pre-understanding is the stance from which we begin our dialectic engagement with the Other of history. In the same vein, Gadamer points out that we do not stand at the end of history, or outside of history, as if we possess some objective vantage point from which to judge the meaning of what has come before. We recognize that we are insuperably part of history (so also Keck 2000:9), that our account of the historical Jesus' meaning will be unavoidably stamped with the image of our own era, as Schweitzer pointed out to be the case with the liberal nineteenth-century scholars, and as Dunn incisively showed with respect to the Jesus Seminar (Dunn 2003:62–64). So if we desire to overcome, at least in part, the limitations of our own historicity, we have to foreground our presuppositions. We are obliged to declare them (Protestant, Orthodox; feminist, chauvinist; atheist, relativist; American, German) from the outset instead of denying that they exist (cf. Johnson 1996:175; Morgan 2004:5), keeping them always before us in remembrance of the fact that they are both vantage points from which we view the past, and that their horizons are limited. In light of our limitations and the limitations of our every human predecessor, we don't get to claim objective knowledge of the "meaning" of history; we can at best say what history has meant (in some degree), what it does mean (in some degree), and what it could mean (in some degree). Thus, as one recent and insightful article averred, *Wirkungsgeschichte* "enables exegesis to regain its interpretive self-consciousness" (Roberts and Rowland 2010:133).

There is little doubt that Gadamer has done a great deal to legitimate the work of confessing scholars in the field of historical Jesus research, as he has reminded us that we must listen to the witness of the Gospels to understand the identity and meaning of Jesus, as he has iterated that the meaning of an event resides in large part in its effects, and as he has admonished us regarding the inexorability and indeed valour of our presuppositions. Small surprise that confessing scholars have integrated Gadamerian insights (generally without articulating the source of those insights) into their historical Jesus work. But even Gadamerian historical hermeneutics will not suffice for Christian historical Jesus scholarship, in so far as the Christian historical Jesus scholar intends to draw theological conclusions from his or her work on the grounds that the historical Jesus (whoever he was) should at least in some way inform and norm our Christian belief.

THEOLOGICAL HERMENEUTICS AND THE HISTORICAL JESUS

3.3 The Limitations of Gadamerian Hermeneutics for Confessional Jesus Scholarship

At this point it bears note that Gadamer himself distinguishes historical hermeneutics from theological hermeneutics. "Scripture is the word of God, and that means it has an absolute priority over the doctrine of those who interpret it. Interpretation should never overlook this" (Gadamer 2004:326–327).[14] Sensitivity to this distinction is salient for investigations of the historical Jesus since the *Christian* historical Jesus scholar combines, in various degrees, the traits of the historian and the theologian (for which reason Wolter describes himself as a theological historian). A Christian historical Jesus scholar is like the historian, for she reads the texts of the New Testament (*inter alia*) not only on their own terms, but for what they betray about history in spite of themselves. Like the historian, she is also interested in describing Jesus' history of effects, seeing what beliefs in and about Jesus arose following his death. Still, the Christian historical Jesus scholar is not just an historian. The Gadamerian historian is only interested in what history was and what it meant; if further research (archaeology, critical reading, etc.) were to show that the significance that an event had in history depended in part on an assumption that things occurred in a way in which they did not, that is not of great hermeneutical importance: the effect of the event did obtain, irrespective of whether it would have obtained if "the facts" of the historical event were more accurately or completely disclosed.

But can the Christian historical Jesus scholar behave so indifferently towards the occurrence-character of the events of Jesus' life and death (and resurrection)? To a degree, we can say that certain events described in the Gospels may not have occurred, but that they nonetheless do portray the character of Jesus truly (cf. Placher 2008:34). Consider, e.g., the account of Jesus' temptation in the wilderness (Matt 4:1–11//Luke 4:1–13) or the story of the woman caught in adultery (John 7:52–8:11). Even if we decide that it seems unlikely that these events did occur, they graphically depict a Jesus who resisted the demonic, refused self-aggrandizement, was committed to the worship of YHWH alone, and who defended and forgave

---

[14] Gadamer was similarly inclined to privilege the incarnation as a unique moment in history, of determinative significance for history in a manner unlike from any other historical moment, precisely because it was a moment in which *God entered history*. "... [F]or the Christian theologian the 'practical purpose' of all universal historical conceptions has its fixed point in the absolute history of the incarnation" (Gadamer 1976:37).

142 CHRISTOPHER M. HAYS

sinners and outsiders; surely these stories illustrate the identity and character of the Jesus who truly was, even if the stories did not occur as such (cf. Keck 2000:20). Francis Watson, perhaps Gadamer's foremost disciple in the New Testament guild, has argued that the development of "legendary" materials is part and parcel of reception/tradition, that reception is a "dialectic of preservation and innovation within the process of tradition" (Watson 2008:107), and that these legends arise from a deep-seated conviction about and traditional knowledge of the Jesus who really was (Watson 2008:107).

3.4 *The Theological Necessity of Occurrence for Hope*

Nonetheless, there are certain things that cannot simply be affirmed at the textual level and disregarded at the historical level. For some items, the confidence of our theological claim, the veracity of the text's function as divine speech, depends on elements of historicity (cf. Placher 2008:35).[15] Acceptance of the distance between what is verifiable and what is believed, or accepting that certain stories can be legendary and still true to the character of Jesus, ought not to lapse into indifference towards fundamental contradictions between the historically probable Jesus and the Jesus of faith. The prioritization of "reception" implies that, because history phenomenologically *is* determined by reception, the occurrence-character is indifferent. But this is insufficient. The Gospels and apostolic tradition interpreted the life of Jesus in a particular way because they were convinced of certain fundamental things about who Jesus was.

In this vein, Francis Watson draws also (however implicitly) on Strauss, saying: "For early Christian storytellers, legend seems to have functioned as a way of communicating nonempirical theological truth" (Watson 2008:109). This approach, however accurate it may be at times, cannot be applied to any and all transcendent texts of the Gospels because the so-called legendary accounts do not just *communicate* a theological belief (cf. Strauss), they also seek to *ground* belief by convincing the reader that such things did in point of fact happen; saying that an event is unhistorical does in fact weaken the foundation of a belief. Christian orthodoxy

---

[15] "An authentic link between Jesus of Nazareth and the exalted Christ is in fact *theologically indispensable* for Christianity. If there are no reasonable grounds for a personal continuity between 'crucified under Pontius Pilate' and 'seated at the right hand of God'... then Christian faith would indeed be a travesty" (Bockmuehl 1994:167).

THEOLOGICAL HERMENEUTICS AND THE HISTORICAL JESUS   143

can bear this to some degree, but let us not pretend that nothing is lost in characterizing certain texts as legendary.

Now one might object at this juncture that I have not learned the lessons taught by Gadamer's notion of the history of effects, pointing out that the only Jesus that matters is the Jesus who *effectively* was, and that the Jesus who *effectively was* is the Jesus of the Gospels. Here, however, we run into one of the limitations of Gadamer's historical hermeneutic: the role of history in *hope*.

It is my contention that the meanings of certain events cannot be exclusively located in the effects of those events, but rather, that their meanings are also bound up with the events' occurrence-character (by which I mean, again, their character as having occurred in time-space history). Consider the following scenario: a squad of soldiers is pinned down in hostile territory, and they are sure to be caught and killed if they are not first rescued. If this squad were to receive word by radio that their battalion had broken through enemy lines and was on its way to rescue them, this good news would provide them with hope, changing their present experience, and perhaps helping them to hold on longer than they would have otherwise had the will to do. These positive effects (hope, perseverance) would obtain in the *present situation* for the soldiers, if they believe the radio news to be true, irrespective of whether or not the news actually were true, irrespective of whether or not their battalion actually were on the way to save them. It is, however, also highly significant for the soldiers' *future experience* that the news of forthcoming help is in fact true, that their rescue is really on the way, that their battalion's victory did actually occur in time-space. If help is not truly forthcoming, they may experience hope or renewed stamina (the effects of the fraudulent news) for a period of time, but in the end they will still be caught or killed.

This scenario illustrates that, in some cases, the traditionary significance of an event is less important than the occurrence-character of the event, or at least that the traditionary meaning of an event is limited in its validity if the event did not occur in time-space. This is especially true in the cases of the most disputed subjects of historical Jesus scholarship, such as the virgin birth and the resurrection. In these cases it is particularly important to inquire about an event beyond the level of describing effective history, because the *religious* significance of Jesus is deeply bound up with eschatology, with hope of Jesus' second coming and the resurrection of the dead.

Now, it should be readily granted that history cannot decisively prove or disprove either of these future expectations. Nonetheless, Christian

144   CHRISTOPHER M. HAYS

hope for these eschatological events is based on the historicity of certain events in the life of Christ.[16] The resurrection of Jesus in particular is of massive importance, for without it, as Paul says, our hope is vain[17] (1Cor 15:17–19). The virgin birth warrants an investigation beyond articulating that the effective history of Jesus' life amounted to a belief in his birth from a virgin,[18] for the virgin birth was traditionally adduced as grounds for the Church's claims concerning deity of Christ (the deity from which the efficacy of his salvific action on the behalf of humanity was assumed to derive).[19]

So also the historicity of miracles should be debated since they are considered to be (and depicted in the Gospels as) evidence of Jesus' messianic and divine identity. Granted, if some or even all miracles did not in fact occur in time-space, that would not falsify who Jesus was and/or will be *pro nobis*,[20] but it attenuates Christian confidence and hope. The same

---

[16] What's more, the texts of the Gospels present themselves as witnessing to an historical reality. While the contours of this witness may indeed differ from, e.g., modern expectations of eye-witness accounts or historiography, within the generic and self-imposed constraints of what the texts themselves claim to be doing we are permitted to and (in the contemporary intellectual environment, for apologetic reasons) obliged to assess the events to which they witnessed, in so far as we are able, considering the other data available to us. One ought not to balk at the idea that we can consider the historical Jesus with a view towards data which are at least partially distinct from the information available to us in the New Testament. There are new pieces of information (archaeological, secular-historical, sociological, and non-canonical) bearing on the events of Jesus' life and era which have not been part of the previous stream of tradition, and yet have the right and power to create their own effects, their own traditions. It is valid for us to supplement our understanding of Jesus from this data, considering the potential differences between events and texts. Though effective history does in one sense lend itself to more conservative sentiments, since it allows one to assess data from the orthodox fathers, Gadamer does not only grant license to assess mainstream data, but also requires that we look at the perspectives of all streams of history, including the heterodox streams, bringing them into dialogue so that the logos can arise from them.

[17] Or: our hope is at best founded only on religious texts which derive their expectations at least in part from an event that they assume to be historical but was in fact not.

[18] Or beyond saying that the virgin birth is part and parcel of the classical tendency to describe a notable figure as being sired by a god in order to express wonderment at the figure's superiority to normal humans, or to honour an exceptional benefactor (so Talbert 2006).

[19] This is not to say that Christ could not be God apart from the virgin birth, or that his work could not benefit humanity apart from his deity; I am merely pointing out that belief in his divinity and atonement are based in part on the assumption that the immaculate conception was historical, such that, apart from the occurrence-character of the virgin birth, one would have to articulate an alternative account of Christ's deity and probably need to provide new historical grounds for that doctrine (as perhaps does Dunn 2003:347–348 with his seemingly adoptionist account of Jesus).

[20] "There may be more things in heaven and earth than are dreamt of in our empiricist philosophies, and we should not be too quick to dismiss reports of religious experience

obtains in the case of Jesus' messianic consciousness. Even though Jesus' effective history is clearly that of being the Messiah who proclaimed (*inter alia*) forgiveness of sins, because Christians believe that sins really require a reckoning before God, it does indeed matter whether Jesus was in fact qualified to declare the forgiveness of sins.[21] Therefore, discussion of *only* the effective history of belief in the transcendent Jesus remains insufficient for Christian study of the historical Jesus. It is valid, and indeed, religiously necessary, to inquire into whether certain events of Jesus' life did happen, whether other evidence corroborates or precludes this, even if we recognize, with Gadamer, that definitive knowledge of these matters is not something that we will ever attain.

So, if the confessional historical Jesus scholar (Wolter's "theological historian") cannot remain indifferent to the transcendent, he finds himself caught in a scissor movement between the two sides of his job. He wants to assent to the claims of Scripture about what the life and deeds of Jesus mean, but the validity of the claim of the text does not reside solely in the text, but at least partly in the event of history itself. He has to find a way to coordinate the assent of the theologian to what the text claims with the inquiry of the historian into what the text expresses and betrays about what was.

On the one hand, recognizing the limitations of our historical knowledge and the incapacity of purely historical research to determine meaning with any type of scientific certainty, with Gadamer the Christian Jesus scholar can recognize that he needs to work from within a given tradition. But, on the other hand, Gadamer does not give him license to work from a fortified theological high-ground without admitting the limitations of the high-ground, in particular through conversation with the historical Jesus

---

different from what we ourselves may have shared, but it is reasonable to be sceptical about the historicity of some gospel traditions on account of what we know about the early churches" (Morgan 2005:219).

[21] Admittedly, he theoretically could have been the Messiah and not known it, but the grounds on which Christians choose to believe that he was the Messiah include not only the fact that the apostles proclaimed Jesus to be the Messiah, but also that they made such claims in part because they understood *Jesus* to have personally articulated or at least implied as much. While Luke and John do sometimes depict the apostles as "putting together the pieces" after the fact (see e.g. Luke 24:8 [the Resurrection]; John 2:17–22 [Cleansing of the Temple]; 12:16 [the Triumphal Entry]; Acts 11:16 [Jesus' prophecy about the disciples being baptized with fire]), unless one wants to adopt a rather sinister view of the apostles' intentions, it seems most fair to say that the apostles really did think that Jesus had indicated that he was the Messiah before his death, whether or not an historian judges it likely that Jesus really did express as much.

146   CHRISTOPHER M. HAYS

as made known in part through the work of secular scholars. It is both valid for people to examine the historical Jesus from a theological viewpoint, and for people not to do so.[22] How, then, can these two groups of scholars discuss the historical Jesus without constantly tripping over their epistemological differences?

4. COORDINATING CRITICAL AND CONFESSIONAL JESUS SCHOLARSHIP

It was precisely this question that sparked a debate in the *Expository Times* between James Dunn and Robert Morgan in 2004–2005. Morgan asserts,

> There are two different kinds of historical pictures of the first-century Jew Jesus, those of New Testament theology, written from a Christian standpoint and presenting a historical biblical Jesus, and those (equally legitimate) written (by Christians or non-Christians) from a non-biblical and non-Christian standpoint. (Morgan 2005:223)

Morgan contends that Dunn allows his theological biases to tilt his historical Jesus project through an unduly credulous assessment of the Gospel traditions (a credulity justified on the basis of Dunn's appeal to conventions of oral performance), or that Dunn "conflates" his unspoken confessional biases with his allegedly methodologically atheological historical Jesus research (Morgan 2005:223). Instead, Morgan urges that confessional inquiries be conducted within the Gospels' christological framework (on which, see further below), in agreement with the apostolic interpretation of the resurrection that both he and Wolter rightly identify as decisive for Christian faith.

Here is the rub: Dunn's historical research, representative as it is in principle of the atheological methodology that Wolter also endorses, provides an excellent framework for conversation with non-confessional scholars, as conflicting faith presuppositions are taken out of the equation. Dunn's work is attractive to confessional scholars because he produces a historical Jesus that looks quite similar to the Jesus of the Gospels (Wolter's "earthly Christ"), but this similitude contributes to other Jesus scholars' suspicions of his methods. On the other hand, Morgan's approach is also capable of producing a Jesus similar to the "earthly Christ" of the Gospels,

---

[22] Although the non-confessing historical critic should not assume that his presupposition is any more privileged than that of his believing colleague. Methodologically naturalist historical criticism is itself just one moment within the reception history of the Bible (Lyons 2010).

all the while being so presuppositionally up-front that he cannot be accused of doing biased historical Jesus research, since he is writing New Testament theology informed by critical historiography. The downside to this approach is that it is easy for historical Jesus scholars to ignore the conclusions of "New Testament theology", since it is, in modern parlance, as distinct sub-discipline.

While being most grateful for the works of both Dunn and Morgan, I am concerned that throwing my hat in with either one method or the other would only perpetuate the tendency of Jesus scholars of different presuppositional allegiances to talk past each other. Might I attempt to propose a *via media*? I would like to suggest that it is possible for confessional historical Jesus scholars to combine theological and atheological methodologies, but to be explicit when transitioning from comments that depend on one set of methods and presuppositions to the other. This sort of procedural sensitivity could act as a prophylactic agent against sweeping dismissals of scholars working from opposite presuppositions, and would also help highlight the degree of compatibility between the Jesus accessible to unbelieving historians and the Jesus accessible by faith.

4.1 *A Five-Staged Taxonomy*

For the sake of methodological clarity, even at the risk of developing an overly artificial rubric, I suggest that confessional historical Jesus researchers might proceed according a particular sequence suggested in the taxonomy depicted below, according to which they would separate their work into five different stages in order to make clear the degree to which discrete components of their conclusions depend upon their religious presuppositions. As a discipline of methodological self-awareness, one could proceed in discrete steps from a more reserved "hermeneutic of suspicion" to a more religious "hermeneutic of consent".[23]

The first stage of the proposed sequence would utilize the critical criteria typical of historical Jesus scholarship (albeit with the caveats that the criteria's vulnerability, limitations, and debts to the caprice of the interpreters be recognized). This stage of research would be accessible even

---

[23] "A hermeneutics of consent will give the gospels the benefit of any doubt, while feeling free to pass negative judgments about their historicity in many places, and on their occasional theological deficiencies (*Sachkritik*)" (Morgan 2004:7). Further on the application of *Sachkritik* in the modern reception of Scripture see Morgan (2010).

148   CHRISTOPHER M. HAYS

Hermeneutic of Suspicion

1. Conventional Critical Indices

2. Orality, eye-witness testimony, and living memory (mundane topics)

Dividing line between belief and non-belief

3. Orality, eye-witness testimony, and living memory (transcendent topics)

Dividing line between event and interpretation

4. Adoption of the Theological Framework of the Gospels

5. Adoption of the Theological Framework of the Christian Tradition

Hermeneutic of Consent

Figure 1. A hermeneutical taxonomy for historical Jesus scholarship.

to scholars who eschew Christian faith and are committed to the most suspicious of hermeneutics.

The second stage of research would take a step in the direction of a hermeneutics of consent (albeit a small one) by bringing to bear the observations of Dunn (*et al.*) on oral performance,[24] Bauckham on eye-witness testimony,[25] and Bockmuehl (2010a:17–30) on living memory. These types of historical inquiry can remain in the realm of what a non-confessional historian would potentially countenance (they encompass Wolter's fourth and fifth images of Jesus), though they rely less on the narratives of

---

[24] Dunn (2003:192–253), notwithstanding the various critiques of Dunn's notion of orality that have surfaced in e.g. Bockmuehl (2010b); Gregory (2004).

[25] Bauckham (2006), though it is important that the confessional stance of Bauckham's thesis has been challenged by *inter alia* James Crossley. A debate between the two scholars is available at http://www.premierradio.org.uk/listen/ondemand.aspx?mediaid=%7Boac b5bb-fcae-432f-8224-960c4ad52a5c%7D. I am grateful to Chris Tilling for drawing this to my attention.

THEOLOGICAL HERMENEUTICS AND THE HISTORICAL JESUS 149

suspicion, suppression, and even subterfuge that characterize the works of scholars like Crossan, Funk, and Lüdemann.

In so far as a scholar is open to the transcendent claims of Christianity, he or she will desire to evaluate the plausibility of those claims, to whatever degree such evaluation might be possible. Thus, a third stage of research could bring to bear the same methodologies as those of the first and second stages (especially attention to "testimony") but for the express purpose of inquiring into early Christian beliefs *in transcendent events* such as the virgin birth, miracles, and the resurrection. Evaluating the transcendent aspects of Jesus' life should be kept distinct from inquiries into other aspects of his teachings and deeds precisely because a stance of belief is the crucial presupposition by which the former such items could be evaluated even as to their *relative* reliability.

Here I would pause to comment on the division I have made between steps two and three on the basis of the latter's attention to the "transcendent claims of Christianity"; this distinction does differ from Wolter's crucial differentiation between theological and non-theological history. For Wolter, the determinative difference between the theological and atheological historian is that the former assents to the apostles' interpretation of the resurrection while the latter does not. Now, I certainly agree with Wolter that belief in the resurrection vindicates "Jesus' 'self-conception'", but I am also inclined to say that one's assent to the occurrence of a miracle of that magnitude what Richard Swinburne calls a "super-miracle" (Swinburne 2003:190) calls into question the *a priori* rejection of other miracles, a theoretical constraint which is characteristic of atheological methodology.[26] Thus, I am not content to say that faith in the resurrection only stimulates historical Jesus research to examine a theological object *via* atheological means, and instead would argue that faith in the resurrection requires a method that is theologically informed.

---

[26] I recognize that Wolter endorses a visionary construal of the apostles' resurrection experiences, and that some have construed those experiences as non-miraculous. Setting aside my disagreement with an account of the resurrection in terms of a subjective (or objective) vision, I do not think one can assent to Wolter's assertion of the truth of the apostles' interpretation of their experiences in 1Corinthians 15 (to use Wolter's example), and then deny that a supreme miracle has occurred. Paul claims that, as a consequence of Jesus' resurrection and entrance into a unprecedented form of post-mortem existence is the initiation of a transformation from mortality to immortality, death has lost its sting (1Cor 15:51–55). Whatever immortality means to Paul, it is a radical transformation of the pre-Easter state of affairs that defies the hegemony of naturalism and throws open the question of whether or not the alteration of lesser natural operations might well have preceded the super-miracle that is Christ's resurrection.

It is only after the first three stages of the proposed taxonomy that we enter into the task of assigning *meaning* to the events previously under investigation.[27] The fourth stage undertakes to interpret Jesus from within the christological and eschatological (or, simply, the theological) framework of the Gospels (and derivatively, the canons of the Old and New Testament), which are the most significant moments in the effective history of Jesus (cf. Watson 1997:54, 110). This perspective accepts Gadamer's argument that taking an initial, prejudiced stance is something that all historians inexorably do, whether Christian or not;[28] it thus accepts that a Christian pre-understanding is as legitimate a starting point as any. The most eloquent advocate for this approach is Bob Morgan (1987:198), who says, "A New Testament theology [ought] to retain the evangelists' own Christological frameworks, but to build into its interpretations further historical information" (see also Watson 2001:164–165). Guarding the theological framework of the Gospels,[29] Morgan suggests that the insights of historical critical research on Jesus be integrated "piecemeal" in that Gospel framework,[30] recognizing that the historical critical results about discrete data related to the life of Jesus are far more secure than their ambitious global reconstructions of the meaning of his life, which at their best can be considered plausible alternatives to the Gospel interpretations of Jesus. This allows us to step beyond the limits of historical research, which generally speaking lacks the philosophical tools to deal with the transcendent. It is this stage which most closely appropriates Wolter's third image of Jesus, the "earthly Christ".

Nonetheless, this approach does not give confessional scholars license to ignore historical Jesus research; we can still evaluate the degree to which the Jesus of stages one and two is compatible with the Jesus of the Gospels. Or put negatively, we can ask if the apparent facts of a construction of the historical Jesus which disagree with the Gospel accounts do indeed *belie* the meaning of Jesus' life offered by the Gospels.

---

[27] This is not to say that non-confessional scholars who would decline this stage of investigation are incapable of assigning meaning to Jesus; rather, in light of my argument that atheological methodologies are unable to provide any sort of historically certain meaning for the life of Jesus this taxonomy is proposed only for confessional scholars interested in a theological construal of the historical Jesus.

[28] A point also made by Allison (1998:36) and Dunn (2004:14).

[29] By which I refer to the fourfold Gospel, since it is John that most explicitly articulates the most profound reality of Jesus: his divinity (cf. Watson 2008:111). John is the canonical climax of Jesus' effective history (so also Allison 2009:29).

[30] See e.g. Morgan (1987:200–201).

THEOLOGICAL HERMENEUTICS AND THE HISTORICAL JESUS

Here Morgan both eschews the wholesale liberal rejection of traditional christology, and avoids retreating into a pre-critical assumption that the Gospels always render the historical events of Jesus' life as they occurred. When Christian Jesus scholars enter the fray of historical Jesus debate from this perspective, then "The conflict is no longer between faith and reason but between a reasonable faith and a faithless reason" (Morgan 1987:199).

Although certain Protestant biblical scholars might be content to stop after the fourth stage, the historical Jesus could also be analysed (fifth and finally) from the vantage point of later Christian Tradition (construed in whatever terms one will: the Niceno-Constantinopolitan creed, Augustine, the Catechism of the Catholic Church, Moltmann, etc.); this is the second image of Jesus in Wolter's typology.[31] Once one is no longer epistemologically confined by the assumptions of an historical criticism governed by naturalist metaphysics, and instead considers the possibility that God might actually reveal truth through Tradition and Scripture, then a theological issue of the utmost importance arises: if Jesus of Nazareth truly is the Second Person of the Trinity, the Divine Word, then he was not that only after the resurrection, but he was that before his crucifixion, irrespective of what historical methodology considers likely or plausible. Given this epistemological and confessional stance, any account of the historical Jesus that neglects attention to Jesus *qua* God in Jewish flesh[32] is seriously failing to describe history as it really was (Jenson 2008:48).

It was exactly this type of theological sensitivity that drove Joseph Ratzinger to write his best-selling and massively controversial *Jesus of Nazareth* (Ratzinger 2007). Conversely, it was his lack of methodological articulacy that caused a vociferous uproar in many quarters of the New Testament guild. The problem was not that Ratzinger wrote a book claiming that the historical Jesus was God, but that he wrote such a book under the pretenses of doing what historical critical scholarship (conventionally

---

[31] I am willing to entertain the full-range of this five-staged taxonomy because I have what might be called a Barthian-Catholic epistemology, believing that God desires to make Godself known in history, that he did so definitively in Christ and concentrically in the people of God throughout time, through the working of the Holy Spirit. Because I believe that God is committed to this extensive work of self-revelation, I am inclined to ask how God revealed Godself in subsequent history, seeing it not as merely an impediment to historical knowledge of the revelation that is Jesus (though it is sometimes that), and not just a traditionary bridge to the revelation that is Jesus (though it is also that) but also as the sphere of continued and further revelation about Jesus.

[32] Cf. Bockmuehl (2008:75), "the Word became *Jewish* flesh".

construed) does. Ratzinger's is an approach to Jesus that is explicitly Christian; it is not a neutral, or better, non-believing, approach to the text of the sort that could be characterized as "historical critical" without massive qualification regarding the pre-understandings operative in a given account of Jesus. It is in order to avoid precisely this sort of indignation, which is bound to arise when one elides what is non-believing and believing in one's approach to the historical Jesus, that I here propose a five-stage hermeneutical taxonomy for historical Jesus scholarship.

As in the fourth stage of interpretation, the fifth and final step is not intended to give the Jesus of Nicaea (for example) license to run roughshod over the Jesus of Nazareth. It remains incumbent upon us to evaluate whether or not the Jesus of Nazareth precludes the Jesus of Nicaea, or if the God of Nicaea is a plausible reckoning of the man from Nazareth (cf. Bockmuehl 1994:167). David Yeago undertook an analogous task in his famous essay, "The New Testament and Nicene Dogma", where he argued that "the ancient theologians were right to hold that the *homoousion* is neither imposed *on* the New Testament texts, nor distantly deduced *from* the texts, but rather describes a pattern of judgments present *in* the texts" (Yeago 1997:88). The present proposal asks that a similar inquiry be undertaken with respect, not to the New Testament texts alone, but to the historical Jesus known outside of, behind, *and* through the New Testament texts.

4.2 *A Fideistic Trump Card?*

Now, I'd wager that even a Christian scholar with a commitment to theologically-informed historical Jesus research may still be uncomfortable with the amount of ambiguity that remains in this five-stage taxonomy. Does this approach pay mere lip service to historical Jesus study, allowing the confessional scholar to sample from a critical palette in order to lend the hue of academic rigour to what is otherwise an exercise in fundamentalist self-congratulation? This might be the case if the interpreter considers the Gospels or, e.g., Nicaea to be such privileged positions that working from them is a matter of relative certainty *vis-à-vis* the historical Jesus. Things are quite different if one considers Nicaea and the Gospels to be no more privileged positions than the scholarly construal of the historical Jesus we endeavour to understand.

Personally, I'm inclined to locate myself somewhere between the two extremes: while I believe that the Gospels and the Church speak truly for God as regards the identity of Jesus, I am not convinced that either the character of the Gospels themselves or the history of the Church warrants or requires that they be given immediate assent on any and every point. Thus I would hope to engage in a Gadamerian hermeneutic experience, first, taking the Gospels or Nicaea as starting points, but then foregrounding those starting points as prejudices, and finally endeavouring to transcend them through a dialectical dialogue.[33] The dual vocational allegiances (historian and theologian) of the Christian historical Jesus scholar requires her to engage dialectically not only with the texts of Scripture/Tradition (like a theologian), nor only with the events of history expressed and betrayed by the texts (like an historian); she must bring the fruits of both of these dialogues into further dialogue with each other.

That is simple enough to say, but in practice "dialogue" is more than a matter of a simple dialectic because the claims of historical criticism and Christian faith are at times squarely opposed to each other. If we take a cue from someone like Allison, we would be given to think that, when in doubt, reason trumps faith; Johnson would assert the opposite, arguing that any Jesus whom historians can construct is a human artifice and thus inferior to the Gospels.

Now, in Johnson's favour, I would agree that Christian faith in the theological Christ certainly precludes the empirically verifiable historical Jesus from dictating the terms of their joint construal. But on the other hand, I don't think that means that any disagreement should be decided in favour of the "theological" Jesus, as if the Christ of faith were a fixed and agreed-upon entity. How much can we pack into (or derive from) the "theological" Jesus? Deity? Dyotheletism? The immaculate conception of Mary?

I would suggest that, rather than giving absolute supremacy to either the theologians' Jesus (Wolter's "Jesus Christ") or the historians' Jesus (Wolter's "historical Jesus"), we approach the problem of contrary Jesuses in the same way that we would approach any case of counter-indicative evidence: by weighing the relative strengths and weaknesses of each body of evidence. In this specific scenario, that would entail assessing:

1) the centrality of a theological tenet to Christian dogma, and
2) the relative certainty of a given historical critical conclusion.

---

[33] It may seem precocious to assert that the Gospels' account of Jesus can be critiqued theologically, but this is perhaps less capricious in so far as they are drawn into dialogue with both history and tradition. If both historical Jesus research and tradition were to fail to corroborate an aspect of a given Gospel's depiction of the man, it would seem reasonable to bring that aspect under scrutiny, and perhaps to transcend it.

On the former count, the "centrality" of a doctrine could be construed in terms of its prominence in the sources considered revelatory (Gospels, Scripture as a whole, Christian creeds, etc.) as well as in terms of a doctrine's systematic theological importance (so that theological derivations from the core of the apostolic *kerygma* could be assessed on a sliding scale). For example, the doctrine of the immaculate conception of Mary (a highly derivative conclusion of later Christian theology without any direct warrant in Scripture) might not merit as much deference as would Jesus' resurrection or deity.

Once the relative centrality of a doctrine has been assessed, it can then be weighed against the probability of a given historical critical conclusion. If a doctrine (say, the deity of Christ) is historically central to the Christian faith, and that doctrine is pitted against a relatively less-certain historical critical perspective (say, that Jesus never construed himself as the Son of Man in terms of Daniel 7; so Vermès 1974:186), then it seems reasonable to favour Christian dogma. Conversely, if a more disputed theological topic (e.g. penal substitutionary atonement) is pitted against an item that is relatively probable on historical critical grounds (e.g. that Jesus did not see his death as being a replacement for the sacrificial system (Dunn 2003:795–960, *pace* e.g. Theissen and Merz 1998:431–437), then perhaps the critical view can be given more credence.

The proposed five-stage taxonomy is not simply a Germanic exercise in schematization; rather, it is a Gadamerian discipline, a commitment to foregrounding our presuppositions so that we can enter genuine dialogue as members of a scholarly community and engage in more clear-headed investigation of the historical Jesus. The benefits of the schema are thus threefold. First, this typology would aid conversation between confessional and non-confessional scholars by permitting the discussion of transcendent topics without blurring presuppositional boundaries. Second, the taxonomy allows us to assess the degree of compatibility between the Jesus of history and the Christ of faith. Third, conversely, and finally, this schema would highlight certain features of Christian doctrine that may need to be reevaluated in conversation with historical Jesus scholarship.

5. Concluding Summary

In the seminal essay of the present collection, Wolter contributes to the current debate on how to talk about "the real Jesus", an endeavour which is both theological in nature and yet insuperably historical. Corroborating Wolter's assessment that historical Jesus research does not safely conduct us to the "real Jesus", I have argued that the conventional approaches of historical Jesus scholars are insufficient for reconstructing the life and teachings of Jesus of Nazareth with any certainty, let alone for determining the theological *meaning* of Jesus.

In what I hope was constructive dialogue with Wolter's work, I made my own suggestions about how to pursue knowledge of the "real Jesus", contending for the importance of both atheological and theological approaches. To this end, I initially addressed the recent incorporation of Gadamerian hermeneutics into historical Jesus scholarship. Gadamer greatly aids confessional Jesus scholarship in demonstrating the legitimacy of beginning from a perspective of faith, and in articulating the fact that meaning is determined in large part by the effects of a person in history; all this buttresses Wolter's case that Jesus be studied in light of the resurrection and the apostles' interpretation thereof. Nonetheless, I contended that the attention to Jesus' effective history remained inadequate for confessional Jesus scholarship, in so far as it leaves outside the pale of discussion the question of the occurrence-character of certain events, such as the resurrection, which are of fundamental significance to the Christian faith.

Finally, with a tip of the hat to Wolter's typology of Jesuses, I proposed my own five-staged taxonomy by which Christian historical Jesus scholarship could engage both in critical and confessional research on Jesus, without neglecting one in favour of the other. I argued that, although this approach would not remove *faith* from its central place in discussion of Jesus, the appeal to faith need not derail effective interaction with non-Christian scholars. Instead, I hope this approach might create a space in which confessing scholars could draw on the productive insights of non-confessing scholars and help demonstrate the historical credibility of the Church's theological Christ, God the Word. This is not an endeavour borne out of positivist optimism. Rather, I enthusiastically agree with Wolter's contention that "The 'real Jesus' beyond the images that people have made of him in his own time and since then is, therefore, none other than the Jesus as God knows him, whose identity came into being through God's knowing him". But I remain hopeful of our ability to say a number of true things about the real Jesus because of my faith that God desires to make this Jesus known to us.

156 CHRISTOPHER M. HAYS

Bibliography

Allison, D.C. 1998. *Jesus of Nazareth: Millenarian Prophet*. Minneapolis: Augsburg Fortress.
———. 2008. "The Historian's Jesus and the Church." Pages 79–95 in B. Roberts Gaventa and R.B. Hays, eds., *Seeking the Identity of Jesus: A Pilgrimage*. Grand Rapids: Eerdmans.
———. 2009. *The Historical Christ and the Theological Jesus*. Grand Rapids: Eerdmans.
Bauckham, R. 2006. *Jesus and the Eyewitnesses: The Gospels as Eyewitness Testimony*. Grand Rapids: Eerdmans.
Bockmuehl, M. 1994. *This Jesus: Martyr, Lord, Messiah*. Edinburgh: T. & T. Clark.
———. 2001. "Resurrection." Pages 102–118 in M. Bockmuehl, ed., *The Cambridge Companion to Jesus*. Cambridge: Cambridge University Press.
———. 2006. *Seeing the Word: Refocusing New Testament Study*. Grand Rapids: Baker.
———. 2008. "God's Life as a Jew: Remembering the Son of God as the Son of David." Pages 60–78 in B. Roberts Gaventa and R.B. Hays, eds., *Seeking the Identity of Jesus: A Pilgrimage*. Grand Rapids: Eerdmans.
———. 2010a. *The Remembered Peter: In Ancient Reception and Modern Debate*. Tübingen: Mohr Siebeck.
———. 2010b. "Whose Memory? Whose Orality? A Conversation with James D.G. Dunn on Jesus and the Gospels." Pages 31–44 in G.R. Habermas and R.B. Stewart, eds., *Memories of Jesus: A Critical Appraisal of James D. G. Dunn's Jesus Remembered*. Nashville: B&H Academic.
Crossan, J.D. 1991. *The Historical Jesus: The Life of a Mediterranean Jewish Peasant*. San Francisco: HarperCollins.
Dunn, J.D.G. 2003. *Jesus Remembered*. Vol. 1 of *Christianity in the Making*. Grand Rapids: Eerdmans.
———. 2004. "On Faith and History, and Living Tradition: In Response to Robert Morgan and Andrew Gregory." *ExpTim* 116, no. 1: 12–19.
Ehrman, B.D. 1999. *Jesus: Apocalyptic Prophet of the New Millennium*. Oxford: Oxford University Press.
Funk, R.W. 1997. *Honest to Jesus: Jesus for a New Millennium*. San Francisco: Harper SanFrancisco.
Gadamer, H.-G. 1976. "On the Scope and Function of Hermeneutical Reflection." Pages 18–43 in H.-G. Gadamer and D.E. Linge, eds., *Philosophical Hermeneutics*. London: University of California Press.
———. 2004. *Truth and Method*. Second, revised ed. London: Continuum.
Gregory, A. 2004. "An Oral and Written Gospel? Reflections on Remembering Jesus." *ExpTim* 116, no. 1: 7–12.
Jenson, R.W. 2008. "Identity, Jesus, and Exegesis." Pages 43–59 in B. Roberts Gaventa and R.B. Hays, eds., *Seeking the Identity of Jesus: A Pilgrimage*. Grand Rapids: Eerdmans.
Johnson, L.T. 1996. *The Real Jesus: The Misguided Quest for the Historical Jesus and the Truth of the Traditional Gospels*. San Francisco: HarperSanFrancisco.
Kähler, M. 1953. *Der sogenannte historische Jesus und der geschichtliche, biblische Christus*. Munich: Chr. Kaiser.
Keck, L.E. 2000. *Who is Jesus? History in the Perfect Tense*. Columbia: University of South Carolina Press.
Lüdemann, G. 1999. *The Great Deception: And What Jesus Really Said and Did*. Amherst: Prometheus.
Lyons, W.J. 2010. "Hope for a Troubled Discipline? Contributions to New Testament Studies from Reception History." *JSNT* 33, no. 2: 207–220.
Minear, P.S. 2002. *The Bible and the Historian: Breaking the Silence about God in Biblical Studies*. Nashville: Abingdon.
Morgan, R. 1987. "The Historical Jesus and the Theology of the New Testament." Pages 187–206 in L.D. Hurst and N.T. Wright, eds., *The Glory of Christ in the New Testament: Studies in Christology*. Oxford: Clarendon.

THEOLOGICAL HERMENEUTICS AND THE HISTORICAL JESUS   157

———. 2004. "James Dunn's *Jesus Remembered*, Review of *Jesus Remembered*." *ExpTim* 116, no. 1: 1–6.

———. 2005. "Christian Faith and Historical Jesus Research: A Reply to James Dunn." *ExpTim* 116, no. 7: 217–223.

———. 2010. "*Sachkritik* in Reception History." *JSNT* 33, no. 2: 175–190.

Placher, W.C. 2008. "How the Gospels Mean." Pages 27–42 in B. Roberts Gaventa and R.B. Hays, eds., *Seeking the Identity of Jesus: A Pilgrimage*. Grand Rapids: Eerdmans.

Ratzinger, J. 2007. *Jesus of Nazareth: From the Baptism in the Jordan to the Transfiguration*. London: Bloomsbury.

Roberts, J., and C. Rowland. 2010. "Introduction." *JSNT* 33, no. 2: 131–136.

Swinburne, R. 2003. *The Resurrection of God Incarnate*. Oxford: Clarendon.

Talbert, C.H. 2006. "Miraculous Conceptions and Births in Mediterranean Antiquity." Pages 79–86 in A.J. Levine, J.D. Crossan, and D.C. Allison, eds., *The Historical Jesus in Context*. Princeton: Princeton University Press.

Theissen, G., and A. Merz. 1998. *The Historical Jesus: A Comprehensive Guide*. London: SCM.

Vermès, G. 1974. *Jesus the Jew: A Historian's Reading of the Gospels*. New York: Macmillan.

Watson, F. 1997. *Text and Truth: Redefining Biblical Theology*. Grand Rapids: Eerdmans.

———. 2001. "The Quest for the Real Jesus." Pages 156–169 in M. Bockmuehl, ed., *The Cambridge Companion to Jesus*. Cambridge: Cambridge University Press.

———. 2008. "*Veritas Christi*: How to Get from the Jesus of History to the Christ of Faith without Losing One's Way." Pages 96–114 in B. Roberts Gaventa and R.B. Hays, eds., *Seeking the Identity of Jesus: A Pilgrimage*. Grand Rapids: Eerdmans.

Wright, N.T. 1996. *Jesus and the Victory of God*. London: SPCK.

Yeago, D. 1997. "The New Testament and Nicene Dogma: A Contribution to the Recovery of Theological Exegesis." Pages 87–100 in S. Fowl, ed., *The Theological Interpretation of Scripture: Classic and Contemporary Readings*. Oxford: Blackwell.

HISTORICAL JESUS RESEARCH AS NEW TESTAMENT THEOLOGY

Robert Morgan

The typical academic qualification, "If I have understood him correctly" must preface my response to Michael Wolter's far-reaching contribution, "Which Jesus is the Real Jesus?". It is possible that philosophical and theological differences, or different views of the relationship between these two disciplines, have led me to misunderstand some details where I thought (and still think) we are in general agreement. The subject is many-sided, and complicated by 250 years of fractious debate and drawing on 2,000 years of relevant religious experience. It is to Dr. Wolter's credit that he simplifies matters less than most. Any lecture-length contribution to so complex a subject is likely to contain simplification, but Wolter avoids over-simplifications as he draws attention to several aspects of the problem that are often overlooked and reaches conclusions which could challenge those who share his commitment to both critical historical scholarship and theological reflection to reconsider the way they study and teach the Gospels. The importance and complexity of the topic and the fertility of Wolter's essay are the only excuses I can offer for the length of this response.

Even stating the problem is a problem; there are clusters of problems, some of them lurking in the vocabulary used to define and address them, others in the different standpoints occupied by participants in the debate. History, theology, religion, and faith are ambiguous, contested, and multi-layered concepts, and differing standpoints prioritize different issues. In asking about the real Jesus we may wonder which question is the real question. It is possible to talk at cross-purposes by addressing rather different questions as well as by addressing them in different ways. After 250 years of debate Reimarus and his English precursors, Strauss in his opposition to Schleiermacher, and Kähler and those who invoke him in the name of a rather different kerygmatic theology remain conversation partners.

Wolter's title, and the analyses and arguments which follow, recall two conflicting ideas about "the real Jesus", both of them spurious. Its conventional meaning is synonymous with "the historical Jesus", underlining the polemical opposition of both phrases to traditional Christianity or "the dogmatic Christ", or more generally "the Christ of faith". That reflects the perception that historical criticism has undermined traditional religious belief. Modern historical methods do not speak of God. Whether or not that implies a naturalistic world-view, the claims of historical reason seem 'harder' than those of faith. Wolter rightly dismisses the equation of "the real Jesus" with "the historical Jesus", but the misunderstanding persists, together with its polemical antithesis to "the Christ of faith" first made current by D.F. Strauss in the title of his 1865 tract *The Christ of Faith and the Jesus of History*.[1] Wolter's argument will be reinforced in what follows by some criticism of the phrase "historical Jesus".

But the phrase "real Jesus" also evokes for theologians Martin Kähler's 1892 pamphlet *The so-called Historical Jesus and the Historic, Biblical Christ*.[2] This title echoes Strauss' polemical contrast, but Kähler reversed Strauss' preference for the historical Jesus and insisted that the Jesus Christians follow is their Christian Jesus, the Christ of faith, the man from Nazareth portrayed in the canonical Gospels, the Christ of the whole Bible, the Redeemer. The question is who is right about Jesus, and while Kähler is glad to see historical criticism demolish the brittle pictures of Byzantine dogma he is not willing to surrender his pietist biblical faith in Jesus to the likes of Renan and Strauss. Their so-called historical Jesuses are more fiction than science. If Christians are right (as Kähler assumed they are) then theirs is the real Jesus: "the real Christ is the preached Christ", the "historic, biblical Christ" (a phrase in need of some elucidation), not the "historical Jesus".

Wolter sees that "the real Jesus" can no more be identified with Kähler's "biblical Christ" or believer's faith-images than with the historian's constructions. The real Jesus is an "ontic reality" behind or beyond all images. This ontological difference between "the real Jesus" and all our images and historical or religious descriptions entails (for him) that the real Jesus is unknowable and inexpressible for humans—be they theologians or historians. I agree on the main point but am doubtful about the apophatic

---

[1] D.F. Strauß, *Der Christus des Glaubens und der Jesus der Geschichte: Eine Kritik des Schleiermacherschen Lebens Jesu* (Berlin: Duncker, 1865); ET: *The Christ of Fatih and the Jesus of History: A Critique of Schleiermacher's Life of Jesus* (transl., ed. and with an introduction by L.E. Keck; Philadelphia: Fortress, 1977). Schleiermacher's semi-traditional christology was Strauss' main target. See below, n. 20.

[2] M. Kähler, *Der sogenannte historische Jesus und der geschichtliche, biblische Christus* (Leipzig: Deichert, 1892; 2nd ed. 1896); ET: *The So-called Historical Jesus and the Historic, Biblical Christ* (trans., ed. and with an introduction by C.E. Braaten; Philadelphia: Fortress, 1964–1988).

HISTORICAL JESUS RESEARCH AS NEW TESTAMENT THEOLOGY 161

entailment. It seems to me that as metaphors may communicate some knowledge about an ontologically different object, so our images of God and religious descriptions of Jesus may approximate or correspond in some small measure to the largely inaccessible reality. We assume (surely rightly) that some statements are more true to "the real Jesus" and to God than others. Both theologians and historians can use this phrase in a regulative way, as an ideal towards which they both strive. By contrast, Wolter is not asking here about the form and identity of the real Jesus, but instead reserves the phrase for a reality in the mind of God which is confirmed as corresponding to Jesus' own self-interpretation by God's vindicating him in what faith calls his resurrection. That may be good theology. It forges a link between historical and theological judgements. But it is remote from current use of the phrase.

We agree that Jesus existed in flesh and blood in first-century Palestine, but is now an idea in many human minds. As Christian theologians we may also agree that Jesus exists in the mind of God (even if we cannot talk about this) because we believe that God determines all reality. Wolter's new meaning for the phrase "the real Jesus", makes it the vehicle of a theological claim about reality. I do not disagree, but want to remain close to ordinary speech—though without accepting the vulgar identification of "the real Jesus" with "the historical Jesus". When non-theologians use the phrase to claim cognitive superiority for their own truth-claims (which conflict with mine) I join Wolter in protesting about their rhetorical sleight of hand, but I also accept the challenge to an argument about who is right about Jesus. Wolter's sophisticated new meaning for the phrase simply discards the way it is used by non-believers and by some liberal protestant theologians. I think the anti-theological usage contains a positive claim which more orthodox liberal theologians have to refute, not simply disregard. Believers disagree among themselves and with non-believers about "the real Jesus", and think their religious descriptions come closer to the reality than non-religious descriptions. They do not dispute the right of others to take a different (non-theological and so anti-theological) view of Jesus, but they do challenge its truth. When Schlatter and Käsemann answer their question "Kennen wir Jesus?" in the affirmative I think (with Kähler) that the implied or intended referent of this Christ of faith is the real Jesus.

This is not to identify the Christ of faith, a generic term for many biblical and other religious descriptions of Jesus, with the barely (but sufficiently) accessible reality. It is to claim that these linguistic trajectories come closer to that reality than secular historical constructions of Jesus.

I therefore resist reserving the phrase "real Jesus" for God's knowledge and Jesus' self-interpretation. Only God knows Jesus wholly. We see through a glass darkly and know only in part as yet. But we (both historians and believers) hope we are in some contact with reality when we construct our images of Jesus. The real Jesus can be known to some degree through some good historical reconstructions, and in more important ways through believers' faith-images of him. Against the view that our images or constructions or representations of Jesus can at all reflect his reality I accept in principle the relative validity of both the historian's and the believer's images, but want to argue that "theological portraiture",[3] constructing the history from a religious standpoint and admitting from 2,000 years of history and experience kinds of evidence which most historians prefer to ignore, can come closer than the secular historian can to the reality of Jesus. That is because believers' accounts of Jesus embrace a wider reality (God and "resurrection") than secular historians can entertain.

This is a Christian theological claim which will not impress those who do not accept resurrection faith as the key to understanding the story of Jesus, but the difference between the believer's and the non-believer's perspectives (both may be historians) is one on which Wolter and I are in full agreement, as we are broadly on the theological conclusion to which Wolter's article leads. Whether our different philosophical assumptions derail that substantial agreement may emerge as I say some of the same things in a slightly different way, elaborating on only a few of them while expressing strong appreciation for such a rich and suggestive paper.

Wolter might well accept the two phrases proposed in my title to facilitate our discussion. It seems clear from his conclusion that his question about the significance for Christian faith of modern historical research is posed by a theologian whose reflection on Jesus is informed by resurrection faith in Jesus as well as by historical research. He speaks of "the theologian" analytically, not autobiographically, but his suggestion on p. 14 that the theologian who is engaged in historical study can go a step further than the historian who is not a theologian is surely not intended hypothetically or ironically. He is a professor of theology developing a theological argument, and although this says nothing about his own faith his argument

---

[3] E. Farley, *Ecclesial Reflection* (Philadelphia: Fortress, 1982), 193–216. Farley notes that the visual metaphor (Kähler's *Bild*) fails to express the temporal mode in which the theological reflection that generates an image occurs.

does hinge on accepting the perspective on Jesus proposed by resurrection faith. He is arguing here from within the Christian theological circle. Some historians will accept his conceptual analysis without going with him his final step in identifying "the real Jesus".

That final theological step in Wolter's identification of "the real Jesus" makes me hesitate over his phrase "the theological historian". It is true that he is himself that kind of historian, but his final argument is that of a theologian engaged in critical historical research. His methods make him a historian, but his aims make him a theologian, and the latter take priority because although his methods have their own integrity and independence, they are employed in the service of his theological aims. I would acknowledge this religious interest (and try to prevent it from corrupting my historical judgement) by calling myself a historical theologian rather than a theological historian. The analogous phrase "political historian" may well express writers' interests as well as their subject-matter, but it indicates their vocation as historians, not politicians (which they may or may not also be). Theologians engaged in historical study should therefore avoid the phrase "theological historian", or reserve it for their colleagues writing ecclesiastical history. Social and political history are important for theology, but Wolter's writing about Jesus, good history though it is, may (like Käsemann's and Bornkamm's) best be classified as New Testament theology, a branch of historical theology.

Several of Bultmann's predecessors wrote Jesus books as volume 1 of their New Testament theologies (e.g. Schlatter).[4] The ways that Kümmel[5] and especially Jeremias[6] made their accounts of Jesus' proclamation part of their textbooks is open to criticism, but these other theologians' reconstructions of Jesus' proclamation belong to the genre New Testament theology, however judicious their historical constructions. The phrase "New Testament theology" is contested but may be taken to mean that those who do it are engaged in Christian theology in and through their biblical

---

[4] A. Schlatter, *Die Theologie des Neuen Testaments*, vol. 1: *Das Wort Jesus* (Calw: Verlag der Vereinsbuchhandlung, 1909; second ed. *Die Geschichte des Christus*, 1920); ET: *The History of the Christ: The Foundation for New Testament Theology* (trans. A.J. Köstenberger; Grand Rapids: Baker, 1997).

[5] W.G. Kümmel, *Die Theologie des Neuen Testaments nach seinen Hauptzeugen Jesus, Paulus, Johannes.* (Grundrisse zum Neuen Testament 3; Göttingen: Vandenhoeck & Ruprecht, 1969); ET: The Theology of the New Testament: According to its Major Witnesses, Jesus, Paul, John (trans. J.E. Steely; Nashville: Abingdon, 1973).

[6] J. Jeremias, *Neutestamentliche Theologie*, vol. 1: *Die Verkündigung Jesu* (Gütersloh: Mohn, 1971); ET: *New Testament Theology*, vol. 1 *The Proclamation of Jesus* (trans. J. Bowden; London: SCM, 1971).

scholarship. They are moved by questions of God and Christ, the Gospel and faith, when writing their history which is historical theology. This history is less neutral and objective than some have claimed—usually out of a proper concern to defend their historical honesty and integrity. A suggestion about how one might do New Testament theology when writing about Jesus, or how to write about Jesus as New Testament theology, will follow. My suggestion goes beyond the scope of Wolter's paper, but is illustrated by his historical argument on p. 17 that the Easter visions would not have generated the belief reflected at Rom 1:4 and Phil 2:9–11 without some point of contact with how Jesus had understood himself in his ministry. This connection between Jesus and early Christian belief is at the heart of New Testament theology. Wolter's *oeuvre* can well be classified as New Testament theology without prejudice to its quality as history.

Wolter does not need to say much about Jesus in this article because he sensibly asks his question about the significance of modern historical research on Jesus for Christian faith in general terms, not by reference to particular historical reconstructions. The "which Jesus" in his title invites elaboration as "which type of image" before rejecting both alternatives. It does not pose choices between different historical reconstructions. Neither does it use the phrase to ask (as I do, following Kähler in this respect) about the relative adequacy of historical descriptions and religious images of Jesus. He has different plans for the phrase. But we agree that historical construction and theological interpretation of Jesus are both legitimate enterprises and that the second requires the first. Wolter brings these two discourses together by identifying Jesus' self-interpretation or self-presentation with God's view of him. By contrast I want to avoid the Nestorian (two Christs) echoes in christological talk of "the historical Jesus and the kerygmatic Christ". Both kinds of image exist, but rather than holding one in each hand most believers are taught and construct for themselves a single narrative or set of pictures of Jesus which they assume correspond roughly to the historical reality as well as to their own needs and aspirations. This picture or narrative fuses its historical and its theological elements, and avoids a christological dualism, by building the few firm conclusions reached in historical Jesus research into a christological faith-image which may then come closer to the reality of Jesus (the real Jesus) than either the secular historians' constructions or those of uncritical Bible believers. In answer to Kähler's objection to a "papacy of professors" one may reflect that theologians might know more about Jesus without knowing him better. Saving knowledge differs from historical and even from doctrinal understanding.

While constructing my christological faith-image differently from Wolter I share his interest in the significance of historical research for faith. His initial formulation of this question seems to me unfortunate, however. He asks about the importance of "this Jesus, reconstructed by means of historical analysis, for Christian faith" (p. 2). Leaving aside the question whether "this Jesus" refers to the class of reconstructions written by historians who are not theologians, or those written by theologians engaged in "serious historical work", and whether there is any perceptible difference, the point here is the significance of *historical Jesus research as such* for Christian faith, not that of any or all actual *reconstructions*. That is not to deny that all historical research involves some reconstruction, but intends to avoid suggesting (against Wolter's intention too) that the main significance of historical Jesus research in theology lies in its actual reconstructions. My alternative formulation ("historical Jesus research as such") leaves open the possibility that its main significance might lie in showing that no total historical reconstructions of Jesus can be *constitutive* for faith. They are highly uncertain and they do not speak of God. Nevertheless, our religiously indispensable faith-images may be reinforced or corrected by historical research. The analysis of details in historical Jesus research can also contribute to larger historical reconstructions, but these tentative reconstructions have little existential import for faith.

The reason for this coolness towards large-scale reconstructions is not only that historical research can deliver only a human Jesus (Christians say more) but that written from a non-religious perspective some of them tend to obscure or compete with Christians' religious perspectives on this earthly, human Jesus of Nazareth. Such a damaging outcome can be avoided by avoiding total historical reconstructions and adopting from historical Jesus research piecemeal only as much as can be justified by the evidence. Theologians can discount the speculation and imaginative leaps which keep historians and biographers in business. They can incorporate some of the historical conclusions they have reached about Jesus' life and teaching into their Christian faith-images of Jesus, perhaps even using them to criticize an evangelist's presentation at certain points, but that contribution of historical research to Christian faith-images is very different from replacing these by new historical reconstructions of Jesus. Some historical reconstructions are religiously valuable, but some satisfy their historical aims at the expense of their religious ones, or *vice versa*.

I think we are in essential agreement here, despite my minor quibble about Wolter's initial formulation, but his apparent conclusion that the only historical enquiry about Jesus that is important for faith concerns Jesus' self-interpretation, and that not even this (as historical information) reflects "the real Jesus", seems to me to undervalue the positive contribution historical study can make to the credibility of believers' faith-images of Jesus, and the critical as well as constructive potential of this theological task. We both, however, agree with Kähler in refusing to replace our historically-informed faith-images with a construction made by secular historiography.

The character of the source material permits believers to decline to probe far into the hidden depths of Jesus' personality or religious consciousness. These hypothetical reconstructions in all their diversity surely have some scholarly validity, considerable economic profitability, and even entertainment as well as devotional value, but after 250 years of disagreement it is hard to accord them the moral, religious, and theological centrality that some of our colleagues have found in them. The on-going activity of historical Jesus research, on the other hand, and the limited hard information it supplies, and the possibilities it judges probable or improbable, are self-evidently of interest to any theologian (including Kähler) who takes the real humanity and historical reality of Jesus seriously. The over-reaction of Barth and Bultmann to some liberal protestant life-of-Jesus research was hyperbole 90 years ago but would be theological eccentricity today.

The rubric "historical Jesus research" implies a theological warning against the inevitable popular historical reconstructions of Jesus. These are in themselves legitimate, however fragile or fanciful, and some of them are more compatible with Christian faith than others. This field therefore became in the late nineteenth century (and again a century later) an often unacknowledged theological and apologetic battleground between constructions thought by their authors compatible with or expressive of Christian faith, and those which tend to undermine or even falsify it. Christians have disputed the latter constructions by working within the parameters of historical research, but no historical accounts of Jesus are "neutral" or objective in a way that excludes their authors' perspectives.

Their Christian perspective has led theologians to emphasize the relationship between their historical images of Jesus and post-resurrection faith, not only to see him as part of his Palestine Jewish context, important as that also is. But relating historical accounts of Jesus to the faith of the early church, including the theological witness of the evangelists, is

HISTORICAL JESUS RESEARCH AS NEW TESTAMENT THEOLOGY   167

already to be engaged in New Testament theology in and through stringent historical and exegetical work, as Bultmann acknowledged when he saw the central problem for New Testament theology as understanding how the proclaimer became the proclaimed.[7]

Secular historians also try to explain that the rise of resurrection faith, and accounts of that which discount the character of Jesus' activity and teaching lack credibility, as do accounts of Jesus which fail to consider what gave rise to that resurrection faith. The disciples' risen Lord was the crucified Galilean whose words and works they remembered and re-interpreted. Whether or not a modern scholar shares that perception, i.e. whether they are historical theologians (and therefore also historians of religion) or nothing more than historians of religion, may not be obvious from their presentations and interpretations of the evidence, but marks a difference of perspective. This becomes clear when the bare bones of both believers' and biographers' pictures of Jesus are expanded by more speculative elements. Believers accept some things about Jesus which they cannot prove historically. The doctrine of his sinlessness implies a historical claim that can never be justified historically and will sound absurd to other historians. Any justification for it will lie elsewhere. But secular historians also offer explanations and connexions which cannot be justified strictly on appeal to the historical evidence and these too may be influenced by the scholar's non- or anti-religious perspective. Deciding between these two types of construction will sometimes depend on what is allowed to count as evidence.

Christological faith-images of Jesus which are historically credible but unproven are preferable to a two-step christology in which a reconstructed Jesus of history and a Christ of faith are not integrated. This neo-Nestorianism reduces both constructions to abstractions remote from the believer's religious thinking. The distinction between the abstractions "Jesus of history" and "Christ of faith" has its place in discussing whether a saying was actually spoken by Jesus or emerged later, but making it constitutive for christology (as often happened in the wake of the powerful historical analyses of the Gospels by Strauss and Baur) has proved a dead end. Ernst Käsemann's essay on "Sackgassen im Streit um den historischen Jesus"[8]

---

[7] B. Jaspert, ed., *Karl Barth—Rudolf Bultmann Briefwechsel: 1922–1966* (Gesamtausgabe 5/1; Zurich: Theologischer Verlag, 1971), 65; ET28. Cf. R. Bultmann, *Theology of the New Testament*, vol. 1 (trans. K. Grobel; London: SCM, 1952), 33.

[8] E. Käsemann, "Sackgassen im Streit um den historischen Jesus", in idem, *Exegetische Versuche und Besinnungen,* vol. 2 (Göttingen: Vandenhoeck & Ruprecht, 1964), 31–68; ET:

168 ROBERT MORGAN

failed to identify this dead end, and that partly explains why the theological "New Quest of the historical Jesus" petered out around 1970.

Bornkamm's noble attempt "to seek the history *in* the Kerygma of the Gospels and in this history to seek the Kerygma"[9] was seldom taken up in what followed and has not been on the agenda of some more recent historical Jesus research. It does not have to be—except where a Christian perspective on this historical figure is shaping a faith-image. In contrast to some recent non-theological pictures Wolter's "earthly Christ" (type 3) is a combination of the "historical Jesus" (type 1) and Kähler's Christ of faith (type 2), such as is found in the Gospels themselves.

This type 3 opposes the tendency in some liberal christology to hold the other two apart and seems to me the best option for Christian theologians among Wolter's seven types, whatever the analytic interest of the others. My own modifications to his typology of images of Jesus would be to call the first type 1 "the historian's Jesus" and to subdivide it between the believing historian's and the secular historian's Jesus, distinguishing between historical Jesus research written from a faith-perspective and that which is not, while recognizing that this division is not always visible to the scholars' readership. Believers' faith-images of Jesus may also be subdivided between those which admit a modern historical critical element and those which do not. Kähler's "historic biblical Christ" could find exemplars on both sides of this divide, or rather all along the spectrum from uncritical, through moderately critical, and on to radically critical use of the Gospels in one's faith-image.

The more critical uses of Scripture may be said to yield "the critical theologian's Jesus", in contrast to the uncritical believer's Jesus, and some of its instantiations (type 2A) will coincide with some believing historians' Jesus (type 1A), and both with Wolter's type 3. His other distinctions among Jesus images (types 4 through 6) may further reduce or clarify the gulf between some historians and some believers. The "real Jesus" is for neither of us an image of Jesus but for me signals the attempts of all constructions to approximate more closely to the reality of the first-century crucified Palestinian Jew confessed as living Lord in the faith of his followers.

"Blind Alleys in the 'Jesus of History' Controversy", in idem, *New Testament Questions of Today* (trans. W.J. Montague; London: SCM, 1969), 23–65.

[9] G. Bornkamm, *Jesus of Nazareth* (trans. I. and F. McLuskey with J.M. Robinson; London: Hodder and Stoughton, 1960), 21 (German 1956).

HISTORICAL JESUS RESEARCH AS NEW TESTAMENT THEOLOGY   169

The integration of history and theology in the construction of faith-images may start by identifying some assured results of historical Jesus research (Jesus' baptism by John, the subject-matter and modes of his teaching, his healing, his disciples and opponents, his arrest and crucifixion), but instead of making this critically assured minimum the foundation of historical constructions and discarding the historically doubtful elements in the tradition one may use them to give more weight to the impact of Jesus and how he was understood and interpreted, as evidenced in the tradition as a whole. Those who identify with this tradition of interpretation may still find some things in it to set aside as they construct faith-images which combine probabilities with possibilities at the historical level. They continue to engage in historical Jesus research, allowing their faith-images to be modified if necessary, but without abandoning the Christian perspective they share with the Gospels even when they make a case by *Sachkritik* to set aside some of that material as no part of their own faith-image.

Doubts about its historicity is not a sufficient reason to reject a tradition. *Sachkritik* is based on a sense of the tradition as a whole, and on what is deemed authentic Christianity, and on the best moral reflection and rational thought available to the critical theological interpreter of Scripture. The temptation to reject too easily material which does not fit our own faith-images must be resisted, and a willingness to be challenged by the tradition cultivated. In practice, the controls provided by the diversity of opinion within the wider faith-community act as a brake on disrespect for the tradition.

For all their exercise of historical imagination and use of historical methods most Christian theologians share something of the Christian perspective of the canonical Gospels and like them interpret Jesus' ministry and passion in the light of their own and their sources' post-resurrection standpoint. This results in many different faith-images, because historical and theological judgements differ, but each believer lives and thinks and acts with the help of one or more of these flexible and provisional faith-images of Jesus. They may encounter two types of construction, one provided by historians, the other by theologians, but their religious and theological impulse will be to combine them in a post-critical appropriation of the Gospels' Christian perspectives.

This discussion has, in accord with Wolter's conclusions, led us into christology. The question of "the real Jesus" posed afresh by modern historical study of the Gospels is bound to be answered by most Christians in terms of christology and by others in terms which reject christological claims about Jesus. That these two camps can nevertheless agree on many things about Jesus confirms that christological belief is compatible with secular historiography—not only over matters of detail, but even in the larger reconstructions treated here with some scepticism. This agreement or convergence stems from Christian apologists not allowing their beliefs to pressurize their readings of the historical evidence, and from much of the data itself being open to different interpretations. Christians' faith-images may owe much to their post-resurrection perspective, but in academic discussion with non-believing scholars believers understand their opponents' standpoints and share their methods and can talk about Jesus without making what they say in any way dependent on Christian belief. For example, a belief in Jesus' resurrection (however understood) does not depend on and should not influence a decision about the authenticity of Jesus' prophesying this—which most consider *vaticinia ex eventu* even if they think Jesus must have expected vindication by God.

Casting the discussion in general terms of the significance of historical Jesus research as such for Christian devotion and theology, while accepting the inevitability and apologetic necessity of historical reconstructions of Jesus, underlines that the question raised by Wolter's title and the answer provided by the article itself concerns a christological argument that has sometimes raged and sometimes simmered in European Protestantism at least since English Deism. It includes the question how Christians should read their Scriptures and what *kinds* of things they say. Christians and non-Christians can agree about many things in their talk of Jesus and that is relevant for apologetics, but it is in addition axiomatic for most Christians that their talk of Jesus must also be at least implicitly christological, or implicitly related to their christologies. One of Kähler's and Schlatter's objections to modern historical reconstructions was that they concealed their implicit christological (or anti-christological) dimensions.

All this does not mean that Christians cannot engage in modern historiography with its secular methods—even though it may not include all that they want to say about Jesus. Their religious perspective need not corrupt their historical judgement. Their christology need not and should not influence particular judgements made in their historical Jesus research. On what date we think Jesus was crucified, and where, and by whom, should not be affected by our religious standpoint (though this has often happened). Modern critical historical reconstructions will (by definition) eschew supernaturalism, but believers' perspectives on Jesus are likely to be influenced by their theological interpretation of what happened after his death, whereas those who think the emergence of Christianity had nothing to do with God, and very little to do with Jesus himself, may take a different view of him, however strongly both sides insist on seeing him in his first-century Palestinian Jewish context. This implies a distinction between issues where the historian's naturalistic procedures rightly operate without regard to the historian's own beliefs, i.e. the nuts and bolts of historical Jesus research, and the total reconstructions where a scholar's perspective makes more of a difference. However historically accurate their framework and some of their content, these constructions often owe more to the perspective and imagination of their believing or unbelieving authors.

That is not to condemn them as brutally as Wrede and (ironically) Schweitzer condemned them, though it perhaps recommends restraint. Historians need their hypotheses and believers their faith-images (some of them informed by historical Jesus research) for different reasons. Different aims, interests, and perspectives will lead to different readings of the Gospels and to different constructions or images of Jesus, and the superiority of one type over another cannot be assumed or demonstrated. Arguments can be adduced to adjudicate between two exemplars of a type, but even these are often inconclusive. They are in any case less helpful in deciding between different types of discourse about Jesus. Historical Jesus research can chip away at both the faith-images of believers and at the constructions of other historians, but competing accounts of Jesus remain in play.

When Christians write about Jesus, whether devotionally, doctrinally, or historically, they might well write differently from non-Christians whose methods and assumptions as historians they share. They might also disagree among themselves over both historical matters and religious perspective. Christians think and speak of Jesus in somewhat different ways, and some Christians' talk of Jesus seems closer to how some non-Christians speak of him than to how some other Christians do. That is because most modern christologies are responding to the modern knowledge and world-views which lead many Christians as well as non-Christians to reject traditional Christian ways of speaking about Jesus. Differences of standpoint can stem from education and background as well as from religious faith.

My question *how Christians should speak or write of Jesus* is different from Wolter's title and his two initial "interesting questions" on p. 2, but his conclusions suggest that we are in the same ball-park singing from the same hymn-sheet. As Christian theologians who spend much of our professional life engaging in modern critical historical research on the New Testament we are both very happy to be doing this alongside colleagues who would not claim to be theologians. We recognize that both theologians and non-theologians can write good books about Jesus, but we share Kähler's scepticism about the value of some of these for religious faith. We go on asking about the historical figure at the centre of Christian faith, but the great differences among historical reconstructions of Jesus—even those made by competent and honest historians—is a fair indication of our learned ignorance. Historical Jesus research remains a necessary discipline for theologians who take seriously the real humanity of Jesus, but its uncertain and changing conclusions are less important for theology than the process which generates them.

Kähler's refusal to be seduced by portraits of Jesus drawn from non-theological (and therefore anti-theological) standpoints had Strauss and Renan particularly in mind, but his (and Schlatter's) warning against anti-Christian polemic disguised as modern historical research is still applicable. Its guesswork, speculation, hypotheses and constructions are legitimate but scarcely knowledge. Believers' faith-portraits of Jesus are also uncertain at the historical level but their historical elements are not necessarily inferior to those of less sympathetic historians. Kähler did not deny that some truth is to be found in most historical reconstructions, but he saw this as at best only a part of the truth about Jesus to which Christians bear witness. He thought that by masquerading as the whole truth about Jesus, or as much of the truth as is available, such reconstructions involve a denial (if only an implicit denial) of orthodox Christian claims.

That may be an oversimplification, resulting from too narrow a view of Christian orthodoxy. Some liberal Christians deny the doctrine of the divinity of Christ but, following Schleiermacher, others merely relativize certain ancient formulations and try to reformulate the doctrine in ways that do not conflict with modern historical research.[10] It is often impossible to distinguish between Christians' and non-Christians' historical reconstructions because their differences in perspective are not always visible, but they are more likely to become so the more they are elaborated in overall historical reconstructions. There is a certain tactical

---

[10] See, for example, my discussion of Macquarrie's christology, "Jesus in History and Faith: A Schleiermacherian Christology", in R. Morgan, ed., *In Search of Humanity and Deity* (London: SCM, 2006), 228–253.

wisdom in theologians restricting their historical observations to what can be verified with some probability, however legitimate it is for devotion to allow the imagination more freedom. Even historians depend on historical imagination, without claiming as much for its conjectures as for their more limited and sober judgements about the evidence, but on this terrain theologians are wise to err on the side of caution.

Kähler's attack on the historical reconstructions produced by liberal life-of-Jesus research is still timely[11] because the phrase "the real Jesus" has become (in some quarters) synonymous with the phrase "the historical Jesus". "Real" is typically used rhetorically to claim validity for one's own preferred type of Jesus image. Both phrases are used polemically against traditional Christian doctrinal accounts of Jesus. Kähler responded, equally polemically, that "the real Christ is the preached Christ". Wolter rightly rejects both and later in his article suggestively uses the phrase in a way that those who deny his resurrection by God (however understood) cannot entertain. Identifying "the real Jesus" hinges on how we understand reality as a whole. Christians who accept the resurrection of Jesus by God (not necessarily in traditional supernaturalist terms, but not in a reductionist way either) evidently understand reality differently from those who do not. But not even our most ambitious christologies are adequate to the reality to which they seek to bear witness—often in terms which dispute alternative Christian accounts of Jesus, and usually disputing accounts of Jesus which decline to acknowledge the reality of God or God's self-identification with Jesus in vindicating him.

Wolter relativizes all our historical and theological images of Jesus, including Kähler's, distinguishing them from the inaccessible "real" Jesus, but finally links his Christian account of the latter to historical reality by reference to Jesus' own self-interpretation and to Christian belief in God's having vindicated him in an event which the first disciples expressed most vividly as his resurrection. The "real Jesus" is beyond all our images—faith, theological, or historical—and cannot be grasped. The phrase does not properly refer to any of the images of Jesus which find expression in the different discourses by which we speak of him. But theologians go further than other historians in identifying the real Jesus (without adequately describing him historically, philosophically or doctrinally), when they acknowledge God's vindication of him. The link to Jesus' own

---

[11] It is echoed (without mentioning Kähler) by L.T. Johnson, *The Real Jesus* (San Francisco: HarperSanFrancisco, 1996).

self-interpretation which is thus confirmed by God invites further elaboration, but is strengthened by the historical argument (on p. 16), that the Easter visions alone do not explain the disciples' interpretation that Jesus has been placed by God in the heavenly sovereign position of Son of God and Lord, and that this pre-Pauline (Rom 1:4, Phil 2:9–11) belief must have some point of contact with how Jesus understood himself in his ministry. This historical argument gives some possible support to Wolter's theological answer to the question raised by his title. He offers a theological argument where most writers (even Kähler) use "real" as a loud-speaker.

Having indicated substantial agreement with what I think Wolter is saying I would like to reinforce it with a few questions and caveats.

After his initial orientation through the history of the debate Wolter generally avoids conducting his argument in terms of the classic figures who commonly provide points of reference or a "framework" (p. 3). Granted the use of these icons as a kind of shorthand, that common practice introduces unnecessary complications that it cannot resolve without taking lengthy diversions. The *frisson* of name or brand recognition is bought at the expense of the clear and distinct concepts that the debate requires. The main value of these references to the ghosts of theologians past is to point out how often nineteenth-century suggestions have been unwittingly recycled on another shore and without much greater light.

For example, the connection made by Wolter between Reimarus and some recent American writing on Jesus is illuminating on more than one level. That eighteenth-century rational Jesus has something in common with some recent de-eschatologized notions of a Galilean cynic or teacher of wisdom or social reformer, and these images of the historical figure have religious appeal for some of their modern authors. But Albert Schweitzer could celebrate Reimarus for recognizing the importance of eschatology for his failed political Messiah. It is therefore surprising (and an unnecessary distraction) to find American anti-Schweitzerians sharing a boat with Reimarus. Rather than using Reimarus as a label for the type of Christian writing about Jesus in which the historians' Jesus is thought adequate for Christian faith ("making the historical Jesus directly into the Christ of faith", p. 7, correcting the translation of *kurzerhand*[12]) I would

---

[12] The translation given above is: "Reimarus' 'historical Jesus' as a short-cut for the 'Christ of faith' ". My translation is based on Wolter's original German article, "Was macht die historische Frage nach Jesus von Nazaret zur theologischen Frage?", in: U. Busse,

HISTORICAL JESUS RESEARCH AS NEW TESTAMENT THEOLOGY   175

suggest as a label for this "the liberal protestant theologian's historical Jesus", or (preferring simplicity to precision) "the liberal protestant Jesus". It matters not that Hans Küng and Dominic Crossan are denominationally Roman Catholics. We have here a type of christology which maximizes the common ground with non-Christian writing about Jesus (a merit) to the point that it risks losing its Christian identity and finding itself no longer christology at all. That it fails to deliver an orthodox christology would perhaps not unduly worry its proponents, but most of them would agree that Christian faith requires some sort of christology.

Reimarus (and his English Deist precursors) can be admired for pioneering the modern historical presentations of Jesus which make no normative use of God-language. They also deserve the mention Reimarus receives from Wolter as an example of the historian's construction of Jesus' teaching (or parts of it) coinciding with the theologian's own preferred modernizing interpretation of Jesus. But if Reimarus can also represent critics who see the importance of eschatology, and also those who see the need to include Jesus' Jewish historical and political context, and can also symbolize the supposed gulf between Jesus and the church's witness to him, and indeed all modern scholars who treat the sources with a hermeneutics of suspicion, and other aspects of the subsequent debate, we should salute him for pioneering "the (modern critical) historian's Jesus", distinct from traditional Christian faith pictures, and let him rest. There is so much wrong (as well as so much right) in his actual historical construction that he is now not much more than a chronological point of reference. Making him a symbol of the liberal protestant Jesus (history serving as religion) also obscures the cultural distance between 1750 and 1900 Germany (or North America *ca.* 2000).

One of Reimarus' many merits is that he did not use the late nineteenth-century phrase "the historical Jesus", best known from Kähler's 1892 title but made familiar to English readers by its frequent occurrence in the translation of Albert Schweitzer's *Von Reimarus zu Wrede* (1906), *The Quest of the Historical Jesus* (1910). This mischievous phrase should be used with care if at all on account of its ambiguity and the misuse of that ambiguity for ideological purposes. It can mean "Jesus as he actually was" (Jesus as part

---

M. Reichardt and M. Theobald, eds., *Erinnerung an Jesus: Kontinuität und Diskontinuität in der neutestamentlichen Überlieferung. Festschrift für Rudolf Hoppe zum 65. Geburtstag* (Göttingen: V & R Unipress, Bonn University Press, 2011), 17–33, here 21: "Für ihn ist charakteristisch, dass man weder den 'historischen Jesus' kurzerhand zum 'Christus des Glaubens' macht...".

of first-century Palestinian and Jewish history—though even that formulation is defective), or it can mean Jesus as reconstructed (or constructed) by modern historians (the historian's Jesus). Confusion of these two meanings is a mistake, as Wolter and others have insisted, and claiming the reality of the inaccessible first in support of modern historians' reconstructions is a naïve absolutizing of one's own relative standpoint. The mistake was understandable because modern historical reconstructions do aim to do justice to the past historical reality, but they often claimed too much for themselves, and the phrase might be better avoided. In its normal, most common, and proper meaning it can easily be replaced by "the historian's Jesus". It is more difficult to find a phrase for the improper use of "the historical Jesus", to refer to the inaccessible "actual" Jesus behind all the images, but I would suggest (resisting Leander Keck's distaste for the Kantian *Ding an sich*) "the *noumenal* Jesus". This can serve to hold a space open for "the real Jesus" until Wolter has persuaded the world to use that phrase in a theologically responsible way. The philosophical objections to Kant's dualism are irrelevant here because all the label is doing in this context is to provide a vocabulary to distinguish between all images of Jesus (phenomena) and a reality beyond our full knowledge.

The phrase "the historian's Jesus" was used by L.E. Keck in *A Future for the Historical Jesus* (1971). He comments that "the historical Jesus is not really an uninterpreted Jesus but Jesus as the historian is able to recover and reconstruct him.[13] Wolter does not use the phrase "historian's Jesus", but his question echoes Keck's: "Is the historian's Jesus, the Jesus reconstructed by critical methods, centrally significant for Christian faith and thought, or is such a Jesus irrelevant or even inimical to it?"[14] Like others in the theologically motivated "New Quest of the historical Jesus", Keck anticipates Wolter's question, but not his innovative answer. Van Harvey in *The Historian and the Believer* (1967) also discusses the ambiguity in the phrase in a section on "The Meanings of 'Jesus of Nazareth'": "As has been often pointed out, 'the historical Jesus' is actually an ambiguous term because it may refer both to the actual Jesus and to the Jesus that is now recoverable by historical means. For clarity's sake I shall use 'the

---

[13] L.E. Keck, *A Future for the Historical Jesus: The Place of Jesus in Preaching and Theology* (Nashville: Abingdon, 1971), 20.

[14] *Ibid.*

historical Jesus' in the latter sense...".[15] Clarity is better served by Keck's "historian's Jesus".

Van Harvey also proposes a new and not really appropriate meaning for Kähler's phrase "the biblical Christ" (his fourth meaning of "Jesus of Nazareth"): "the transformation and alteration of the memory-impression (or perspectival image) under the influence of the theological interpretation of the actual Jesus by the Christian community".[16] This definition, or the use of that label for this aspect of the Christ of faith, is surely open to criticism ("biblical Christ" should refer more directly to the biblical texts), but it indicates the complexity of our issue. Adding this sub-category of the Christ of faith to Wolter's typology would add to the can of worms.

My reservations about using individuals to identify types are reinforced when like many others Wolter makes Martin Kähler the other pole of his initial "framework". Kähler's 1892 tract, *Der sogenannte historische Jesus und der geschichtliche, biblische Christus*, rejects what is represented by the first half of his title in favour of the second half, but the subsequent history of the debate wrongly elided Kähler's position with Bultmann's. These theologians do share a reaction against liberal lives of Jesus, and also a Pauline-Lutheran kerygmatic emphasis. However, they sit on opposite sides of the liberal-conservative divide, fashionable though it became in the 1920s to avoid the self-designation "liberal". Had Kähler, who died in 1912, lived to read Bultmann's *Jesus* (1926) he would surely have liked it even less than Hoskyns[17] and Barth (in his correspondence) did. Kähler could play the historical scepticism card against modern quasi-historical reconstructions of Jesus, but his assessment of the historical veracity of the Gospels was surely closer to Schlatter's than to Bultmann's, and he would never have agreed that the mere *Daß* of Jesus' historical existence (and the cross) are all that is theologically relevant about the historical figure. The Gospel narratives and their general reliability were important to this pietist theologian.

Reimarus and Kähler can be used to identify or illustrate several different facets of the debate, and that tells against using them as ciphers for one issue or one position. These icons are too complex and also too elusive to sharpen the profile of any single aspect of the issue. That is better done by concepts. There are in any case some unclarities in Kähler's

---

[15] V.A. Harvey, *The Historian and the Believer: The Morality of Historical Knowledge and Christian Belief* (London: SCM, 1967), 266.

[16] *Ibid.*, 267.

[17] E.C. Hoskyns, Review of R. Bultmann, *Jesus*, *JTS* 28 (1927): 106–109.

description of his Christ of faith as *der geschichtliche, biblische Christus*, which may explain the absence of "the biblical Christ" from Wolter's seven types of image. It is not obvious what, beyond the contrast itself, is achieved in this context by the murky German distinction between *historisch* and *geschichtlich*. It is also far from clear what exactly *biblischer Christus*, or "Christ of the whole Bible" might mean, and the contrast between Jesus and Christ, however rhetorically effective, actually subverts Kähler's own position. He would himself surely have endorsed both the two titles and the aims of Schlatter's "New Testament Theology", vol. 1: *Das Wort Jesu* in 1909, and then in the second edition (1920) *Die Geschichte des Christus*.[18] In 1912 Bultmann combined admiration with criticism of Schlatter's book,[19] and later he relegated the historically presented proclamation of Jesus to the presuppositions of New Testament theology, but he must have preferred Schlatter's original 1909 title to his 1920 insistence on history which was perhaps provoked by Barth's anti-historical *Epistle to the Romans* (1919). The English title of Bultmann's own Jesus book (1926), *Jesus and the Word* (1934) was appropriate, despite Bultmann's appropriation of Dilthey's novel conception of history.

The difficulties of the concept of "history" in Gospel study are illustrated not only by Kähler's contrasting the two German words, but also by the recent attraction of the word "story" which has no precise German equivalent. Wolter (or his translator) chooses "story of Jesus" (p. 5) for "Jesusgeschichte". Granted that "history of Jesus" will not do (the context excludes both meanings of "historical Jesus" here), "story" nevertheless risks obscuring the historical reality of Jesus' ministry and passion. Would the meaning of Dr Wolter's all-important third type not be more accurately expressed if *Jesusgeschichte* were rendered "life and work of Jesus" here?

Wolter's introductory use of Reimarus and Kähler leads into his own sevenfold typology of Jesus images. This shows that the contrast between "the Christ of faith and the Jesus of History"[20] is over-simple. There are more distinctions to be made. But expanding the list risks obscuring the

---

[18] ET, *The History of the Christ: The Foundation for New Testament Theology* (trans. A. Köstenberger; Grand Rapids: Baker, 1997).

[19] His review ("Vier neue Darstellungen der Theologie des Neuen Testaments", in *Monatsschrift für Pastoraltheologie* 8 [1912]: 432–443) is reprinted in R. Bultmann, *Theologie als Kritik* (ed. M. Dreher and K.W. Müller; Tübingen: Mohr Siebeck, 2002), 41–52.

[20] See above, n. 1. Schleiermacher had died in 1834, but his 1832 lectures on the life of Jesus were not published until 1864, perhaps because (as Strauss observed) they had been rendered obsolete by the young Strauss' 1835 *Life of Jesus*. Jack Verheyden's American

HISTORICAL JESUS RESEARCH AS NEW TESTAMENT THEOLOGY 179

all-important distinction between images of Jesus which want to speak normatively of God in relation to him, and those which do not. Neither the distinction nor its expression as Christian *versus* non-Christian images of Jesus is crystal-clear, because both Godtalk and Christianity (not to mention "religion") are fuzzy, but this does represent some fundamental intentions even though they are often combined and overlapping, as in Wolter's "third possibility" which consists in preparing a way which was between the other two ways (the historian's Jesus and the Christ of faith). This third way describes (p. 6, modifying the translation) the ministry and passion of Jesus by historical methods, but in the light of Easter faith. Here, as Wolter rightly says, "enquiring into the historical Jesus (*sic*) gets its distinctive characteristic to stand out over against the questions posed by the other two paths" (p. 6, correcting and varying the translation). It is, he thinks, clear why theologians will be dissatisfied with the approaches of both Reimarus and Kähler, but less easy to say what makes historical enquiry into Jesus (which is methodologically untheological) into a theological enquiry. The point to be emphasized here is that (in contrast to much English historical Jesus research) Wolter is theologically motivated and interested as he does his historical research. That is what makes his work New Testament theology, as I understand it. Classifying it in this way may throw light on what historical Jesus research by theologians using historical methods might involve.

In so far as different constructions or images of Jesus are in dispute or competition it is worth clarifying how far these differences arise from different assessments of the evidence and how far from interpreters holding different views about what counts as evidence. The former type of disagreements is part and parcel of historical research and presents no problem. On the other hand, conservative theological attempts to change the procedures of historical research, to allow it to speak of God explicitly, exclude themselves from New Testament theology as normally understood, since this operates within those conventions. This latter type of disagreement may result from different philosophical or theological world-views and does not normally arise in historical research. It is not a factor in Wolter's typology and can therefore be excluded from consideration here.

Wolter's first and second types of Jesus image have been sufficiently discussed with reference to Reimarus and Kähler. One may prefer the

---

translation appeared in 1975, following Peter Hodgson's edition of Strauss' 1835 work in 1973, and followed in 1977 by Leander Keck's translation of Strauss' critique.

180   ROBERT MORGAN

phrase "historian's Jesus" for the first, and "Jesus Christ of faith" for the second while agreeing with what he says about them. Kähler recognized that his "historic, biblical Christ" was a *Bild*[21] and he would agree that it exists only in Christian confession. At least, it exists *in re* only in Christian faith; it exists *in intellectu* wherever an analyst tries to distinguish different types of images of Jesus, but it is "unattainable" (*unerreichbar*) *in re*, except *in intellectu fidelium*.

Wolter's all-important third type seems to me to conflate two subtypes in which historical memory and faith-perspective are combined. The evangelists themselves are innocent of Reimarus' and other modern historians' type 1. One might therefore distinguish between their combination of faith and history and that of modern theologians who do the same thing in a modern context. The attraction of calling both these accounts of Jesus which combine historical study (type 1) and a faith perspective (type 2) "the earthly Christ" is that this echo of the traditional theological language of Jesus' two "states" makes clear that it is Christian theological portraits (see n. 3 above) that are being attempted here. Most Christian faith pictures of Jesus conform to this mixture of history and theology.

For type 4 Wolter borrows James Dunn's suggestive title *Jesus Remembered* (2003). He rightly points out that the category is not new, and that it has been used in different senses. Older English and American readers will recall John Knox's writings on Jesus in the memory of the Church, especially *The Church and the Reality of Christ* (1962), and the astute use made of them by Archbishop Peter Carnley in *The Structure of Resurrection Belief* (1987). Dunn uses the category for historiographical rather than theological purposes, though an apologetic theological aim may be seen in the background. It remains for Christians an important and inescapable category, as the eucharist indicates, and there is a distinction to be made between the memory of the first disciples and that of the subsequent church, but whereas Wolter's earlier distinction (between the earthly and the heavenly "states" of Jesus) is essential to Christian thinking it is less clear to me whether Wolter's fourth or fifth types serve any practical purposes of history, theology or piety—or are purely analytic (as may be implied by calling the difference of type 4 from type 3 a matter of "medium"—literary and non-literary). One may nevertheless welcome type 4 as holding a space open for further reflection. If type 5 exists now only in the mind of the analyst there is not much to say about it.

---

[21] See H.-G. Link, *Geschichte Jesu und Bild Christi* (Neukirchen: Neukirchener Verlag, 1975).

Wolter's sixth type, Jesus' self-interpretation, is theologically all-important—up to a point. It is surely a truth-condition of orthodox Christianity that Jesus thought himself sent by God with a mission and a message. How or whether he conceptualised this precisely, e.g. by thinking of himself as Messiah, Son of God, son of man, eschatological prophet, wisdom teacher or whatever, and how he interpreted his impending death, are questions whose uncertainty is more troubling to historians and would-be biographers than to most theologians. Whether his self-interpretation developed over the course of his ministry is also theologically irrelevant if historically impossible to ascertain, but it does raise the theoretical possibility of more than one instantiation of this type. Despite the reaction against nineteenth-century historians' and theologians' over-confidence about this category, even Bultmann was prepared to speak of "implicit christology" in Jesus' words and deeds, and the relation of Jesus' self-interpretation (so far as it can be known) to the early church's christology remains a central question for New Testament theology, though apparently of little interest to some secular historical Jesus research.

Jesus' self-interpretation provides a bridge between historical reality and Wolter's theological answer to the question posed by his title. For Christians the resurrection confirms that Jesus is and was the One sent by the Father to do God's will by proclaiming and in some sense enacting God's in-breaking rule. That link does not require more than most historians will concede about Jesus' self-consciousness. It does not depend on Jesus choosing for himself a title or title-role—though the latter may be implied by what he said and did. Most Christians accept the resurrection of Jesus (in some sense) as God's vindication of what he said and did—and who he thought he was, but historians may offer their own very different accounts of the rise of Christian resurrection faith. The Christian hypothesis (or certainty) about Jesus is by no means guaranteed, not even by what followed his death, since the theological account of this is not public knowledge.

That is not to deny that historical research has a major role in Christian theology. Reflecting on the tradition as a whole includes trying to get the record straight—in self-criticism as well as gratitude and fellowship in the communion of saints. Schleiermacher's dictum that "historical theology is the actual corpus of theological study"[22] has not been rendered obsolete by postmodernity. But the positive role of historical study of Christian

---

[22] F.D.E. Schleiermacher, *A Brief Outline on the Study of Theology* (trans. V.A. Richmond; Louisville: John Knox Press, 1966), 26 (German 1811, 2nd ed. 1830).

origins for Christian faith is limited by the character of both the sources and the subject-matter. Schleiermacher's corresponding comment that "historical theology attempts to exhibit every point of time in its true relation to the idea of 'Christianity' "[23] is essential here. It stands behind Farley's notion of "theological portraiture" drawn on in this essay. Some faith-images draw on historical study less than others and are no less valid on that account, however urgent this study has become in apologetic contexts. Indirectly it has contributed substantially to restatements of Christian faith and sensibility in the modern world, but its main contribution to theology lies in clarifying early Christian witness to Jesus, not in forging an alternative (historical) means of access to him. Perhaps that is why Wolter's answer to the question of "the real Jesus" and the most appropriate ways to speak of him is like mine finally more about resurrection faith than about what modern secular historians say about him.

In concluding this appreciation of Wolter's paper, a suggestion about its implications for the study of the Gospels in ecclesial and secular contexts may be drawn from it.

As was the case in the ministry of Jesus, so today. His followers and opponents and observers can agree on many points about this first-century Galilean, including that he was a Galilean Jew. But their fundamental differences about his significance lead them to produce or adopt very different images of him. The points of agreement, clarified by historical Jesus research, can be built into various conflicting hypothetical reconstructions—or they can be integrated into Christian faith's "retrospective image of the earthly ministry of the risen Son of God" (Wolter's type 3). Since this is a matter of perspective, not necessarily disagreement on matters of historical detail, it is possible for some historians' reconstructions to correspond closely to some faith-images of Jesus. Hence "the liberal protestant Jesus" offers some valid modern instantiations of Wolter's type 3.[24] They should not be tarred by the mistakes and hubris of some nineteenth-century life-of-Jesus research and its successors.

Believers' religious priorities allow them to be fairly relaxed about historical study. Some simply assume that their faith-images, shaped by the Gospels, are historically as well as religiously reliable. Christians acknowledge that Jesus was the human historical figure he was, and can welcome

---

[23] *Ibid.*

[24] E.g. recently D. Allison, *Constructing Jesus: Memory, Imagination, and History* (London: SPCK, 2010), and (in my opinion still the best) G. Theissen and A. Merz, *The Historical Jesus* (London: SCM, 1997), 185–563.

modern historical investigation (as Kähler did) as protection against the docetism or Apollinarianism which often beguiles those who worship him as living Lord. Modern historical sensibilities sometimes now lead to faith-images that are closer to the synoptic portraits than to the Johannine.

However relaxed most believers can be (since historical Jesus research is not a requirement of faith as such and Christians are at most influenced by it indirectly in their thought and speech about Jesus) critical theology must nevertheless take it seriously, and engage in it rigorously, in its reflection on and correction of Christian faith-images. This need not and should not undermine faith perspectives as total historical reconstructions of Jesus can do when pitched against traditional perceptions. That danger is best averted by limiting historical Jesus research to the on-going process of challenging or reinforcing those perceptions piecemeal. In general outline the Gospels' and historians' pictures of Jesus are close enough to provide a framework open to both a faith-perspective and to historical investigation.

The necessary but subordinate place of historical Jesus research in Christian theology is secured by doing it in a context of New Testament theology. This discipline combines criticism and theological reflection, and makes the relationship of its conclusions to post-resurrection faith a central concern. The implication for Christian study of the New Testament is that in contexts where the New Testament is functioning as a norm of Christianity (i.e. in most theological contexts) critical historical exegesis is now essential, as it may not be in other religious contexts. Textual intention and where possible even authorial intention have to be considered for there to be any realistic hope of consensus about the implications of the New Testament texts within the churches that read them as part of their task of discerning what is authentic and what inauthentic in Christianity. New Testament theology, guided by theological interests and assumptions but subject to the conventions of critical historical and exegetical methods, should therefore provide the substance if not the whole of Christian biblical study. Even the study of the Old Testament which has its own integrity and independence belongs within this framework of New Testament theology when the nature of Christianity is at issue.

Outside this ecclesial context many others also want to know about Jesus for a variety of reasons. Christians who want to share their knowledge and love of Jesus more widely will welcome these conversations. In a post-Christian society the boundaries between Christian and non-Christian readings of the Gospels are often fluid. The market for responsible historical reconstructions is kept buoyant by this wider cultural interest in Jesus, as is the appetite for sensational hypotheses with little or no basis in the sources. In face of the latter, Christian theologians should value their alliance with serious secular historians, only without allowing this to obscure their own proper and legitimate religious interest in Jesus, and their aims in studying the Gospels.

IN WHICH SENSE HAS THE CONVICTION THAT JESUS WAS RESURRECTED THE "CERTAINTY OF FACT"?[1]

Notger Slenczka

For a systematic theologian, it is an honour to be asked to contribute to a scholarly discussion of the prestige lecture delivered by my distinguished and esteemed colleague Michael Wolter. Rarely among theologians do historians and systematicians interact with each other. Systematic theologians are seen by most historians as turning a blind eye to the intricacies of the debates historians are involved in, when they refer to Scripture and to church history; and by many systematic theologians, New Testament scholars and church historians are regarded as hermeneutically naive positivists. So most of the systematicians put forward their quotations from Scripture with a (I admit: slightly) guilty conscience. And the scholars of the New Testament hide their hermeneutical reflections in the introductions or in the epilogues of their commentaries, hoping they will not be read by their colleagues either of the historic or of the systematic department.

There are few New Testament scholars who are considered coequal by systematicians and at the same time esteemed highly by their New Testament colleagues. Michael Wolter is one such. In his brilliant text, he deals with the subject both groups of scholars are supposed to be interested in and on which they are supposed to share their insights with each other: the traditionally so-called "quest for the historical Jesus". In a first paragraph (I.), I'll give a short outline of his paper and present a few critical comments, culminating in the question raised in the title of this paper; in the second paragraph (II.), I present a systematician's view on the quest for the so-called historical Jesus, and in the course of that, I will try to put forward an answer to the question posed in the title.

---

[1] I am very grateful to Jacob Corzine, M. Div., for translating most of this text. All mistakes are mine.

186

NOTGER SLENCZKA

1. The Position of Michael Wolter

1.1 Outline of Wolter's Position

1.1.1 The "Anti-Docetic Option"

Michael Wolter seeks to surpass the antithesis of the "historical Jesus" and the "Jesus Christ" as an object of Christian faith (the risen Christ etc.) established in the positions of Reimarus on the one hand and, for instance, Martin Kähler or Rudolf Bultmann on the other. He suggests a third path beyond these alternatives by pointing out, first, that the Christian Easter confession identifies one particular historical person as the "kyrios" and as risen and being placed at the right hand of the Father; and second, therefore, that Christian faith is interested not only in the risen Christ experienced as present in the Church but is interested in the continuity and identity of this heavenly person with the specific human being that led this particular life of a rabbi raised in Galilee, who travelled through Judea to Jerusalem and was crucified there around the year 28.

1.1.2 Images of Jesus

Wolter shares this anti-docetic option with Ernst Käsemann and his Second Quest for the historical Jesus; I will return to that (pp. 195–196). Since then, the crucial question has been how to fit these two aspects of the person of Christ together. In order to avoid the old trenches, Wolter suggests distinguishing different "images" of Jesus Christ resp. types of images (pp. 1–17)—all of these images are different kinds of constructions of Christ on different levels corresponding to different interests in or approaches to this person. Wolter stresses the fact that there is no approach to Jesus Christ that is not an image and in this sense a construction—this is true for an historical approach as well as for the different levels of religious interpretation, for the remembrance of contemporaries and for the own self-understanding of Jesus of Nazareth. Wolter is not a radical constructivist but assumes that all the images refer to one and the same reality beyond all images. But at the same time he holds that we have this reality only in constructed images and by constructing images.

1.1.3 The Truth of Images?

Wolter then asks if there is a criterion which enables us to decide whether or not the truth claims of these constructions are valid, and links to that the question of whether there is a specifically theological approach to the person of Jesus Christ: This approach, according to Wolter, lies in the fact that a Christian theologian not only distinguishes different images of Jesus Christ, but in fact distinguishes all of them from the image God has of this person, which image the Christian theologian refers to as the ultimate truth of this person or the equivalent of the "real Jesus" beyond (human) images. In God's image, the "real" Jesus and the true knowledge of Jesus converge because the creator's knowledge of Jesus Christ is the foundation of his being.

For Christians, this image that God has of Jesus (and thus "the real Jesus") is accessible: The Easter faith constituted by the certainty of resurrection includes the conviction that by this resurrection God vindicates Jesus. This would be an empty affirmation if there were no way to determine with regard to which claim Jesus is vindicated by the resurrection;[2] this question Wolter answers by asserting that the resurrection vindicated the image Jesus had of himself, or: The Easter faith includes the certainty that the self-understanding of Jesus Christ and the image that God has of him are identical. That means that we have to determine how Jesus saw himself, or better: who he was remembered as claiming to be. Wolter points out that the apparitions of Christ in the visions mentioned by Paul in 1Cor 15:5–7 would not in themselves have been a sufficient foundation for the Christian conviction that Jesus is the Son of God ruling the world as the "*kyrios*" (p. 15). Without grounds in the self-interpretation of Jesus himself as the ultimate representative of God and His coming Kingdom, remembered by his disciples, the early Church, even after the resurrection, would not have dared to proclaim him as Lord. So it is this claim of Jesus as a part of the image of "Jesus remembered" that is vindicated by God through the resurrection.

1.1.4   *The Image-Concept and the Quest for the "Real" Jesus*
Thus, the different images of Jesus presented by Wolter are linked together when it comes to answering the question Wolter raises in the title of his presentation: "Which Jesus is the Real Jesus?" The first answer, limitative:

---

[2] The function of the resurrection reminds one of W. Pannenberg, *Grundzüge der Christologie* (6th ed.; Gütersloh: Gütersloher Verlagshaus Gerd Mohn, 1982), § 3; ET: *Jesus: God and Man* (trans. L.L. Wilkens and D.A. Priebe; London: SCM, 2002).

The real Jesus is accessible only through images formed through different perspectives on him. So to ask for the real Jesus can mean nothing else than to raise the question of which images of Jesus are true. Second answer, negative: The so-called "historical Jesus" is not in itself the real Jesus but an image formed by an historian and within the hermeneutical implications of a methodological perspective. Third step, beyond the conflict of images: There is a way out of the mere conflict of images open only for the theologian: For him, the true perspective on Jesus is the knowledge God has of Jesus; being the knowledge of the creator, this image constitutes the reality of Jesus. Fourth step, normative: The Christians (and they only) claim to have access to this image through the apparitions of Christ interpreted as evidence for the resurrection of Jesus Christ by God who thereby vindicates the self-image of Jesus. This self-image of Jesus, again, is accessible only through the images formed by the persons who have met him during his life-time (Wolter's image of "Jesus remembered") and, perhaps also through the perspective of "the earthly Christ". But, as Wolter, now speaking as a historian, points out: The disciples of Jesus and the early believers would not have formed an image of the king residing at the right hand of God had there not been a claim of Jesus himself as being the ultimate representative of the coming Kingdom of God. So, for the Christians, this self-image of Christ is vindicated by the resurrection, and this is "the real Jesus". So the question about the "real Jesus" in the sense of the quest for the "true image" of Jesus is answered neither by going back to the self-understanding of Jesus nor by going back to the "historical Jesus" beyond all images. The question about the "real" Jesus is answered by a combination of images and perspectives, and it implies a constant shift from the perspective of an historian to the perspective of a theologian and vice versa. And at the core of that answer lies the concept of "God's perspective" on Jesus on the one hand, the Christian's conviction of the reality of the resurrection on the other hand, and on the nonexistent third hand a thesis on the self-understanding of Jesus.

1.2 *Critical Remarks and Questions*

1.2.1 *The Historian's and the Theologian's Perspective*

That leads to a first critical question: Given that all the answers to the question of who Jesus really is or was reflect a certain perspective and, thus, form a certain image of Christ: Who is the one who combines them into the answer Wolter suggests? As far as I can see, Wolter changes from the perspective of an historian to that of a theologian and back again, and at one crucial point the question of who is speaking remains unsolved.

It is, explicitly, the theologian, who refers to the image God has of Jesus Christ. But that is, I presume, a certain way of distinguishing all the images from a reality all the images refer to: something along the lines of "Jesus in himself", a distinction only hard-core constructivists would refuse to make. By referring to the image God has, the theologian holds that this "Jesus in himself" is more than a boundary-concept without content, but that there is a way of knowing what exactly Jesus is in himself, namely: He is what he is known to be and thus created to be by God. This knowledge God has is accessible to human beings through the apparitions, interpreted as proofs for the resurrection, interpreted again as proof for God vindicating the truth-claim of Jesus—and here it becomes very difficult to distinguish the perspectives and the images: *That* the disciples of Christ *claimed* to have experienced an apparition of Christ is a historical statement. *That* the disciples of Christ and the Christians of all times *claim* that these apparitions were real and that they give evidence for the resurrection is an historical statement. But *that claim in itself* is a constitutive part of the image of "Jesus Christ" formed by the Christian faith and "unattainable by the methods of pure historical investigation" (p. 9). And that by this God vindicates the claim Jesus Christ is remembered as having asserted is a constitutive part of this very same image and thus a non-historical statement. On the other hand: that the Christians would not have called Jesus of Nazareth "the Lord" without grounds in the claims Jesus himself made is an historical statement that leads to an insight into the self-image of Jesus as it was remembered by his disciples: He must have been remembered as understanding himself as the representative of God announcing the coming Kingdom.

1.2.2 *The Crucial Point*

The crucial point, therefore, of this image of Jesus Christ the disciples of Jesus and the Church maintain, is constituted by the apparitions of Christ and, derived from that, by the conviction that the resurrection is fact: "Therefore there can be no Christian faith, whose concept of reality does not contain certainty about the fact of the resurrection of Jesus" (p. 16). The question arises: What kind of statement is this—historical? statement of faith?—and what does "certainty about the fact of the resurrection" as a part of the Christian "concept of reality" mean? As the statement of an historian, the following is uncontroversial: As far as we know, till recently, there is no evidence of Christians who explicitly denied "the reality" of the resurrection. But since the nineteenth century, at the latest, there have been Christians who have asked what "certainty of fact" regarding the apparitions or with reference to the resurrection could mean. Under the conditions of modern thought, "certainty of fact" is methodically restricted to truth-claims grounded in or deduced from reason or based on experience, be that the experiment in the sciences or the search for and critique of the historical sources in the humanities. So the historical statement, for a systematic theologian, includes the question, whether or how, under the conditions of modernity, we can indulge in a "certainty of fact" regarding the apparitions or the resurrection: In which sense can we say that the apparitions and thus the resurrection of Jesus is a conviction that has, for us, the certainty of a fact?[3]

2. THE SYSTEMATICIAN'S VIEW

With this question in mind, I go back to the question Wolter raised and present a systematician's perspective on the "real Jesus" and on the reason for the certainty that Christ is risen and is at the right hand of the Almighty:

I will present six theses and explain or ground them in the requested brevity. It will turn out that I learned a lot from the paper of Michael Wolter, and that I merely suggest to find a way to deal with the "certainty of fact" regarding the apparitions and the resurrection.

Thesis 1: *The origin and historical provocation of the quest for the historical Jesus or of the "Confession of Jesus" is originally the endeavour of faith to achieve certainty.*

---

[3] For W. Pannenberg, for instance, the certainty of a fact can be established by historical reasoning: Pannenberg, *Grundzüge* (n. 2), 85–103 = *Jesus: God and Man*, 88–105; cf. J. Ratzinger, *Jesus von Nazareth* (2 vols.; Freiburg et al.: Herder; vol. 1: *Von der Taufe am Jordan bis zur Verklärung*, 2007; vol. 2: *Vom Einzug in Jerusalem bis zur Auferstehung*, 2011), 2:265–302 (chap. 9) (ET: *Jesus of Nazareth*, vol. 2: *Holy Week: From the Entrance into Jerusalem to the Resurrection* [London: Incorporated Catholic Truth Society, 2011]). On that: N. Slenczka, " 'Wahrhaftig' auferstanden? Ein kritischer Dialog mit Joseph Ratzinger", in T. Söding, ed., *Tod und Auferstehung Jesu: Theologische Antworten auf das Buch des Papstes* (Freiburg et al.: Herder, 2011), 179–201.

JESUS WAS RESURRECTED THE "CERTAINTY OF FACT"?   191

This thesis is banal. The quest for the historical Jesus was originally oriented around the classical reformational model of the certainty-seeking return from human traditions to Scripture, which the reformers and the post-Reformation theologians characterized as the contamination-free pure source of the divine word.[4] The insight, that one is dealing, also in the honourable tradition of the christological dogmas, not with the infallible agency of the Holy Spirit, but with the work of men, motivates the reformers initially to return to Scripture; at first it is read as verification of the early church council decisions, then as a critique of them.[5] The blossoming insight, first from Petrus Abaelard, then in Luther, that the boundary between word of God and fallible word of men is not identical with the boundaries of the canon, in other words that Scripture offers texts from the error-capable human pen,[6] awakens in the nineteenth century in many theologians the hope that the methodically historical return to the Gospels and to a proclamation free of the special interests of the disciples will mean being at the sources.[7] The inquiry into original Jesus sayings, one initially to be answered quantitatively, was to allow for the distinction between what grows out of religious special interests and what precedes every such special interest and is thus normative. Further, in the case of most theologians, of both historical and systematic persuasion, this return to Jesus' original message was bound together with the expectation of finding a message from Jesus himself, which would elicit such immediate evidential experiences among one's contemporaries as were no longer expected from the constructions of the dogmatic tradition

---

[4] In the following, I'll offer only characteristic examples. Here: *Formula Concordiae: Solida declaratio*, "Vom summarischen Begriff", in *Bekenntnisschriften der Evangelisch-Lutherischen Kirche* (8th ed.; Göttingen: Vandenhoeck & Ruprecht, 1979), 834:16–22; *Confessio Helvetica Posterior*, Art. I, in E.F.K. Müller, *Die Bekenntnisschriften der reformierten Kirche* (Leipzig: Deichertsche Verlagsbuchhandlung, 1903), 170–171.

[5] See, for example, M. Luther, "Von den Konziliis und Kirchen" (1539), in *D. Martin Luthers Werke: Kritische Gesamtausgabe*, vol. 50 (Weimar: Herrmann Böhlaus Nachfolger, 1914), 524:12–526:10.

[6] Petrus Abaelard, *Sic et Non* (ed. E.L.T. Henke et al.; Marburg: Elwert, 1851), here esp. the hermeneutical foundation in the *prologus*: 1–17, esp. 3–5; M. Luther, "Thesen für die Promotionsdisputation von Hieronymus Weller und Nikolaus Medler" (1535), in *D. Martin Luthers Werke: Kritische Gesamtausgabe* 39/1 (Weimar: Herrmann Böhlaus Nachfolger, 1926), 40–59, here from the theses "De fide", theses 49–57, see however theses 58–62!

[7] For example also J. Jeremias, *Abba: Studien zur neutestamentlichen Theologie und Zeitgeschichte* (Göttingen: Vandenhoeck & Ruprecht, 1966), who is of the opinion that he is at the truth foundation of the Christian faith, when he is at the *ipsissima vox Christi*.

192   NOTGER SLENCZKA

or from Paul's justification theology. Harnack's *Wesen des Christentums* (*What is Christianity?*) is an example of this hope.[8]

Thesis 2: *All recollections of the historical Jesus, that means: of the life, that Jesus of Nazareth led between birth and death on the cross, are not minutes drafted by unbiased archivists, but recollections by persons who—in whatever manner—ascribe salvation-historical meaning to this man and his life.*

This thesis summarizes the result of this hopeful return of dogmatics to a history apparently free of human interpretations.[9] The result was, on the one hand, an insight into the complexity of historical understanding—I'll come back to this; on the other hand, the result of the historical inquiry into the life of Jesus was a related insight into the character of the documents collected in the New Testament: We are dealing with *christologies* no less in the Gospels than in the Pauline epistles, and no less in the Gospels than in old or still present dogmatic texts. This should be beyond debate. It says the following: In the Gospels, we are dealing with texts whose authors report about Jesus of Nazareth because they have experienced him as Son of Man, as Messiah, as Son of David, or as Son of God, and thus predicate such of him—this is the concept Wolter relates to as the image of "Jesus Christ". Whatever each of these predicates say: They say each in their own way, that the authors and those who transmitted the texts are convinced that they are not dealing simply with a man who failed on the cross, even more: that they are dealing with more than just a man. With respect to the Gospels as biographies of Jesus that means: The authors presume as the subject of this life led by Jesus this very title-bearer. This is the concept Wolter relates to as the image of

---

[8] See A. von Harnack, *Das Wesen des Christentums* (ed. K.-D. Osthövener; Tübingen: J.C.B. Mohr [Paul Siebeck], 2005), 15–30, here esp. 17–18, 37 (ET: *What is Christianity?* [trans. T.B. Saunders; 5th ed.; London: Benn, 1958]). On Harnack, see A. Schweitzer, *Geschichte der Leben-Jesu-Forschung* (5th ed.; Tübingen: J.C.B. Mohr [Paul Siebeck], 1933), 631–632; ET: *The Quest of the Historical Jesus: A Critical Study of its Progress from Reimarus to Wrede* (trans. J. Bowden; Minneapolis: Fortress, 2001).

[9] I regard M. Kähler, *Der sogenannte historische Jesus und der geschichtliche, biblische Christus* (ed. E. Wolf; Munich: Kaiser, 1961; ET: *The So-called Historical Jesus and the Historic, Biblical Christ* [trans., ed., and with an introduction by C.E. Braaten; foreword by P.J. Tillich; Philadelphia: Fortress, 1964])—besides the "Schlußbetrachtung" A. Schweitzer, *Geschichte* (n. 13), 631–642—as the successful and not yet satisfying summary of this line of questioning. On the history of the life of Jesus research, see also R. Slenczka, *Geschichtlichkeit und Personsein Jesu Christi: Studien zur christologischen Problematik der historischen Jesusfrage* (Göttingen: Vandenhoeck & Ruprecht, 1967), 25–175.

"the earthly Christ". It is on this account that the texts describe Jesus' majesty (although it was hidden to most contemporaries) already during his lifetime. This majesty is suggested in his authoritative teaching, in his wondrous deeds, in his transfiguration, and it is verified in the fulfillment of Old Testament promises and last, but not least, in his resurrection—I am speaking out of the perspective of these texts. The authors of the texts read the recollection of Jesus as recollection of a majesty-bearer, because they have experienced him in their own individual presence as the resurrected saviour. In this way, the texts are, on the one hand, product and witness of the Easter faith; and, on the other hand, they are transmitted in order to awaken this faith. The texts—all of the texts of the Gospels—are, as Paul says, ἐκ πίστεως εἰς πίστιν—their source is faith, and their goal is to awaken faith.

This thesis on the character of the New Testament texts is the most fundamental insight of critical exegesis, and has by no means remained hidden from modern dogmaticians; rather, dogmaticians have decisively argued for it. Examples are Friedrich Schleiermacher, the phenomenal David Friedrich Strauss, whom I deeply revere, Albrecht Ritschl, Wilhelm Herrmann and Martin Kähler; and among the exegetes: of course Rudolf Bultmann, Herbert Braun, and most of the other members of the Bultmann school.[10]

This means that the return from theological-historical and dogma-historical christological definitions to the Gospels, as expected of every dogmatician, clearly cannot lead to the insights on which a modern-day judgement about Jesus of Nazareth could draw as on positive historical facts that form the foundation of every interpretation. Much more, the

---

[10] Most of the texts are known—only a few examples: Kähler, *Jesus* (n. 14); E. Käsemann, "Das Problem des historischen Jesus", in idem, *Exegetische Versuche und Besinnungen*, vol. 1 (4th ed.; Göttingen: Vandenhoeck & Ruprecht, 1968), 187–214 (ET: "The Problem of the Historical Jesus", in idem, *Essays on New Testament Themes* [trans. W.J. Montague; SBT 41; London: SCM, 1968], 15–47); R. Bultmann, "Das Verhältnis der urchristlichen Christusbotschaft zum historischen Jesus", in idem, *Exegetica: Aufsätze zur Erforschung des Neuen Testaments* (ed. E. Dinkler; Tübingen: J.C.B. Mohr [Paul Siebeck], 1967), 445–469 (ET: "The Primitive Christian Kerygma and the Historical Jesus", in C.E. Braaten and R.A. Harrisville, trans. and ed., *The Historical Jesus and the Kerygmatic Christ: Essays on the New Quest of the Historical Jesus* [New York: Abingdon, 1964], 15–42); H. Braun, "Der Sinn der neutestamentlichen Christologie", in idem, *Gesammelte Studien zum Neuen Testament und seiner Umwelt* (Tübingen: J.C.B. Mohr [Paul Siebeck], 1962), 243–282 (ET: "The Meaning of New Testament Christology", *JTC* 5 [1968]: 89–127). Cf. also: L.T. Johnson, *The Real Jesus: The Misguided Quest for the Historical Jesus and the Truth of the Traditional Gospels* (San Francisco: Harper, 1996); D.C. Allison, *The Historical Christ and the Theological Jesus* (Grand Rapids and Cambridge: Eerdmans, 2009).

194 NOTGER SLENCZKA

Gospels offer an *interpretation* of Jesus' life—an "image" according to Wolter—the origin of which is not the greatest possible freedom from special interests in the perception of facts, but rather the proclamation of Jesus of Nazareth as salvation and meaning of the world—and only on that account are his person and the facts of his life central topics.

In addition to all of this, the hermeneutical insight, formulated by Albert Schweitzer and underlined by Wolter, must be mentioned: even the apparently historical inquiry into the life of Jesus is not free of contextual pre-understandings, rather only blind to their effect. I'll return to this.

These insights mean that the hope of coming, by means of historical research, to the "matter itself" that lies at the foundation of all interpretations, is a ruse. The texts do not provide that. The New Testament documents are so structured, that one could certainly write a history of theology of the beginning of Christianity using them as a basis, but not a history of the life of Jesus that goes beyond the basic facts—that he was born somewhere, lived in Galilee, gathered disciples, and died on the cross in Jerusalem at the end of the third decade of the first century. All this information can be gained by an interpretation of the texts because these texts represent—in the terminology of Wolter—the image of "Jesus remembered" as well as the image of "Jesus of Nazareth"; but these images are embedded into the leading image of the earthly Christ and can only be identified by an exegetical process that methodically tries to distinguish these images. We learn nothing about his religious worldview that stands up to scrutiny, and we are not able to grasp his self-understanding. Also, Wolter goes back to the self-image of Jesus only by a conclusion on the basis of the image of the "earthly Christ", as described above. And that means: deciding, on the basis of these results of historical work, to reflect anew on the history of the life of Jesus, demands a foundation.

With that, I come to my third thesis:

Thesis 3: *The so-called "New" Quest for the historical Jesus—the thesis, that this inquiry is indispensable—proceeds not from some necessity of historical research, but presents itself rather to the inquiring exegete as the result of* dogmatic presuppositions.

I omit the debate on the "Third Quest" for the historical Jesus for the moment[11] because it is only another variation on the question being

---

[11] See also: G.S. Oegema, "Der historische Jesus und das Judentum", in U.H.J. Körtner, ed., *Jesus im 21. Jahrhundert* (Neukirchen-Vluyn: Neukirchener Verlag, 2001), 63–90; G. Theissen

JESUS WAS RESURRECTED THE "CERTAINTY OF FACT"?

posed here—the "New Quest for the historical Jesus".[12] This so-called "New Quest for the historical Jesus" does not challenge the sketched distinctiveness of the texts assembled in the Gospels—rather it presumes them; Käsemann, whose famous essay coined this question, points out that although all of the evangelists, especially John, read the history of Jesus' earthly life as history from the perspective of the resurrection experience, the subject of which is the present Lord, they still fail to separate the revelation connected with the resurrection of Jesus of Nazareth and the importance of Jesus as Son of God connected with it from the life history of the earthly individual—this is an insight shared by Wolter, as mentioned above; rather they transmit it in the form and with inclusion of his life history. Thus the texts present the claim that a continuity exists between the earthly individual and the Lord of the world present to the congregation; and he identifies the following background motif:

> They want to...show that the *extra nos* of salvation is 'given' (*Vorgegebenheit*) to faith. To cleave firmly to history is one way of giving expression to the *extra nos* of salvation.[13]

"They": that are the evangelists or the ancient Christian congregations who do not separate the existential importance of Jesus comprehended in the Easter experience from the life he led and thus proclaim Christian faith as a general and generally valid truth. Instead they connect it with the recollection of his life history and thus assert that the salvation of the world is not an idea that is realized in each present in pious subjectivity, but rather was realized once such as is valid for all time. The eschewal by Bultmann and in existential theology of the inquiry into the historical Jesus breaks with the basic anti-docetic decision of the New Testament, according to which the revelation occurs not in each particular moment, but in the flesh and thus once for all in the contingency of a historical place. The Second Quest for the historical Jesus as suggested by Käsemann is—in the terminology of Wolter—a way to distinguish the image of the earthly Jesus from the image of "Jesus remembered" and of "Jesus of Nazareth".

---

and A. Merz, *Der historische Jesus* (3rd ed.; Göttingen: Vandenhoeck & Ruprecht, 2001), here esp. § 1: "Die Geschichte der Leben-Jesu-Forschung", 21–30 (ET: *The Historical Jesus: A Comprehensive Guide* [Minneapolis: Fortress, 1997]); J. Schröter and R. Brucker, eds., *Der historische Jesus: Tendenzen und Perspektiven der gegenwärtigen Forschung* (Berlin and New York: Walter de Gruyter, 2002). From the English debate cf. J.D.G. Dunn, *Jesus Remembered* (vol. 1 of *Christianity in the Making*; Grand Rapids and Cambridge: Eerdmans, 2003).

[12] See the contribution of Ernst Käsemann mentioned (n. 10) above as well as the answers from Rudolf Bultmann as also Herbert Braun.

[13] Käsemann, "Das Problem" (n. 10), 202 = idem, "The Problem", 33.

Out of this follows that it is in no way the ethos of scientific research, that calls out of dogmatic encrustations and leads to the renewed inquiry into the historical Jesus; much rather, there are dogmatic motifs, the dogma-historical decision against docetism, which lead Käsemann and other exegetes to inquire into the earthly Jesus, regardless of the exegetical insight, that the texts provide nothing reliable for a biography of Jesus: The proclamation of the resurrected one as Lord cannot—and for dogmatic reasons!—be indifferent about the assertion that there exists a relationship of discontinuity between the earthly life led by, and self-understanding of, Jesus and the Christ-proclamation of the congregation. There though—this is decisive for Käsemann—it is neither possible to draw the soteriological importance of Jesus as faith comprehends it out of a contemplation of the earthly life he lead and to emphasize it, nor, on the other hand, to separate the soteriological importance from the inquiry into the life Jesus led between birth and tomb.

This describes the problematic issue that lies at the foundation of the question posed by this conference: On the one hand, Christian faith has to do with an historical occurrence accessible to historical research, at its centre the life led by Jesus of Nazareth. Even if we take into account that we have this life only as presented in images (Jesus remembered; Jesus of Nazareth; the self-image of Jesus): the way of compiling these pictures is through historical research. This life is, for one, a path to the cross and a story of failure—either of a beautiful soul or of a too thinly stretched religious and/or political claim. On the other hand, the Christian faith deals with the fact that this occurrence is transmitted with the claim that it is not only in the past, but rather that the subject of this human history sits at the right hand of God, rules the world, and is present and salvifically experienced in the congregation. The missing link between these two is—according to Wolter as well as Käsemann—the ominous experience of Easter, an experience which is interpreted as the appearance of the crucified one who, therefore, must have been resurrected. As a result, the question of the continuity between the life led on earth and the proclamation of the congregation in the debates within the Bultmann school is transformed into the question of the continuity between the historical life led by Jesus and the resurrected Lord[14]—or

---

[14] For example, Käsemann, "Das Problem" (n. 10), 203 = "The Problem", 33–34; Bultmann, "Verhältnis" (n. 10), 445–449, esp. the bottom of 449. Compare the discussion that followed in the 60s, for example, in the documentation: H. Ristow and K. Matthiae, eds.,

better, according to Wolter, the question of the continuity between Jesus remembered and Jesus Christ. The hermeneutical question is meaningfully asked in this manner, because the dilemma becomes evident in the biblical texts, which are quite carefree in presuming the resurrected one as the subject of the historical life led by Jesus; likewise, they call the post-Easter experience of the presence of the resurrected and exalted one the experience of the presence of the earthly Jesus of Nazareth. And this relationship is connected in more recent discussion with the supposition that the connection back to the historical "one-time-ness" (*Einmaligkeit*) guards the Christian faith against the danger of making the subjectivity of individual or collective—but at any rate limited—experience absolute, by incorporating it uncritically into the historical material. Recalling the historical distance means recalling the non-arbitrary nature of the interpretative perspectives, which are to prove themselves on the basis of what is already given.

> ...the very process of taking the historical source in all its historicity (and that means in its distance from the present) and making it luminous by means of a critical examination that penetrates to the uttermost limits of its explicability, and thereby at the same time also critically correcting the prejudices of the expositor himself and making clear to him the historical conditionedness of his own preconceptions—that very process creates the necessary basis for a genuine encounter with the text...Then the transformation and interpretation of historic events in order to illumine our own existence ceases to be arbitrarily and naively reading things into the source. Rather, the way is now open to genuinely historic, personal encounter and discussion...[15]

Thesis 4: *The attempt to grasp the historical life of Jesus apart from the congregation's ascription of meaning leads to no clear result, but instead into the conflict situation that, according to the witness of the Gospels, marked his life.*

Der historische Jesus und der kerygmatische Christus: Beiträge zum Christusverständnis in Forschung und Verkündigung (2nd ed.; Berlin: Evangelische Verlagsanstalt, 1961).

[15] G. Ebeling, "Die Bedeutung der historisch-kritischen Methode für die protestantische Theologie und Kirche", in: idem, *Wort und Glaube* (Tübingen: J.C.B. Mohr [Paul Siebeck], 1960), 1–49, here 36; ET: "The Significance of the Critical Historical Method for Church and Theology in Protestantism", in idem, *Word and Faith* (trans. J.W. Leitch; 2nd ed.; London: SCM, 1984), 17–61, here 49.

At any rate, the accounts of the life of Jesus make this very clear—and this is underlined by the fact that Wolter connects his distinction of "images" to the way personal identity is shaped and defined by the images persons construct of themselves and of one another (pp. 11–12): the meaning of this person during his life was most disputed, and the dispute surrounding him carried on after his death. The dispute surrounding Jesus of Nazareth presents itself as a variety of interpretations of his person, as is more or less recognizable in the Gospels. He is understood to be one of the salvation-bearers expected in the Judaism of his day (Mark 8:27–28), a political insurgent in his trial (Mark 14), or—by his disciples—as a compass which provided direction for their entire lives, in that they gave up everything and followed him. It is completely unnecessary to ask whether, and if so, then which of Jesus' titles can be traced back to the pre-Easter situation or to a claim made by Jesus himself; the point I want to make, which may be regarded as an accurate historical recollection, is that the effect of his teaching and preaching was ambiguous.

The proclamation of the church as it is comprehensible in the Gospels takes up a position in the dispute about the identity of Jesus in a manner that leads the church itself back to the appearances of the resurrected one: they are themselves the reason for describing Jesus of Nazareth as the centre of the whole history of God with humanity. The accounts of the Gospels reflect this position just as much as its disputed nature, which means: The authors of the Gospels are aware that the insight into Jesus' majesty is not won by simply observing the life Jesus led. Much more, all of the New Testament writings presume—unavoidably in the face of the unbelief of the majority of their contemporaries—that this insight into Jesus' majesty is anything but a matter of course; admittedly, they explain this unbelief not with the contrafacticity of their assertions, but with God's hardening of hearts.

A return to the historical Jesus by clearing away the Christian construction is therefore not able to legitimize this position of the church or to provide it greater probability. Instead, such a return to the historical Jesus, apart from the churchly interpretation of his person, leads necessarily back into the pre-Easter situation of the dispute about his identity. This is why it is in no way surprising that the attempts in the nineteenth and twentieth centuries to reconstruct the life and self-understanding of Jesus have led to such a variety of exegetical results. This is not just because, as Schweitzer writes in the famous concluding reflection of his *Geschichte der Leben-Jesu-Forschung*, the person of Jesus always becomes a mirror of the perspective of the interpreter,[16] but indeed also because there is no clear delineation on the level of the historical texts, but rather—in so far as they even allow one to return to the pre-Easter situation—only a reflection of the "dispute surrounding the person of Jesus".

Thesis 5: *"The" difficulty that practical and systematic theology have with the results of the historical inquiry into the life of Jesus of Nazareth is not, then, an outgrowth of a lacking reception of these results grounded in dogmatic concerns. Rather, it stems from the fact that "Scripture" is only "taken seriously" when one takes into account that it only intends to and only does transport information about Jesus of Nazareth in a minimal manner. Indeed, beside the Gospels stand the (Pauline) epistles, in which the transformation process of the human self-understanding manifests itself on the basis of the message of the crucified as risen. This transformation of human self-understanding, evoked by the proclamation of the Gospel, is the origin of the confession that Jesus of Nazareth is the Son of God, and this experience of transformation is the foundation for the proclamation that Jesus is risen and has appeared to his disciples.*

It is the special character of the New Testament, that none or only very few of the texts transmitted in it understand themselves or want to be understood as accounts of the life of Jesus—that may be true, more or less, for the four Gospels. Much more, the New Testament provides texts that are the expression of the human self-understanding which is established via the encounter, not directly with the person, but rather with the proclamation of Jesus of Nazareth as the risen Lord. In the first case, this means the Pauline epistles, but then also the Johannine epistles— in the following I will concentrate on the Pauline epistles. The point in these texts is not simply that the person of Jesus presented in the Gospels is comprehended dogmatically and provided with more or less dubious predicates of honour. Much more, Paul speaks in his letters, especially in both Corinthian letters and in Philippians (despite 1Cor 2:2), mostly of himself. He describes that—and thereby also how—he understands himself and reaches a new understanding of his own existence in light of the person and fate of Jesus of Nazareth. The letters present what it means to be "in Christ" or again: that Christ lives ἐν ἐμοί. What do I mean by that? A unique correspondence of Paul's own experience on the one hand and

---

[16] Schweitzer, *Geschichte* (n. 8), 631.

the earthly life led by Jesus, focused on the cross-event, on the other hand, can be followed through the Pauline letters. I would just call to mind 1 and 2Corinthians, in which the question is whether the feebleness of Paul's existence falsifies his claim of being an apostle of Jesus Christ (see 2Corinthians 10–12). In the Corinthian letters, Paul interprets his own life, his ills, and his persecution as a depiction and manifestation of the humility and cross of Christ, such that the suffering of the apostle and the suffering of Christ are indistinguishable ("I always carry the suffering of Christ in my body"; 2Cor 4:10). That means, regarding the debate with his opponents: particularly the humility of the apostle proves him to be an apostle of Jesus Christ (2Cor 11:16–12:10); here and in Galatians, he identifies the external life of Christ with his own life ("Christ lives in me"; Gal 2:19). This process is not limited to his apostolic existence; rather, Paul leads the recipients of his letters into this self-interpretation; I'm thinking here of Rom 8:17 and especially Romans 6, where he helps the Roman Christians to understand themselves and the lives they lead in light of the life led by Jesus of Nazareth, which was focused on the cross and suffering: on the basis of baptism, they are to understand themselves (λογίζεσθε ὑμᾶς!) as those who have died in Christ for sin and live for God (Rom 6:11). This new self-understanding also directs the mutual judgements of Christians toward one another and is to direct the relationship of the Corinthians to Paul: Because all have died in Christ—so he says in 2Cor 5:14–15—and because they are all new creatures in Christ (2Cor 5:16–17), they should concur with Paul's self-judgement and not judge him κατὰ σάρκα, but instead see in him the new creature, that he is in Christ (2Cor 5:16). And the Christians in Philippi are called to build a new community in which they all serve each other—with the rationale that Christ humbled himself unto death on the cross (Phil 2:5ff).

The Pauline epistles document the process of self-interpretation which perfectly corresponds to the approach to the recollections of the historical life led by Jesus as given in the Gospels: Even as there the failed life led by Jesus—especially in John—is interpreted as the hidden story of the power of the son (Wolter's "earthly Christ"), so Paul interprets his own life story as the realization of the same "power in weakness", or "strength, that is powerful in the weak" (2Cor 12:9); he interprets his whole life as a reevaluation initiated by the encounter with the risen one, in which what was once valuable is shown to be refused (Phil 3:7–11), and in which feebleness becomes understood as valuable (see 1Corinthians 1–3).

Paul himself bases this insight in the appearance to him of the crucified one as resurrected—possibly on the road to Damascus. But this particular

JESUS WAS RESURRECTED THE "CERTAINTY OF FACT"?   201

encounter with the resurrected one is not constitutive for Paul, rather important is the commission to preach (Gal 1:11–12), which allows others to see what he saw in the Damascus experience. The central text for this is 2Cor 4:6: "For God who called the light to shine out of darkness, has shone brightly into our [apostolic, plural!] hearts, so that, through us, the light of the knowledge of the glory of God in the face of Jesus Christ might shine forth" (2Cor 4:6).

In a manner of speaking, the Damascus experience, which Paul is playing off here with the phrase "[who] has shone brightly into our hearts...", is a repeatable event, an enlightening, which is not for Paul alone, but which comes to be in others through the work—the preaching—of the apostle: "to shine forth...". The equivalent of the Damascus event occurs wherever the preaching of the crucified one as resurrected—"of the glory of God in the face of Jesus Christ"—becomes the origin of a new self-understanding, when the addressee recognizes himself and his life in the light of the unity of weakness and strength presented in Jesus Christ.

Precisely this is the experience that is meant by the phrase "Easter experience" or "appearance of the resurrected one": that the proclamation of the resurrected one begins to make sense in that it becomes the origin of a new self-understanding, in which the addressee experiences his own weakness as the place of the presence of God. It is not the demonstrable continuity between the proclamation of the one who is resurrected and the earthly life led by Jesus, or even the self-understanding of Jesus, that verifies the proclamation of the church, but rather that a light appears to a person by means of the assertion that precisely the crucified one is also the resurrected one. And that a "light shines forth" means: he can recognize his own humble existence as a manifestation of the cross and understand himself anew as borne by the resurrection life.

Why do I describe all of this? For the sake of the concluding thesis:

Thesis 6: The interaction of the New Testament texts—Gospels on the one hand and Pauline and Johannine letters on the other—makes clear wherein the interest in the earthly life led by Jesus lies: not namely (merely) in an anti-docetic "once for all", but rather in the power of a life, that in its humility is "found in fashion as a man". The interest in the earthly life lies therein: that in this feeble life human beings are able to recognize their own feebleness. But of this feeble life, however, contrafactually, something new must be said: namely that this very person is "the Lord". The power of this proclamation is one of comprehension: this life of Jesus opens up, for the one who hears it proclaimed, paths of self-interpretation: As he, the crucified Jesus, is the Lord and Son of God, so the one who hears the Gospel is to understand his own feebleness as the presence of the risen Christ.

There is no path that leads from the life of Jesus and the little bit, that can be determined about it historically, to the church's christology. Churchly christology is not interested in the path of the earthly life of Jesus on account of and conditioned by this earthly life-path somehow being seen in terms of the great formulations and honour-titles, which the first congregations ascribed to him; rather, the church's christology is interested in the path of his life because of its exemplary nature—not in that it invites imitation, but in that it leads one to *find oneself* and one's own feebleness in this life-path leading to the cross, and to understand oneself anew in light of the message that the crucified one is the one who was resurrected.

The special character of the New Testament is not that it tells the story of the path of Jesus' life in the Gospels, and also not that it loads the active subject of this life with honour-predicates. The special character of the New Testament documents is, much more, that they show wherein the continuity between the path of the earthly life and the honour-subject lies, namely not in a historically identifiable claim of the earthly Jesus, but in that the contrafactual opposition of humility and honour in ecclesial proclamation initiates and effects a recognition and redefinition of self-understanding in one contingent person, namely Paul, which is then evident in his epistles. The insight, that the earthly one is the resurrected one, grows out of the intangible and undeducible evidence of the invitation to understand oneself and to understand oneself anew, that is present in Jesus' life-path. The later—that is, chronologically later than the letters to the Corinthians—developed justification theology of Paul unfolds the person of Jesus of Nazareth and his cross as a means of comprehending the problematic nature of the *condition humaine* and as an option for an interpretative approach to this problematic condition.[17] Where then for a person from the narrative of Jesus Christ a light *on himself, the hearer,* appears, he is, as Paul says "in Christ" and "Christ in him". Precisely this

---

[17] This would have to be demonstrated in all its parts, which is not possible here. The reader is referred to a text, in which I have attempted to do that: N. Slenczka, "Entzweiung und Versöhnung: Das Phänomen des Gewissens und der Erlösung in Shakespeares 'King Richard III.' als Hintergrund eines Verständnisses der 'imputativen Rechtfertigung' bei Luther", *KuD* 50 (2004): 289–319. See also: idem, "Problemgeschichte der Christologie", in K. Stock, ed., *Christologie* (Marburger Jahrbuch Theologie XXIII; Leipzig: Evangelische Verlagsanstalt, 2011), 59–111.

insight is the apparition and the presence of Christ, which is announced in the discussion of the resurrection. The determination, that "this truly was the Son of God" (Mark 15:39), points one toward nothing else than this process of founding one's own existence.

In summary: *The interest in the historical Jesus cannot be attributed to a peculiar and finally abstract anti-docetic motif; it also cannot be attributed to the hope of verifying the continuity of the earthly Jesus and the proclamation; it also cannot be attributed to the interest in developing a supposedly better founded christology on the basis of what is historically determinable. Rather, the interest in the earthly Jesus is to be attributed to the insight, that the Gospels speak about each person's individual existence resp. transform his self-understanding, when he hears and begins to understand, that an earthly life led by a humbled person is encompassed with honour-predicates, thus: that this crucified one is more than is visible: the Lord. This insight comprehends, that in the statements about the humility of that man, it is the hearer of the word who is being discussed, and that, in the honour-predicates, he is also being contrafactually redefined.*

Perhaps this would be a way to show how, nowadays, the claim that the apparition and resurrection of Christ has "certainty of fact" might be reconstructed without the misunderstanding, that this "certainty of fact" is derived from reason or experience. Or better: This certainty is derived from experience, but from an experience that has the character of a transformation of self-understanding evoked by the promulgation of the crucified one as the Lord.

IM GLAUBEN ZUM ‚WIRKLICHEN' JESUS?
ÜBERLEGUNGEN ZU MICHAEL WOLTERS UMGANG MIT DER HISTORISCHEN JESUSFRAGE[1]

Martin Laube

1.

Seit Lessings Veröffentlichung der „Fragmente eines Ungenannten" in den Jahren 1774 bis 1778[2] hält die historische Frage nach Jesus von Nazareth die Theologie in Atem. In immer wieder neuen Anläufen wird darum gestritten, welche verlässlichen Erkenntnisse sich über diesen Jesus gewinnen lassen und wer er wohl ‚wirklich' war. Die Folgen sind hinlänglich bekannt: Ging es zunächst darum, das christologische Dogma vom inkarnierten Gottessohn als metaphysische Spekulation zu entlarven, erhielt bald auch das Bild, welches die Evangelien vom Leben und Wirken Jesu zeichnen, deutliche Risse.

Trotzdem liegt die eigentümliche Brisanz der historischen Jesusfrage weniger in den Ergebnissen, zu denen sie geführt hat und immer noch führt, als vielmehr in der Art der Fragestellung selbst. Davon zeugen die weitgespannten Auseinandersetzungen um die theologische Legitimität des Unterfangens, sich mit den Mitteln der historischen Forschung der Gestalt Jesu zu nähern. Sie beziehen sich sowohl auf die *religiöse Bedeutung* als auch auf die *theologische Funktion* der historischen Jesusfrage. Beides steht zwar in engem Zusammenhang, ist aber sorgsam voneinander zu unterscheiden. Im einen Fall steht die Relevanz der historischen Jesusforschung für den *Glauben* zur Debatte: Können bestimmte Ergebnisse der historischen Rückfrage den Glauben gefährden, und wird der Glaube so auf problematische Weise abhängig von der jeweiligen Forschungslage? Verführt die historische Jesusfrage den Glauben, indem sie ihm suggeriert, zu objektiven Fundamenten gelangen zu können? Oder

---

[1] Im Folgenden beziehen sich die ohne weitere Angaben angeführten Seitenverweise im Fließtext und in den Anmerkungen auf die Abhandlung von Michael Wolter, „Which Jesus is the Real Jesus?" (oben S. 1–17).

[2] Vgl. vor allem H.S. Reimarus, „Von dem Zwecke Jesu und seiner Jünger" (1778), in: G.E. Lessing, *Werke*, Bd. VII: *Theologiekritische Schriften I und II*, hg. von H. Göpfert, München 1976, 492–604.

ist es vielleicht ein berechtigtes Bedürfnis des Glaubens selbst, danach zu fragen, wer Jesus wirklich war? Im anderen Fall geht es um die Folgen, die mit dem methodischen Ansatz der historischen Jesusfrage für das überkommene Selbstverständnis der *Theologie* verbunden sind. In welchem Verhältnis steht die dogmatische Reflexion zur historischen Fragestellung? Was bedeutet es für den Geltungsanspruch und die Reichweite theologischer Aussagen, wenn sie der relativierenden Dynamik der historischen Jesusforschung ausgesetzt werden? Was macht eigentlich umgekehrt die historische Frage nach Jesus zu einer theologischen Frage?

Zugespitzt formuliert: Die historische Frage nach Jesus mag zwar nach Jesus fragen. Ihre Brisanz jedoch liegt darin, dass sie—am Beispiel der Person Jesu—den Finger in eine offene Wunde der Theologie legt. Diese Wunde betrifft das noch immer ungeklärte Verhältnis der Theologie zum historischen Bewusstsein und zum modernen Umgang mit dem Problem der Geschichte. Das aufgeklärte Auseinandertreten von Tradition und Gegenwart einerseits, der historistische Bruch zwischen Genese und Geltung andererseits haben die Theologie in eine Grundlagenkrise gestürzt, von der sie sich bis heute nicht erholt hat. Diese Grundlagenkrise findet ihren Ausdruck zunächst darin, dass es noch immer nicht gelungen ist, das Verhältnis von Glaube und Geschichte befriedigend zu bestimmen. Auf der einen Seite ist die Bindung des persönlichen Glaubens an eine ‚objektive‘ Heilsgeschichte unter modernen Bedingungen nicht mehr erschwinglich. Weder geht es im Glauben um die Feststellung historischer Tatsachen, noch eignet er sich ein historisch Vorgängiges nachträglich an: „Die Erlösung ist nicht etwas ein für allemal im Werke Christi vollzogenes und den Einzelnen dann erst Zuzueignendes, sondern ist ein jedesmal neuer, in der Wirkung Gottes auf die Seele durch Erkenntnis Gottes sich vollziehender Vorgang.“[3] Auf der anderen Seite wäre es ein Trugschluss, daraus nun eine grundsätzliche Geschichtslosigkeit des Glaubens abzuleiten. Denn *erstens* steht der Glaube immer schon in einem geschichtlichen Kontext, ist geschichtlich geworden und hat geschichtliche Folgen; *zweitens* bezieht er sich seinerseits auf bestimmte geschichtliche Gegebenheiten—bis dahin, dass er offenkundig für sich selbst an der Frage interessiert ist, wer Jesus wohl ‚wirklich‘ war.

---

[3] E. Troeltsch, „Die Bedeutung der Geschichtlichkeit Jesu für den Glauben" (1911), in: F. Voigt (Hg.), *Ernst Troeltsch Lesebuch: Ausgewählte Texte*, Tübingen 2003, 61–92, hier 64.— Vor diesem Hintergrund erscheint das Vorgehen Michael Wolters überaus problematisch, den Glauben an die Auferstehung Jesu als „a *certitude of fact*" (S. 16) zu beschreiben und rundheraus zu dekretieren, dass „there can be no Christian faith, whose concept of reality does not contain certainty about the fact of the resurrection of Jesus" (S. 16).

IM GLAUBEN ZUM ‚WIRKLICHEN‘ JESUS?

Die genannte Grundlagenkrise beschränkt sich aber nicht nur auf das Verhältnis des *Glaubens* zur Geschichte, sondern betrifft auch das Selbstverständnis der *Theologie* im Umgang mit der Geschichte.[4] Die bittere Ironie besteht hier darin, dass die Theologie über die Ausbildung der Bibelwissenschaften zunächst selbst an der Durchsetzung der historischen Denkweise beteiligt war. Doch einmal auf die Erforschung der biblischen Schriften angewandt, durchdringt sie in der Folge wie ein „Sauerteig“[5] alle Bereiche der Theologie und sprengt ihre bisherigen Grundlagen. Dem Rückzug auf eine übernatürliche ‚Heilsgeschichte‘ wird ebenso der Boden entzogen wie der Berufung auf ein dem geschichtlichen Wandel entzogenes absolutes Geltungsfundament. Mit dem Zusammenbruch der alten ‚dogmatischen Methode‘ gerät dann aber überhaupt die Möglichkeit ins Wanken, im Fluss des geschichtlichen Werdens bleibende Maßstäbe und Werte ausfindig zu machen. Die relativierende Dynamik der historischen Kritik untergräbt den Aufbau normativer Perspektiven und Verbindlichkeiten—ohne dass es der Theologie gelingt, diese Spannung in ein produktives Wechselverhältnis umzumünzen. Stattdessen brechen beide Seiten in einen unüberbrückbaren Gegensatz auseinander. Das Ergebnis zeigt sich im gegenwärtigen Zustand des theologischen Fächerkanons: Das Gegenüber von historischen und systematischen Disziplinen ist geradezu bis zur Sprachlosigkeit erstarrt. Wo früher immerhin noch miteinander gestritten wurde, herrschen heute weithin Schweigen und Desinteresse. Die Spannung von historischer Kritik und systematischer Konstruktion wird nicht mehr als Aufforderung zu fächerübergreifender Zusammenarbeit und Vermittlung begriffen; stattdessen setzt sich mehr und mehr die Tendenz durch, eines der beiden Momente absolut zu setzen. So gibt es in den *exegetischen Disziplinen* eine starke Strömung, welche einseitig das historisch-kritische Profil betont und so—unter Preisgabe des eigenen theologischen Charakters—den Anschluss an das herrschende Wissenschaftsparadigma erstrebt. Das andere Extrem bilden solche Ansätze, die unter Ausblendung aller Regeln des historischen Bewusstseins den normativen Übersprung von den biblischen Texten in die Gegenwart vollziehen. Die *Dogmatik* wiederum irrlichtert zwischen den beiden Extremen hin und her, sich entweder auf bloße Theologiegeschichtsschreibung zurückzuziehen oder

---

[4] Vgl. dazu ausführlicher M. Laube, „Theologische Selbstklärung im Angesicht des Historismus: Überlegungen zur theologischen Funktion der Frage nach dem historischen Jesus“, in: *KuD* 54 (2008), 114–137.

[5] E. Troeltsch, „Ueber historische und dogmatische Methode in der Theologie“, in: ders., *Gesammelte Schriften*, Bd. 2, Tübingen 1913, 729–753, hier 730.

208 MARTIN LAUBE

zu einem übersteigerten Gestus assertorischer Positionalität anzusetzen. Im einen Fall regiert eine geltungsvergessene Historisierungsmethodik, im anderen Fall eine geltungsversessene Gewissheitsrhetorik.

2.

Es zeichnet nun das Denken und Arbeiten Michael Wolters aus, dass er sich mit dieser Entwicklung nicht abfinden will. Er protestiert gegen die Tendenz einer schleichenden 'Enttheologisierung' seines Fachs im Namen der historischen Methode; zugleich verwahrt er sich gegen das umgekehrte Bemühen, eine 'theologische' Exegese jenseits der historischen Methode zu etablieren. Historische Methode und theologischer Anspruch gehören für ihn untrennbar zusammen. Die neutestamentliche Exegese sei nicht nur *trotz*, sondern *in* ihrem historisch-kritischen Profil eine dezidiert *theologische* Wissenschaft—mit diesem Appell ruft er nachdrücklich in Erinnerung, dass die disziplinäre Aufteilung von Genese und Geltung lediglich ein trügerisches Manöver darstellt, um die Abgründigkeiten des historischen Denkens zu entschärfen.

Damit ist zugleich das zentrale Anliegen benannt, das Wolter mit seinen Überlegungen zur historischen Jesusfrage verfolgt. Ihm ist daran gelegen, den inhaltlich *theologischen* Charakter dieser methodisch *historischen* Frage aufzuweisen. „Was macht die historische Frage nach Jesus von Nazareth zu einer theologischen Frage?", so lautet der Titel, unter den Wolter die deutsche Vorfassung seines Aufsatzes gestellt hat. Am Beispiel der historischen Jesusforschung sucht er zu zeigen, wie sich historisch-kritische Methode und theologisches Interesse schlüssig miteinander verbinden lassen. Insofern nimmt Wolter den skizzierten theologiereflexiven Strang im Umgang mit der historischen Jesusfrage auf. Auch wenn der englische Titel: „Which Jesus is the Real Jesus?" zunächst anderes vermuten lässt, geht es ihm doch *nicht unmittelbar* darum, diese Frage zu beantworten und ein Bild des 'wirklichen' Jesus zu zeichnen. Sein eigentliches Interesse besteht vielmehr darin, die *historische* Frage nach Jesus als eine zugleich *theologische* Frage zu formatieren. Erst im weiteren Verlauf macht er diesen theologischen Charakter dann darin fest, dass der Glaube eine Antwort auf die Frage nach dem 'wirklichen Jesus' zu bieten vermag.

Die Pointe liegt also in dem 'Zugleich' von historischer Methode und theologischem Anspruch: Wolter hebt nicht darauf ab, der historischen Frage nach Jesus eine theologische Frage nach Christus zur Seite zu stellen oder sie unter der Hand in eine solche zu überführen. Das würde letztlich bedeuten, historische und theologische Fragestellung gegeneinander auszuspielen—und so die Krise um den theologischen Charakter der historischen Forschung nur verschärfen. Stattdessen packt er den Stier bei den Hörnern und sucht zu zeigen, in welchem Sinne die historisch angesetzte Rückfrage nach Jesus *als solche* zugleich ein theologisches Unterfangen darstellen kann. Mithin bestehe die Aufgabe darin, „to identify the manner of the historical search for Jesus of Nazareth, which makes this inquiry a theological one, even though it is *methodologically* quite atheological. What characterizes such an investigation since it is not pursued purely out of historical interest, but also aims at *theological* cognition? In what way do these issues coincide?" (S. 7).

Nun wäre es durchaus denkbar gewesen, sich in der Bearbeitung dieser Aufgabe an der klassischen Lösung Friedrich Schleiermachers zu orientieren. Dieser hatte in seiner *Kurzen Darstellung des theologischen Studiums* die Theologie als eine ‚positive Wissenschaft' bestimmt, „deren Theile zu einem Ganzen nur verbunden sind durch ihre gemeinsame Beziehung auf eine bestimmte Glaubensweise, d. h. eine bestimmte Gestaltung des Gottesbewußtseins; der christlichen also durch die Beziehung auf das Christenthum".[6] Vergleichbar der Medizin oder Jurisprudenz sei die Theologie mithin durch einen externen Zweckbezug gekennzeichnet. Die vielgestaltige Glaubenspraxis des Christentums stelle die Kirchenleitung vor eine Reihe anspruchsvoller Steuerungsaufgaben. Der Theologie obliege es, der Kirchenleitung dafür die notwendigen „wissenschaftlichen Kenntnisse und Kunstregeln"[7] an die Hand zu geben. Erst und allein durch diesen funktionalen Bezug auf die Belange der Kirchenleitung gewinne die Theologie ihren disziplinären Zusammenhalt.[8] Abgesehen davon zerfalle sie in ein disparates Nebeneinander unzusammenhängender Einzelfächer; zudem verlören die jeweiligen Methoden und Wissensbestände ihren theologischen Charakter: „Dieselben Kenntnisse, wenn sie ohne Beziehung auf das Kirchenregiment erworben und besessen werden, hören auf

---

[6] F. Schleiermacher, *Kurze Darstellung des theologischen Studiums zum Behuf einleitender Vorlesungen* (1811/1830), hg. von D. Schmid, Berlin 2002, § 1, 139.

[7] A.a.O. (1830), § 5, 142.

[8] Vgl. a.a.O., § 1, 140: „Eine positive Wissenschaft überhaupt ist nämlich ein solcher Inbegriff wissenschaftlicher Elemente, welche ihre Zusammengehörigkeit nicht haben, als ob sie einen vermöge der Idee der Wissenschaft nothwendigen Bestandtheil der wissenschaftlichen Organisation bildeten, sondern nur sofern sie zur Lösung einer praktischen Aufgabe erforderlich sind."

theologische zu sein, und fallen jede der Wissenschaft anheim, der sie ihrem Inhalte nach angehören."[9] Es gibt mithin weder einen spezifisch theologischen Gegenstand noch eine spezifisch theologische Methode; zudem verfügt die Theologie nicht über spezifische, nur ihr zukommende Erkenntnisse. Stattdessen bedient sie sich des allgemeinen Methodenspektrums und erarbeitet auf dieser Grundlage Wissensbestände, deren theologischer Gehalt an den kirchenleitenden Funktionsbezug gebunden ist. Die Theologie erweist sich als ein interdisziplinärer Verbund unterschiedlicher fachwissenschaftlicher Einzelperspektiven, deren Wissen kein anderes ist als in anderen Wissenschaften, sondern lediglich in anderen Zusammenhängen steht.[10]

Daraus folgt: Die historischen Bibelwissenschaften bedienen sich der historisch-kritischen Methode und erwerben vermittels ihrer keine qualitativ anderen Kenntnisse als andere historisch-philologische Disziplinen. Theologische Dignität erhalten diese Wissensbestände allein durch ihren funktionalen Bezug auf die Belange der Kirchenleitung: Da das praktische „Interesse am Christenthum"[11] ein entsprechendes „Wissen um das Christenthum"[12] notwendig voraussetzt, gehört auch „die geschichtliche Kenntniß des Christentums"[13]—mitsamt der exegetischen Aufarbeitung der Geschichte des Urchristentums—zu den unerlässlichen Aufgaben der Theologie. Das schließt die historische Rückfrage nach Jesus ein. Ihr kommt sogar eine besondere Stellung zu, da Schleiermacher das Wesensprinzip der christlichen Frömmigkeit gerade darin festmacht, „daß alles in derselben bezogen wird auf die durch Jesum von Nazareth vollbrachte Erlösung".[14] Freilich gelange die historische Methode allein nicht zu gehaltvollen Erkenntnissen. Dazu bedürfe es vielmehr der kritischen Einordnung ihrer Ergebnisse in ein spekulativ gewonnenes Begriffsnetz. Doch auch

---

[9] A.a.O., § 6, 142.

[10] Vgl. dazu auch C. Albrecht, „Kulturverstehen als theologische Bildungsarbeit: Wissenschaftsgeschichtliche und religionshermeneutische Aspekte einer ‚Kulturgeschichte des Christentums' ", in: ders., *Bildung in der Praktischen Theologie*, Tübingen 2003, 51–98, hier 58.

[11] F. Schleiermacher, *Kurze Darstellung* (1830) (siehe Anm. 6), § 8, 143.

[12] A.a.O., § 10, 144.

[13] A.a.O., § 70, 167.

[14] F. Schleiermacher, *Der christliche Glaube nach den Grundsätzen der evangelischen Kirche im Zusammenhange dargestellt: Zweite Auflage* (1830/31), hg. von Rolf Schäfer, Berlin und New York 2003 (Kritische Gesamtausgabe I/13), § 11, 93.—Zu Schleiermachers Umgang mit der historischen Jesusfrage vgl. die vorzügliche Studie von M. Schröder, *Die kritische Identität des neuzeitlichen Christentums: Schleiermachers Wesensbestimmung der christlichen Religion*, Tübingen 1995.

das daraus resultierende deduktiv-induktive Vermittlungsverfahren, mit dem Schleiermacher die Geschichte des Christentums zu erfassen sucht, wird erst dadurch zu einem theologischen Unterfangen, dass es auf die Belange der Kirchenleitung ausgerichtet wird: Die *historische* Beschäftigung mit dem Christentum weist genau dann einen *theologischen* Charakter auf, wenn sie im Dienste des Interesses an der praktischen Gestaltung des Christentums steht. Mehr kann nicht gefordert werden, mehr braucht aber auch nicht gefordert zu werden, um die historische Methode als Teil der Theologie betrachten zu können.

So weit Friedrich Schleiermacher. Michael Wolter geht jedoch einen anderen Weg. Er argumentiert nicht mit dem funktionalen Charakter theologischer Erkenntnis, sondern greift auf den persönlichen Glauben des forschenden Wissenschaftlers zurück. Die historische Frage nach Jesus wird für ihn dadurch zu einer theologischen Frage, dass sie aus der Perspektive des Osterglaubens eine definitive Antwort zu erhalten vermag. So spitzt Wolter die historische Jesusfrage auf die Erhebung des Selbstverständnisses Jesu zu. Im breiten Spektrum der Jesusbilder handle es sich zunächst nur um ein weiteres Bild von Jesus—„the image that Jesus had of himself" (S. 12). Doch in der Perspektive des Osterglaubens ändere sich das. Denn seine Pointe bestehe gerade darin, dass Gott durch die Auferweckung Jesu dessen Selbstbild bestätigt und ins Recht gesetzt habe. Mithin eröffne sich dem *glaubenden* Historiker eine Antwort auf die historische Jesusfrage, die dem *nichtglaubenden* Historiker verschlossen bleibe—ohne dass der Rahmen der historischen Methode gesprengt worden sei: „In both cases, one and the same question is asked—namely: ‚Who was Jesus really?' The historians—be they theologians or not—can only confess that they don't know—at least if they are honest. The theological historians furthermore know that this question will be answered by the self-interpretation of Jesus" (S. 17).

Bei näherem Hinsehen sind es also vor allem zwei Grundentscheidungen, welche Wolters Umgang mit der historischen Jesusfrage prägen: Zum einen nimmt er den *Glauben* des Historikers in Anspruch, um die historische Frage nach Jesus als eine zugleich theologische Frage auszuweisen, zum anderen soll dieser Glaube dazu dienen, eine *Antwort* auf die historische Jesusfrage geben zu können. Es hat geradezu den Anschein, als wollte Michael Wolter darauf hinaus, dass der theologische Mehrwert der historischen Jesusfrage genau darin besteht, sie *im Glauben beantworten* zu können. Anders formuliert: Was macht die historische Frage nach Jesus zu einer theologischen Frage? Dass der Osterglaube sie durch die Selbstauslegung Jesu beantwortet sieht.

Der Rückgang auf den Glauben des Historikers ist nun jedoch alles andere als unproblematisch. Er verdankt sich zwar dem berechtigten Anliegen Wolters, die beiden Ebenen von Theologie und Frömmigkeit nicht gänzlich beziehungslos auseinanderfallen zu lassen. Doch im Gegenzug droht nun die Gefahr, dass die Errungenschaften der neuzeitlichen Unterscheidung beider Seiten[15] hinterrücks preisgegeben und nivelliert werden: Die Theologie ist nicht selbst Vollzug des Glaubens, sondern hat diesen zu ihrem Gegenstand. Sie ist als Theorie der Religion von dieser ebenso unterschieden wie auf sie bezogen. Nur so lassen sich beide Seiten vor gegenseitigen Übergriffen schützen und in ihrer jeweiligen Selbständigkeit bewahren.

Durch seine Verschleifung der Unterscheidung von Theologie und Religion vermengt Wolter sodann die beiden zu Beginn skizzierten Ebenen der historischen Jesusfrage. Es ist eines, das Problem der ‚Theologizität‘ der historischen Jesusfrage zu bearbeiten, ein anderes, dem Interesse des Glaubens daran nachzugehen, wer Jesus ‚wirklich‘ war. Im einen Fall geht es um das Verhältnis des Glaubens zu seinem geschichtlichen Grund, im anderen Fall um das Verhältnis der Theologie zur historischen Methode. Beides ist voneinander zu unterscheiden, wird jedoch von Michael Wolter kurzgeschlossen: Der Rekurs auf den Glauben soll dazu helfen, die ‚Theologizität‘ der historischen Jesusfrage aufzuweisen. Im Ergebnis droht freilich die Gefahr, nun auf beiden Ebenen in eine Sackgasse zu geraten. Der Rückzug auf den persönlichen Glauben des Historikers entwertet faktisch die Bedeutung des historischen Denkens und vertieft den Hiatus zwischen historischer Methodik und theologischem Anspruch der Bibelwissenschaften. Die Fixierung des Glaubens auf die Anerkennung einer wie immer gearteten Tatsächlichkeit der Auferstehung Jesu wiederum macht es diesem letztlich unmöglich, das eigene Interesse an der Person Jesu in ein konstruktives Verhältnis zur historischen Jesusfrage zu setzen. Das gilt es nun in einem kurzen Durchgang durch Wolters Gedankenführung zu zeigen.

3.

Michael Wolter setzt ein mit der methodischen Grundeinsicht moderner historischer Forschung: „[T]here is no written history that reconstructs

---

[15] Vgl. dazu grundlegend B. Ahlers, *Die Unterscheidung von Theologie und Religion: Ein Beitrag zur Vorgeschichte der modernen praktischen Theologie im 18. Jahrhundert*, Gütersloh 1980.

the past as it was in a real or factual sense" (S. 8). Historische Erkenntnis kann nicht als abbildhafte Darstellung der Vergangenheit begriffen werden, sondern weist einen unhintergehbar konstruktiven Charakter auf. Die geschichtliche Wirklichkeit ,entsteht' gleichsam erst unter dem konstruierenden Zugriff des Historikers und ist dessen Tätigkeit nicht schon unabhängig ,vorgegeben'. Mithin liegt das Ziel der historischen Forschung weniger in der *Rekonstruktion von Vergangenheit* als vielmehr in der *Konstruktion von Geschichte*: Es geht um die sinnstiftende Erinnerung und Deutung vergangener Ereignisse.

Im Blick auf die historische Jesusfrage folgt daraus, von der Vorstellung des einen ,wahren' oder ,wirklichen' Jesus *hinter* den vielfältigen Zeugnissen von ihm Abschied nehmen zu müssen. Das gilt freilich nicht allein in dem methodischen Sinne, dass der ,wirkliche' Jesus hinter den Texten nicht mehr *zugänglich* ist, sondern grundsätzlich: Nimmt man die neuzeitliche Einsicht in den konstruktiven Charakter historischer Erkenntnis ernst, ist es *sinnlos*, fernerhin an der Vorstellung eines ,wirklichen' Jesus hinter den Texten festzuhalten.[16] Auch das Postulat eines Jesus ,an sich'—gleichsam als Substrat oder Fluchtpunkt aller historischen Konstruktionen— stellt selbst nur wieder das Konstrukt eines Historikers dar und vermag der grundsätzlichen Perspektivität aller Erkenntnis nicht zu entrinnen. Stattdessen tritt nun an die Stelle des einen ,wirklichen' Jesus die Vielfalt unterschiedlicher Jesusbilder. Entsprechend lautet der Grundsatz der neueren Jesusforschung „that on every level of our investigation only certain *images* of Jesus are available to us, and that we can always *produce* only certain images of Jesus" (S. 8).

Wolter nimmt diesen Grundsatz auf und gibt ihm eine originelle Wendung, indem er verschiedene Typen solcher Jesusbilder unterscheidet. Dabei kommt er auf insgesamt sieben Bildtypen, die ihrerseits in sich verschiedene Gestalt annehmen. Als *ersten Bildtyp* führt er den *historischen Jesus* an und versteht darunter das Konstrukt der historischen Jesusforschung: „It is the image that the researchers of the historical Jesus conceptualize in their books on him" (S. 8–9). Den *zweiten Bildtyp* nennt er *Jesus Christus*. Hier geht es nun—im Unterschied zum historischen Jesus—um den dogmatischen Christus. Es handelt sich um das Bild, mit dem der christliche Glaube Jesus charakterisiert und das auch nur vom

---

[16] Wolter selbst hält freilich am ,wirklichen' Jesus im Sinne einer „ontic reality" (S. 14) fest, über den wir keinerlei Aussagen machen können: „He (the real Jesus) existed, but no one can know him as such or even make statements about him" (S. 14). Er bricht damit dem von ihm selbst bemühten geschichtstheoretischen Konstruktivismus absichtsvoll die Spitze ab.

214 MARTIN LAUBE

christlichen Glauben aus zugänglich ist. Der *dritte Bildtyp* stellt gleichsam
eine Kombination der ersten beiden dar. Wolter nennt ihn den *irdischen
Christus* und bezieht sich damit auf das Bild, welches die Evangelien von
Jesus zeichnen: „this is the retrospective image of the earthly ministry
of the risen Son of God" (S. 10). Der Unterschied zum Bildtyp des historischen Jesus besteht darin, dass dessen Darstellungen mit dem Bericht
seines Todes enden, während „the works and fate of the ‚earthly Christ'
are onle the pre-history for the proclamation of Jesus Christ' after Easter"
(S. 10). Den *vierten Bildtyp* nennt Wolter den *erinnerten Jesus*. Im Unterschied zur literarischen Gestalt des irdischen Christus handelt es sich hier
um das nachösterliche Erinnerungsbild derer, die Ohren- und Augenzeu-
gen des Wirkens Jesu gewesen waren. Im Mittelpunkt steht „the ‚impact'
that Jesus left on his disciples" (S. 10). Der *fünfte Bildtyp—Jesus aus Nazareth—*umfasst die verschiedenen Bilder derer, mit denen es Jesus im Laufe
seines Lebens zu tun bekommen hatte. Dazu zählen die Adressaten seiner
Verkündigung und die Zeugen seines Wirkens ebenso wie diejenigen, die
Jesus kritisch bis ablehnend gegenüberstanden. Der gedankliche Schwer-
punkt der Bildtypologie liegt nun allerdings auf den beiden letzten Bildtypen. Als *sechsten Bildtyp* nennt Wolter die *Selbstauslegung Jesu* und zielt
damit auf das, was in anderen Zusammenhängen als Selbstbewusstsein,
Selbstverständnis oder Sendungsanspruch Jesu bezeichnet wird. Anders
als bei den vorangegangenen Bildtypen soll es sich hier nur um ein ein-
ziges Bild handeln: „the image that Jesus had of himself, of the meaning
and significance of his teaching and actions" (S. 12). Den Abschluss bildet
der *siebente Bildtyp*. Wolter nennt ihn durchaus provokant den *wirklichen
Jesus*. Damit sei nun gerade nicht der historische Jesus gemeint, vielmehr
so etwas wie der Jesus ‚an sich' hinter den pluralen Jesusbildern. In historischer Perspektive sei er zwar nicht zugänglich. Wohl aber könne er in
der Perspektive des christlichen Glaubens als derjenige Jesus bestimmt
werden, wie er von Gott erkannt und so als Person konstituiert worden
sei. Mithin gehe es auch hier um ein Bild—um das Bild, welches Gott sich
von Jesus gemacht habe: „The ‚real Jesus' beyond the images that people
have made of him in his own time and since then is, therefore, none other
than the Jesus as God knows him, whose identity came into being through
God's knowing him" (S. 15).[17]

---

[17] Hier und an anderen Stellen beruft sich Michael Wolter auf ein spezifisch christliches ‚Wirklichkeitsverständnis', welches dem Glauben zu eigen sei und beinhalte, in dieser markant theistischen Weise von Gott reden zu können. Allerdings ist gegenüber der
Proklamation eines solchen ‚Wirklichkeitsverständnisses' Vorsicht geboten. Zu sehr steht

IM GLAUBEN ZUM ,WIRKLICHEN' JESUS?

Diese Typologie von Jesusbildern mag auf den ersten Blick wie eine harmlose Klassifikation wirken, die sich dem Ziel verdankt, endlich ein wenig Klarheit in die notorische Sprachverwirrung der historischen Jesusforschung zu bringen. Doch bei näherem Hinsehen ändert sich dieser Eindruck. Sie beinhaltet ebenso weitreichende wie zugleich unausgewiesene Vorentscheidungen, mit denen sich Wolter den Weg für seine eigene Lösung der Jesusfrage bahnt. So tritt die anfänglich zugestandene unaufhebbare Pluralität der Jesusbilder mehr und mehr in den Hintergrund. Stattdessen scheint die Rede vom Selbstbild Jesu plötzlich doch die Möglichkeit zu bieten, vom störenden Plural in den gesuchten Singular wechseln zu können. Zwar handelt es sich immer noch um ein *Bild*, aber *erstens* nur noch um *ein* Bild und *zweitens* um ein solches Bild, das, wie Wolter zu unterstellen scheint, der historischen Erschließung zugänglich ist. Nun bleibt nur noch die Frage zu klären, ob und wie dieses Bild in seinem Bildcharakter aufgehoben und als Darstellung des ,wirklichen' Jesus einsichtig gemacht werden kann. Hier kommt jetzt der Glaube ins Spiel. Er bietet zunächst die Möglichkeit, an der Annahme eines Jesus ,an sich' hinter seinen Bildern festzuhalten. Denn in der Perspektive des Glaubens ist der ,wirkliche' Jesus derjenige Jesus, den Gott erkannt hat und in diesem schöpferischen Erkennen hat wirklich werden lassen. Mithin fehlt nur noch ein Zwischenstück, das es erlaubt, diese beiden ,Bilder'—das Selbstbild Jesu und Gottes Bild von Jesus—übereinanderzulegen. Auch dazu verhilft nun Wolter zufolge der Glaube. Denn er sei seinem Wesen nach Auferweckungsglaube und schließe als solcher die Gewissheit in sich, dass Gott durch sein österliches Handeln an Jesus dessen vorösterliches Auftreten bestätigt und ins Recht gesetzt hat. Anders formuliert: In der Perspektive des Osterglaubens werde sichtbar, „that the ,real Jesus', in the sense presented above, is none other than how Jesus understood himself, or, in other words, that the ,real Jesus', as constituted by the judgement of God, had taken a concrete form in the self-interpretation of Jesus within the human life-world" (S. 16–17). Damit hat die historische Jesusfrage für Wolter eine definite Antwort gefunden. Wer Jesus wirklich ist, wird

---

dieser Ansatz in der Gefahr, unter dem Deckmantel des hermeneutischen Verständnisbegriffs ein substanzialistisch-gegenständliches Verständnis christlicher Glaubensaussagen zu repristinieren und zugleich für unangreifbar zu erklären. Einen exemplarischen Beleg dafür bietet Wolters rigide Behauptung, dass „there can be no Christian faith, whose concept of reality does not contain certainty about the fact of the resurrection of Jesus" (S. 16). Die christlichen Glaubensgehalte *konstatieren* jedoch nicht etwas, was sein soll, sondern *deuten* das, was ist. Es handelt sich bei ihnen nicht um kognitive Propositionen, sondern um symbolische Deutungsfiguren.

216 MARTIN LAUBE

sichtbar in seiner Selbstauslegung, die in der Perspektive des christlichen Osterglaubens von Gott bestätigt worden ist. Kurz gefasst: Jesus ist der, als der er sich verstanden hat.

Wolters Zugangsweise zur historischen Jesusfrage ist zweifellos originell, und auch seine eigene Lösung zeugt von einem beeindruckenden theologischen Scharfsinn und Witz. Dennoch lassen sich die gravierenden Probleme seines Gedankengangs nicht übersehen. Vor allem zwei markante Punkte seien hier herausgehoben.

1. In seiner Typologie der Jesusbilder arbeitet Wolter mit einem unklar schillernden *Bildbegriff*. Er beginnt zunächst mit einem hermeneutisch gefassten Verständnis, um den konstruktiven Deutungscharakter historischer Erkenntnis zu betonen. An die Stelle der Fiktion eines Jesus ‚an sich' tritt das Faktum unterschiedlicher Bilder von Jesus. Die historische Rückfrage stößt auf eine irreduzible Pluralität solcher Jesusbilder. Wolter benennt sie mit den Typen *irdischer Christus, erinnerter Jesus* und *Jesus aus Nazareth.* Umgekehrt produziert auch die heutige Beschäftigung mit Jesus nur wieder bestimmte Jesusbilder—handle es sich nun um die Suche nach dem *historischen Jesus* oder das dogmatische Nachdenken über *Jesus Christus.* Dieses hermeneutische Bildverständnis bricht jedoch bei dem Versuch, auch Jesu Selbstverständnis als *Selbstbild Jesu* in die Typologie einzufügen. Denn Wolter geht es hier nicht um *Bilder* des Selbstverständnisses Jesu, sondern um das *eine* Selbstverständnis Jesu: „From this type of image, only one single specimen exists since it is produced by only one person: by Jesus himself" (S. 12). Dieser Wechsel in den Singular kann weder methodisch noch psychologisch überzeugen; vor allem aber kommt dem Bildbegriff hier keine Deutungsfunktion, sondern nur mehr eine—zudem linear bestimmte— Darstellungsfunktion zu. Nochmals anders stellt sich die Sachlage schließlich beim Übergang zum Bildtyp des *wirklichen Jesus* dar. Dabei handle es sich um das Bild Gottes von Jesus in dem Sinne, dass Gott ihn im Zuge seines schöpferischen Erkennens wirklich werden lasse. Mithin eignet dem Bild hier keine hermeneutische Deutungsfunktion, sondern eine strikte Konstitutionsfunktion: Das Bild Gottes von Jesus *deutet* Jesus nicht, sondern *erschafft* ihn überhaupt erst. Damit aber ist der anfängliche Richtungssinn des Bildbegriffs geradezu auf den Kopf gestellt. Anders formuliert: Wolters Typologie der Jesusbilder beruht auf einer heimlichen Äquivokation im Bildbegriff und suggeriert eine methodische Analogie, wo faktisch ein gedanklicher Bruch besteht.

IM GLAUBEN ZUM ‚WIRKLICHEN‘ JESUS?

2. Ein weiteres Problem verbindet sich mit der Figur des *Selbstbildes Jesu*. Wolter scheint davon auszugehen, dass dieses Selbstbild der historischen Forschung zugänglich ist. Denn nur so kann er sein anspruchsvolles Argumentationsziel erreichen, im Glauben auf der Grundlage der historischen Jesusforschung über deren Grenzen hinauszugelangen. Es geht ihm ja nicht darum, die Perspektive des Glaubens einfach *gegen* die historische Methode auszuspielen. Vielmehr sucht er zu zeigen, dass die Perspektive des Glaubens *inmitten* des Spektrums historischer Jesusbilder den ‚wirklichen‘ Jesus zugänglich werden lässt. Das *missing link* bildet hier die Figur des Selbstbildes Jesu: Aus *historischer* Perspektive handelt es sich zwar lediglich um ein Bild; doch in der Perspektive des *Osterglaubens* hat dieses Bild durch die Auferweckung Jesu seine Bestätigung erhalten. Mithin lässt das—historisch eruierbare—Selbstbild Jesu erkennen, wer Jesus ‚wirklich‘ war. Allerdings schweigt sich Wolter nun darüber aus, wie ein solcher Zugang zum Selbstbild Jesu mit den Mitteln der historischen Forschung soll gelingen können. Ohnehin fällt auf, dass er diesem so zentralen—und exegetisch doch umstrittenen—Teilstück seiner Argumentation irritierend wenig Aufmerksamkeit widmet. In der Folge kommt es daher zu einer problematischen Verschleifung. Natürlich ist es möglich, nach dem Selbstbild Jesu zu fragen. Doch für diese Frage gilt dasselbe, was für die Jesusfrage überhaupt gilt: Historisch zugänglich sind nur verschiedene *Bilder* des Selbstbildes Jesu, wie auch die historische Forschung ihrerseits nur wieder *Bilder* dieses Selbstbildes zeichnen kann. Indem Wolter diese Differenz zwischen Jesu Selbstbild und den historisch zu gewinnenden Bildern von Jesu Selbstbild einzieht, verlässt er *de facto* den Boden dessen, was—seinem eigenen Urteil nach—mit den Mitteln der historisch-kritischen Forschung erreicht werden kann. Zugespitzt formuliert: Der argumentative Kunstgriff, über die im Osterglauben erschlossene Bestätigung des Selbstbildes Jesu einen Zugang zum ‚wirklichen‘ Jesus zu gewinnen, verdankt sich einer zuvor vollzogenen Sistierung der historisch-kritischen Methode.

Die beiden genannten Kritikpunkte zeigen, dass Wolters Typologie der Jesusbilder eine heimliche Tendenz aufweist, die vorderhand zugestandene Konstruktivität historischer Erkenntnis unter der Hand wieder zu unterlaufen. Der Überschritt von den historisch zugänglichen Jesusbildern zur göttlichen Bestätigung des Selbstbildes Jesu gelingt nur unter der Voraussetzung einer faktischen Entwertung des historischen Denkens für die Belange der Theologie. Damit aber wird der Graben zwischen Theologie und historischer Methode, den Wolter zu überwinden angetreten war, im Ergebnis nur nochmals vertieft.

Am Beispiel der historischen Rückfrage nach Jesus sucht Wolter zu zeigen, wie eine der historischen Methode verpflichtete Fragestellung zugleich als theologisches Unterfangen ausgewiesen werden kann. Zur Lösung verweist er auf den persönlichen Glauben des forschenden Historikers. Denn in der Perspektive des Glaubens finde die historisch unbeantwortbare Jesusfrage eine Antwort—und zwar so, dass der Glaube den Rahmen des Historischen nicht lediglich überspringe, sondern eines der historischen Jesusbilder als Korrelat des ‚wirklichen‘ Jesus zu benennen erlaube. Bei näherem Hinsehen jedoch weist diese Verknüpfung von Glaube und Geschichte verdächtige Risse auf. Das entscheidende Scharnier bildet die Figur des Selbstbildes Jesu; sie aber vermag die ihr zugedachte Funktion erst zu erfüllen, wenn sie zuvor historisch entkernt worden ist. Anders formuliert: Inwiefern die historische Jesusfrage gerade *als* historische Frage theologisch von Interesse ist, zeigt Wolter gerade *nicht*. Stattdessen bleibt er dem Paradigma verhaftet, ihren theologischen Mehrwert an der Aussicht auf eine – wie immer geartete—Überwindung der historischen Methode festzumachen. Wolter reiht sich damit in die lange Reihe von Versuchen ein, das Verhältnis von Theologie und historischem Denken so zu bestimmen, dass die Theologie eine Erlösung vom Fluch der historischen Relativität verspricht.

4.

Nun darf aber das kritische Urteil über die inhaltliche Durchführung nicht vergessen lassen, dass das methodische Anliegen Michael Wolters rückhaltlose Zustimmung und Unterstützung verdient. Es zeichnet ihn aus, dass er sich mit der gegenwärtigen Sprachlosigkeit zwischen den theologischen Fächerkulturen nicht abfinden will, sondern einen neuen Anlauf unternimmt, um—am Beispiel der Jesusfrage—historische Methode und theologischen Anspruch miteinander zu verknüpfen. Wolter rührt damit an ein ungelöstes Grundproblem der Theologie: Sie hat die moderne Herausforderung des historischen Denkens noch immer nicht zufriedenstellend gemeistert.

Die aufgewiesenen Schwierigkeiten lassen es allerdings geraten erscheinen, gegenüber Wolters Lösungsvorschlag zwei grundsätzliche Umstellungen vorzunehmen. *Zum einen* gilt es, auch im Umgang mit der historischen Jesusfrage die neuzeitliche Grundunterscheidung von Theologie und Religion zur Geltung zu bringen. Damit entfällt die Möglichkeit, auf den persönlichen Glauben des forschenden Historikers zurückzugreifen, um die ‚Theologizität‘ der Rückfrage nach Jesus sicherzustellen. Es ist ein gefährlicher Irrweg, die theologische Dignität historischen Arbeitens an die unausweisbare Zusatzbedingung einer persönlichen Glaubenshaltung binden zu wollen. Auf diese Weise wird nicht nur die disziplinäre *Selbständigkeit* der Theologie im universitären Fächerkanon gefährdet; die These eines konstitutiven ‚Surplus‘ im Glauben bedeutet zugleich Gift für den *Wissenschaftsanspruch* der Theologie. Vor allem aber verkehrt sich das Anliegen, zwischen historischer Methode und theologischem Anspruch zu vermitteln, geradewegs ins Gegenteil: Das ‚Theologische‘ wird nun erst recht zum ganz Anderen der wissenschaftlichen Forschungsarbeit. Friedrich Schleiermacher entgeht diesen Schwierigkeiten, indem er mit seiner Bestimmung der Theologie als ‚positiver Wissenschaft‘ die Theologie als Reflexions- statt Ausdrucksgestalt des Glaubens fasst und ihre disziplinäre Einheit in der funktionalen Ausrichtung auf die Belange der Kirchenleitung begründet sein lässt. Zu dieser klassischen Lösung gibt es bis heute keine überzeugende Alternative: Die Theologizität einer theologischen Erkenntnis hängt nicht an einem—wie immer gearteten—methodischen, inhaltlichen oder religiösen ‚Surplus‘, sondern allein an ihrem Funktionsbezug auf die Aufgabe der Förderung des Christentums. Damit ist eine weitreichende Entlastung im Blick auf die theologische Dignität der historischen Jesusfrage verbunden. Vor allem wird es nun möglich, deutlich zwischen den beiden Ebenen der *theologischen Funktion* und der *religiösen Bedeutung* der historischen Frage nach Jesus zu unterscheiden. Es geht dann nicht mehr darum, was die historische Frage nach Jesus zu einer theologischen Frage macht. Wohl aber lässt sich danach fragen, warum gerade die historische Jesusforschung—seit ihrem Aufkommen in der Neuzeit—die Theologie so in den Bann schlägt. Und erst recht interessant ist die andere Frage, was es für den Glauben bedeutet, sich mit historischen Mitteln der Gestalt Jesu zu nähern.

Um diese Fragen bearbeiten zu können, ist zuvor jedoch noch eine *zweite Umstellung* vonnöten. Sie betrifft den Umgang mit der unhintergehbaren Konstruktivität, Pluralität und Relativität des historischen Denkens. Bisher lautete die Parole der Theologie auf ‚Überwindung‘ dieser Abgründe des Historischen. Allenthalben ging es um die Rückgewinnung verlorener Eindeutigkeiten und absoluter Gewissheiten. Auch Wolter steht noch in dieser Tradition: Er macht den theologischen Mehrwert der historischen Jesusfrage gerade daran fest, im Glauben die irritierende Vielfalt der Jesusbilder auf den einen, ,wirklichen' Jesus hin durchsichtig machen zu können. Doch es ist an der Zeit, diesen theologischen Fluchtreflex im Umgang mit dem historischen Denken hinter sich zu lassen. Die Theologie hat keine höheren Wahrheiten zu bieten, welche der Reichweite des historischen Bewusstseins entrückt wären oder ihrerseits dazu ermächtigten, im Namen absoluter Gewissheiten den Rückzug aus der Geschichte anzutreten. Das bedeutet, die Vorstellung einer schlichten *Diastase* von Normativität und Geschichte verabschieden zu müssen. Natürlich stellt das historische Denken eine Herausforderung für das überkommene, an eindeutige Offenbarungen und Dogmen gewöhnte theologische Denken dar. Gleiches gilt für den Glauben, dessen persönliche Unbedingtheit nicht mehr an die vorgängige Autorität vermeintlicher Geschichtswahrheiten entlastet werden kann. Dennoch besteht die entscheidende Aufgabe darin, Normativität und Geschichte als einander widerstreitende Pole eines zirkulären Wechselverhältnisses zu begreifen. Es gibt keine theologischen oder auch religiösen Gewissheiten, welche ihr geschichtliches Bedingtsein abzustreifen und zu einer absoluten Warte jenseits der Geschichte aufzusteigen vermöchten. Doch daraus folgt nicht, dass im Gegenzug alle Orientierungspunkte und Geltungsansprüche im Strudel des geschichtlichen Wandels versinken. Kontingenz bedeutet nicht Beliebigkeit, sondern Geschichtlichkeit—in dem Sinne, dass hier die *Relativität* allen geschichtlichen Werdens und die *Unhintergehbarkeit* des faktischen Gewordenseins unauflöslich ineinanderliegen.

Für den Umgang mit der historischen Jesusfrage ergeben sich daraus folgende Konsequenzen.[18] Ihre *theologische Funktion* besteht gerade nicht darin, sie zu beantworten und hinter den vielfältigen Jesusbildern nach dem Bild des einen, ,wirklichen' Jesus zu suchen. Stattdessen hält sie auf exemplarische Weise innerhalb der Theologie das Bewusstsein für die Geschichtlichkeit und Pluralität ihrer Gehalte wach. Ihr kommt so eine „Korrekturfunktion"[19] zu, indem sie vorschnelle dogmatische „Eindeutigkeitskonstruktionen"[20] verhindert und dafür Sorge trägt, dass sich die Theologie der eigenen Geschichtlichkeit nicht durch den Rückzug

---

[18] Vgl. dazu auch C. Danz, „Der Jesus der Exegeten und der Christus der Dogmatiker: Die Bedeutung der neueren Jesusforschung für die systematisch-theologische Christologie", in: *NZSTh* 51 (2009), 186–204; A. von Scheliha, „Kyniker, Prophet, Revolutionär oder Sohn Gottes", in: *ZNT* 2 (1999), Heft 4, 22–31; sowie F. Wittekind, „Christologie im 20. Jahrhundert", in: C. Danz und M. Murrmann-Kahl (Hg.), *Zwischen historischem Jesus und dogmatischem Christus*, Tübingen 2010, 13–45.

[19] C. Danz, *Einführung in die evangelische Dogmatik*, Darmstadt 2010, 140.

[20] Ebd.

IM GLAUBEN ZUM ‚WIRKLICHEN‘ JESUS?

auf ein ahistorisches Konstrukt – handle es sich nun um den ‚wirklichen‘ Jesus oder den dogmatischen Christus—entziehen kann. Anders formuliert: Die historische Jesusfrage leitet die Theologie zu einer kritischen Dauerselbstreflexion ihres eigenen Tuns an. Gerade in diesem Sinn ist sie für die Theologie ebenso unabschließbar wie zugleich unverzichtbar.

Die *religiöse Bedeutung* der historischen Frage nach Jesus hingegen bezieht sich auf das Bedürfnis des Glaubens, das eigene Jesusbild als zumindest kompatibel mit den Einsichten der historisch-kritischen Forschung ausweisen zu können. Doch dieses Interesse ist von dem fehlgeleiteten Bemühen um eine historische Begründung des Glaubens strikt zu unterscheiden; mithin lässt es sich auch nicht schon durch die Unterstellung eines solchen Bemühens erledigen. Zwar gilt unter modernen Bedingungen die Feststellung Kants: „Der Geschichtsglaube ist ‚tot an ihm selber‘.“[21] Es geht im Glauben nicht um die Anerkennung vermeintlicher Geschichtstatsachen. Im Mittelpunkt steht nicht eine objektive Heilstat der Vergangenheit, sondern das gegenwärtige Erleben der heilvollen Gegenwart Gottes. Zugespitzt formuliert: Nicht Jesus, sondern der Glaube selbst ist die Erlösung. Dennoch bleibt dieser Glaube notwendig auf seinen geschichtlichen Grund bezogen. Es gibt keinen Glauben, der sich ohne jede Rückbindung an die Geschichte rein als Idee entfalten würde. Insofern kommt auch dem Bild Jesu—als des Ursprungs und Maßstabs christlicher Frömmigkeit—eine unverlierbare Bedeutung für den Glauben zu. Im Medium dieses Bildes bringt sich der Glaube den fortdauernden ‚Wirkgrund‘ seiner eigenen Lebendigkeit zur Darstellung; gerade in der Anschaulichkeit eines plastischen Jesusbildes wird die erlösende Kraft des Christentums als dynamische Lebensmacht—statt in der Form eines dogmatischen Lehrprinzips—zugänglich.[22] Dabei erscheinen historische Objektivität und religiöse Subjektivität eigentümlich miteinander verschränkt. Auch wenn historische Tatsächlichkeit und religiöse Deutung streng zu trennen sind, hat der Glaube doch durchaus ein Interesse an der historischen Jesusfrage—freilich nicht, um sich durch die historische Forschung seinen Gegenstand des Glaubens vorgeben zu lassen, sondern um sein eigenes Jesusbild als religiöse *Deutung* eines geschichtlichen *Faktums* verstehen zu können. In seiner *Glaubenslehre* hat Ernst Troeltsch dieses Wechselverhältnis von Glaube und Geschichte so zu bestimmen

---

[21] I. Kant, *Die Religion innerhalb der Grenzen der bloßen Vernunft*, hg. von B. Stangneth, Hamburg 2003, B 161.

[22] Vgl. dazu J.H. Claussen, *Die Jesus-Deutung von Ernst Troeltsch im Kontext der liberalen Theologie*, Tübingen 1997, 261.

versucht, dass historische Jesusforschung und religiöse Jesusdeutung weder auseinander- noch ineinanderfallen:

> Gewiß darf das Vergangene nicht zum Glaubensobjekt gemacht werden; aber das Vergangene, um das es sich hier handelt, ist zu betrachten als etwas in seinem eigenen Wesen Übergeschichtliches enthaltend. Wir haben es nicht zu tun mit einer Unterwerfung unter ein einmal gewesenes Geschichtsfaktum, sondern um ein sich kundmachendes Übergeschichtliches, das im Geschichtlichen liegt und niemals von ihm zu trennen ist. Indem es in uns Geschichtlichkeit gewinnt, ist es Gegenwärtiges. Dabei wird es aber nie möglich sein, Idee auf der einen und Geschichte auf der anderen Seite zu sehen. Was uns heute als reifste Autonomie erscheint, wird für Späterkommende ein in bestimmte Kulturgrenzen gebanntes Geschichtliches sein. Wir können nun einmal das Zeitlose nicht ganz abstrakt fassen, denn das Leben ist nirgends abstrakt. Es gibt keine Idee der Religion, die ohne Historisches zu ergreifen wäre; aber es gibt auch nichts Historisches, das nur Historisches wäre. [...] Wir beziehen uns auf den *Sinn* des Faktums, der aber nie vom Faktum selbst abzulösen ist.[23]

Vielleicht bringt Troeltsch hier von einem ganz anderen theologischen Ausgangspunkt aus eine Einsicht zur Sprache, die dem Anliegen von Michael Wolter letztlich gar nicht so fernsteht.

---

[23] E. Troeltsch, *Glaubenslehre: Nach Heidelberger Vorlesungen aus den Jahren 1911 und 1912*. Mit einem Vorwort von M. Troeltsch, München 1925 (Nachdruck Saarbrücken 2006), 92–93.

ACADEMIC CURRICULUM VITAE

Michael Wolter

1969–1973	Theological Studies in preparation for *Erstes Theologisches Examen*
	Kirchliche Hochschule, Berlin (1969–1970)
	Ruprecht-Karls-Universität, Heidelberg (1970–1973)
	Georg-August-Universität, Göttingen (1973)
1973	Erstes Theologisches Examen (equivalent to M. Div.)
1977	Dr. theol. at the University of Heidelberg
1977–1983	Editor of the *Theologische Realenzyklopädie* (TRE) (Verlag Walter de Gruyter)
1983–1988	Wissenschaftlicher Assistant at the Dept. of Protestant Theology of the University of Mainz
1986	Habilitation at the University of Mainz
1988–1993	Professor for Biblical Theology at the University of Bayreuth
since 1993	Professor for New Testament at the University of Bonn
1996–1998	Dean of the Protestant Faculty at the University of Bonn
since 2004	Honorary Professor at the Theological Faculty of the University of Pretoria

LIST OF PUBLICATIONS: PROF. DR. MICHAEL WOLTER

1978
- *Rechtfertigung und zukünftiges Heil. Untersuchungen zu Röm 5,1–11*, Berlin/New York 1978 (BZNW 43).

1980
- Art. Bekehrung. I.1.1.2. Zur jüdischen Bekehrungsterminologie, in: *TRE* 5 (1980) 442–443.
- *Aus dem Archiv des Verlages Walter de Gruyter. Briefe – Urkunden – Dokumente*, Berlin/New York 1980 [mit Doris Fouquet-Plümacher].

1981
- ἔχθρα/ἐχθρός, in: *EWNT* 2 (1981) 233–237.
- ἵστημι/ἱστάνω, in: *EWNT* 2 (1981) 504–509.
- Art. Brent, Charles, Henry, in: *TRE* 7 (1981) 168–170 [mit Stephen C. Neill].
- μᾶλλον, in: *EWNT* 2 (1981) 939–941.
- ὀφειλέτης/ὀφείλημα, in: *EWNT* 2 (1981) 1344–1346.
- ὀφειλή, in: *EWNT* 2 (1981) 1346–1347.
- ὀφείλω, in: *EWNT* 2 (1981) 1347–1350.

1982
- (Rez.:) Th. Baumeister, Die Anfänge der Theologie des Martyriums, Münster 1980, in: *ZKG* 93 (1982) 362–364.
- (Rez.:) Kirche. Festschrift für Günther Bornkamm, Tübingen 1980, in: *ThR* NF 47 (1982) 99–102.

1983
- παράβασις/παραβαίνω, in: *EWNT* 3 (1983) 32–35.
- παράπτωμα, in: *EWNT* 3 (1983) 77–79.
- πόσος, in: *EWNT* 3 (1983) 337–338.
- στήκω, in: *EWNT* 3 (1983) 659.
- τολμάω, in *EWNT* 3 (1983) 873–875.
- φέρω, in: *EWNT* 3 (1983) 1000–1003.
- Φῆλιξ, in: *EWNT* 3 (1983) 1004–1005.

1984
- *Theologie und Kirche im Wirken Hans von Sodens. Briefe und Dokumente aus der Zeit des Kirchenkampfes 1933–1945*, Göttingen 1984 (AKZ 2/2).
- Art. Gewissen. II. Neues Testament, in: *TRE* 13 (1984) 213–218.

1986
- *Theologie und Kirche im Wirken Hans von Sodens. Briefe und Dokumente aus der Zeit des Kirchenkampfes 1933–1945*, Göttingen 2. Aufl. 1986 (AKZ 2/2).

1987
- Apollos und die ephesinischen Johannesjünger (Act 18,24–19,7), in: *ZNW* 78 (1987) 49–73.

226 LIST OF PUBLICATIONS: PROF. DR. MICHAEL WOLTER

– Verborgene Weisheit und Heil für die Heiden. Zur Traditionsgeschichte und Intention des ‚Revelationsschemas‘, in: *ZThK* 84 (1987) 297–319.

1988
– *Die Pastoralbriefe als Paulustradition*, Göttingen 1988 (FRLANT 146).
– Die anonymen Schriften des Neuen Testaments. Annäherungsversuch an ein literarisches Phänomen, in: *ZNW* 79 (1988) 1–16.

1989
– Akklamation, in: *NBL* Lieferung 1 (1988) 69–70.
– 'Christus und Adam' oder 'Adam und Christus'? Karl Barths und Rudolf Bultmanns Interpretation von Römer 5,12–21, in: *Existenz und Sein. Karl Barth und die Marburger Theologie*, hg.v. W. Schmithals, Tübingen 1989, 15–36.
– Arznei, in: *NBL* Lieferung 2 (1989) 177–178.
– Arzt, in: *NBL* Lieferung 2 (1989) 178–179.
– Paulus, der bekehrte Gottesfeind. Zum Verständnis von 1.Tim 1,13, in: *NovTest* 31 (1989) 48–66.
– Heiliger Abend: 1.Timotheus 3,16, in: *Gottesdienstpraxis*, hg.v. H. Nitschke, Serie A, 6.Perikopenreihe, Bd. IV: Ergänzungsband Exegesen, Gütersloh 1989, 21–23.
– Invocavit: Jakobus 1,12–18, in: *Gottesdienstpraxis*, hg.v. H. Nitschke, Serie A, 6.Perikopenreihe, Bd. IV: Ergänzungsband Exegesen, Gütersloh 1989, 57–60.
– 6.Sonntag nach Trinitatis: 1.Petrus 2,2–10, in: *Gottesdienstpraxis*, hg.v. H. Nitschke, Serie A, 6.Perikopenreihe, Bd. IV: Ergänzungsband Exegesen, Gütersloh 1989, 127–130.
– 9.Sonntag nach Trinitatis: 1.Petrus 4,7–11, in: *Gottesdienstpraxis*, hg.v. H.Nitschke, Serie A, 6.Perikopenreihe, Bd. IV: Ergänzungsband Exegesen, Gütersloh 1989, 135–138.
– Die Pastoralbriefe als Paulustradition, in: *Jahrbuch der Akademie der Wissenschaften zu Göttingen 1988*, Göttingen 1989, 25–27.

1990
– 4.Advent: Lukas 1,(39–45)46–55(56), in: *Gottesdienstpraxis*, hg.v. H. Nitschke, Serie A, 1.Perikopenreihe, Bd. IV: Exegesen, Gütersloh 1990, 15–17.
– 1.Sonntag nach Trinitatis: Lukas 16,19–31, in: *Gottesdienstpraxis*, hg.v. H. Nitschke, Serie A, 1.Perikopenreihe, Bd. IV: Exegesen, Gütersloh 1990, 105–108.
– 4.Sonntag nach Trinitatis: Lukas 6,36–42, in: *Gottesdienstpraxis*, hg.v. H. Nitschke, Serie A, 1.Perikopenreihe, Bd. IV: Exegesen, Gütersloh 1990, 113–115.
– 10.Sonntag nach Trinitatis: Lukas 19,41–48, in: *Gottesdienstpraxis*, hg.v. H. Nitschke, Serie A, 1.Perikopenreihe, Bd. IV: Exegesen, Gütersloh 1990, 128–130.
– 22.Sonntag nach Trinitatis: Matthäus 18,21–35, in: *Gottesdienstpraxis*, hg.v. H. Nitschke, Serie A, 1.Perikopenreihe, Bd. IV: Exegesen, Gütersloh 1990, 157–159.
– Art. Leiden. III. Neues Testament, in: *TRE* 20 (1990) 677–688.
– Der Apostel und seine Gemeinden als Teilhaber am Leidensgeschick Jesu Christi. Beobachtungen zur paulinischen Leidenstheologie, in: *NTS* 36 (1990) 535–557.

1991
– (Rez.:) G.Gerleman, Der Heidenapostel. Ketzerische Erwägungen zur Predigt des Paulus, Lund 1989, in: *Gymnasium* 98 (1991) 286–288.
– Heiliger Abend: Titus 2,11–14, in: *Gottesdienstpraxis*, hg.v. H. Nitschke, Serie A, 2.Perikopenreihe, Bd. IV: Exegesen, Gütersloh 1991, 18–20.
– 1.Weihnachtstag: Titus 3,4–7, in: *Gottesdienstpraxis*, hg.v. H. Nitschke, Serie A, 2.Perikopenreihe, Bd. IV: Exegesen, Gütersloh 1991, 21–23.
– Rogate: 1.Timotheus 2,1–6, in: *Gottesdienstpraxis*, hg.v. H. Nitschke, Serie A, 2.Perikopenreihe, Bd. IV: Exegesen, Gütersloh 1991, 95–97.

LIST OF PUBLICATIONS: PROF. DR. MICHAEL WOLTER   227

- 3.Sonntag nach Trinitatis: 1.Timotheus 1,12–17, in: *Gottesdienstpraxis*, hg.v. H. Nitschke, Serie A, 2.Perikopenreihe, Bd. IV: Exegesen, Gütersloh 1991, 119–122.
- Evangelium und Tradition. Juden und Heiden zwischen solus Christus und sola scriptura (Gal 1,11–24; Röm 11,25–36), in: *Sola Scriptura*, hg.v. H.H. Schmid, Gütersloh 1991, 180–193.

1992
- Das Judentum in der Theologie Rudolf Bultmanns, in: *Erinnern – Verstehen – Versöhnen*, hg.v. B.Jaspert, Kassel 1992 (Didaskalia 10) 15–32.
- (Rez.:) J. Martin/B. Quint (Hrsg.), Christentum und antike Gesellschaft, Darmstadt 1990, in: *Gymnasium* 99 (1992) 56–58.
- Johannes von Gischala, in: *BBKL* 3 (1992) 372–374.
- Judas (Bruder Jesu), in: *BBKL* 3 (1992) 761–762.
- Judas der Galiläer, in: *BBKL* 3 (1992) 763–764.
- Judas Makkabäus, in: *BBKL* 3 (1992) 766–768.
- Justus von Tiberias, in: *BBKL* 3 (1992) 899–901.
- Der Gegner als endzeitlicher Widersacher. Die Darstellung des Feindes in der jüdischen und christlichen Apokalyptik, in: *Feindbilder. Die Darstellung des Gegners in der politischen Publizistik des Mittelalters und der Neuzeit*, hg.v. F. Bosbach, Köln u.a. 1992, 23–40.
- Inschriftliche Heilungsberichte und neutestamentliche Wundererzählungen. Überlieferungs- und formgeschichtliche Beobachtungen, in: *Studien und Texte zur Formgeschichte*, hg. v. K. Berger u.a., Tübingen/Basel 1992 (TANZ 7) 135–175.
- Art. Pastoralbriefe, in: *Ev. Kirchenlexikon* 3 (1992) 1067–1070.
- (Herausgeber:) *Im Zeichen des Kreuzes*. Aufsätze von Erich Dinkler mit Beiträgen von C. Andresen, E. Dinkler-v. Schubert, E. Gräßer, G. Klein, Berlin/New York 1992 (BZNW 61) (zusammen mit O. Merk).

1993
- *Der Brief an die Kolosser. Der Brief an Philemon*, Gütersloh/Würzburg 1993 (ÖTK 12).
- Das frühe Christentum und die Vielfalt der Konfessionen, in: *GlLern* 8 (1993) 120–132.
- 1.Weihnachtstag: 1. Johannes 3,1–6, in: *Gottesdienstpraxis*, hg.v. H. Nitschke, Serie A, 4.Perikopenreihe, Bd. IV: Exegesen, Gütersloh 1993, 21–24.
- 3.Sonntag nach Trinitatis: 1. Johannes 1,5–2,6, in: *Gottesdienstpraxis*, hg.v. H. Nitschke, Serie A, 4.Perikopenreihe, Bd. IV: Exegesen, Gütersloh 1993, 121–123.
- Nikomedes, in: *BBKL* 6 (1993) 935–936.
- Noët von Smyrna, in: *BBKL* 6 (1993) 984–985.

1994
- Erinnerung an Paulus: Die Pastoralbriefe, in: *Zs. f. Gottesdienst u. Predigt* 12/2 (1994) 21–22.
- Polykrates, Bischof von Ephesus, in: *BBKL* 7 (1994) 815–817.

1995
- 'Was heisset nu Gottes reich?', in: *ZNW* 86 (1995) 5–19.
- 'Reich Gottes' bei Lukas, in: *NTS* 41 (1995) 541–563.
- Ekklesia: Versammlung–Gemeinde–Kirche. Neutestamentliche Anmerkungen für die protestantische Orientierung, in: *GlLern* 10 (1995) 104–111.
- (Rez.:) B.W. Winter/A.D. Clarke (Ed.), The Book of Acts in Its First Century Setting. I. The Book of Acts in Its First Century Setting, in: *ThLZ* 120 (1995) 38–42.
- (Rez.:) B.W.Winter (Ed.), The Book of Acts in Its First Century Setting. II. The Book of Acts in Its Graeco-Roman Setting, Grand Rapids, Mich./Carlisle 1994, in: *ThLZ* 120 (1995) 1005–1008.

228   LIST OF PUBLICATIONS: PROF. DR. MICHAEL WOLTER

1996
- Wort Gottes. 2. Neues Testament, in: *EKL* 4 (1996) 1326–1329.
- Zwölf, die, in: *EKL* 4 (1996) 1431–1432.

1997
- 'Der altböse Feind'. Der Umgang mit dem Bösen im Neuen Testament, in: *GlLern* 12 (1997) 22–30.
- Ethos und Identität in paulinischen Gemeinden, in: *NTS* 43 (1997) 430–444.
- Art. Pseudonymität. II. Kirchengeschichtlich, in: *TRE* 27 (1997) 662–670.
- Israels Zukunft und die Parusieverzögerung bei Lukas, in: *Eschatologie und Schöpfung*. FS Erich Gräßer, Berlin/New York 1997 (BZNW 89) 405–426.
- Art. Recht/Rechtstheologie/Rechtsphilosophie. II. Recht/Rechtswesen im Neuen Testament, in: *TRE* 28 (1997) 209–213.
- Art. Kolossä, in: *LThK³* 6 (1997) 202.
- Art. Kolosserbrief, in: *LThK³* 6 (1997) 202–203.
- (Herausgeber:) *Eschatologie und Schöpfung*. Festschrift für Erich Gräßer zum 70. Geburtstag, Berlin/New York 1997 (BZNW 89) (zusammen mit M. Evang, H. Merklein).

1998
- Wann wurde Maria schwanger? Eine vernachlässigte Frage und ihre Bedeutung für das Verständnis der lukanischen Vorgeschichte (Lk 1–2), in: *Von Jesus zum Christus*. FS Paul Hoffmann, Berlin/New York 1998 (BZNW 93), 405–422.
- Die Juden und die Obrigkeit bei Lukas, in: *Ja und Nein. Christliche Theologie im Angesicht Israels*. FS Wolfgang Schrage, Neukirchen-Vluyn 1998, 277–290.
- Interaktive Erzählungen. Wie aus Geschichten Gleichnisse werden, und was Jesu Gleichnisse mit ihren Hörern machen, in: *GlLern* 13 (1998) 120–134.
- Art. Onesimus, in: *LThK³* 7 (1998) 1054.
- 'Jesus Messias'?, in: *Welt und Umwelt der Bibel* 10 (1998) 35–37.

1999
- 'Zeremonialgesetz' vs. 'Sittengesetz'. Eine Spurensuche, in: *Recht und Ethos im Alten Testament. Gestalt und Wirkung*. FS Horst Seebass, Neukirchen-Vluyn, 1999, 339–356.
- Israel's Future and the Delay of the Parousia, according to Luke, in: *Jesus and the Heritage of Israel*, ed. D.P. Moessner, Harrisburg, PA 1999, 307–324.
- Die Unscheinbarkeit des Reiches Gottes, in: *Marburger Jahrbuch Theologie. XI. Reich Gottes*, hg.v. W. Härle/R. Preul, Marburg 1999 (MThSt 53), 103–116 [mit Michael Welker].
- 'Apokalyptik', in: *GlLern* 14 (1999) 11–22 [mit Christofer Frey].
- Zu diesem Heft, in: *VuF* 44 (1999) 1.
- Art. Philemon, Philemonbrief, in: *LThK³* 8 (1999) 210–211.
- Art. Spruch, Sprichwort, in: *NBL* Lieferung 13 (1999) 665–666.
- Art. Dinkler, Erich, in: *RGG⁴* 2 (1999) 856.

2000
- Die Hirten in der Weihnachtsgeschichte (Lk 2,8–20), in: *Religionsgeschichte des Neuen Testaments*. FS Klaus Berger, Tübingen/Basel 2000, 501–517.
- Erstmals unter Quirinius! Zum Verständnis von Lk 2,2, in: *Bibl. Notizen* 102 (2000) 35–41.
- 'Offenbarung' und 'Geschichten' in der jüdischen und christlichen Apokalyptik, in: *Offenbarung und Geschichten*, hg. v. J. Barton und G. Sauter, Frankfurt a.M. 2000, 175–194.
- 'Revelation' and 'Story' in Jewish and Christian Apocalypticism, in: *Story and Revelation*, ed. by G. Sauter and J. Barton, Aldershot u.a. 2000, 127–144.
- Art. Soden, Hans Freiherr von, in: *TRE* 31 (2000) 420–423.

LIST OF PUBLICATIONS: PROF. DR. MICHAEL WOLTER   229

- Art. γῆ, in: *ThBNT²* 2 (2000) 1887–1891.
- Art. κόσμος, in: *ThBNT²* 2 (2000) 1891–1898.

2001
- 5. Esra-Buch/6. Esra-Buch (*JSHRZ* III/7), Gütersloh 2001.
- Die ethische Identität christlicher Gemeinden in neutestamentlicher Zeit, in: *Woran orientiert sich Ethik?* Marburger Jahrbuch Theologie. XIII, hg.v. W. Härle/R. Preul (MThSt 67), Marburg 2001, 61–90.
- 'Dumm und skandalös'. Die paulinische Kreuzestheologie und das Wirklichkeitsverständnis des christlichen Glaubens, in: *Das Kreuz Jesu. Gewalt – Opfer – Sühne*, hg. v. R. Weth, Neukirchen-Vluyn 2001, 44–63.
- (Herausgeber und Editorial:) *Paulus. Ein unbequemer Apostel*, Stuttgart 2001 (Welt und Umwelt der Bibel 19).
- Neues Testament, in: *Evangelischer Taschenkatechismus*, hg.v. W.C.-W. Clasen/M. Meyer-Blanck/G. Ruddat, Rheinbach 2001, 130–132.
- Jesus von Nazareth, in: *Evangelischer Taschenkatechismus*, hg.v. W.C.-W. Clasen/M. Meyer-Blanck/G. Ruddat, Rheinbach 2001, 133–136.
- Paulus, in: *Evangelischer Taschenkatechismus*, hg.v. W.C.-W. Clasen/M. Meyer-Blanck/G. Ruddat, Rheinbach 2001, 142–145.
- 'Wandelt nur würdig des Evangeliums Christi!' (Phil 1,27). Die ethische Identität christlicher Gemeinden nach dem Neuen Testament, in: *epd Dokumentation* 50/2001, Frankfurt 2001, 12–20.
- (Rez.:) Geschichte – Tradition – Reflexion. FS für Martin Hengel zum 70. Geburtstag (3 Bde., Tübingen 1996), in: *ZAC* 5 (2001) 161–167.

2002
- Lk 15 als Streitgespräch, in: *EThL* 78 (2002) 25–56.
- 'Gericht' und 'Heil' bei Jesus von Nazareth und Johannes dem Täufer, in: *Der historische Jesus. Tendenzen und Perspektiven der gegenwärtigen Forschung*, hg.v. J. Schröter/R. Brucker (BZNW 114), Berlin/New York 2002, 355–392.

2003
- (Herausgeber:) *Die Einheit der Schrift und die Vielfalt des Kanons. The Unity of Scripture and the Diversity of the Canon* (BZNW 118), Berlin/New York 2003 (zusammen mit John Barton).
- Einleitung, in: *Die Einheit der Schrift und die Vielfalt des Kanons. The Unity of Scripture and the Diversity of the Canon* (BZNW 118), Berlin/New York 2003 1–9 (zusammen mit John Barton).
- Die Vielfalt der Schrift und die Einheit des Kanons, in: *Die Einheit der Schrift und die Vielfalt des Kanons. The Unity of Scripture and the Diversity of the Canon* (BZNW 118), Berlin/New York 2003 45–68 (zusammen mit John Barton).
- Der Brief des so genannten Unzuchtsünders, in: *Liebe, Macht und Religion. Interdisziplinäre Studien zu Grunddimensionen menschlicher Existenz*. Gedenkschrift für Helmut Merklein, Stuttgart 2003, 323–337.
- Ethisches Subjekt und ethisches Gegenüber. Aspekte aus neutestamentlicher Perspektive, in: *Diakonie in der Stadt. Reflexionen–Modelle–Konventionen*, hg. v. H. Schmidt/R. Zitt, Stuttgart u.a. 2003, 44–50.
- Friedrich Bleeck (1793–1859), in: *Theologie als Vermittlung. Bonner evangelische Theologen des 19. Jahrhunderts im Porträt*. FS Friedrich Wintzer, Rheinbach 2003, 61–66.
- Kolosser 1,24–2,23 (3,4), in: *'Le Christ tout en tous' (Col 3,11). L'epître aux Colossiens*, éd. par B. Standaert (SMBen.BE 16), Rom 2003, 29–68.

230   LIST OF PUBLICATIONS: PROF. DR. MICHAEL WOLTER

- Der Exeget als Leser und Interpret der Bibel, in: *Neutestamentliche Wissenschaft. Autobiographische Essays aus der Evangelischen Theologie*, hg.v. E.-M. Becker, Tübingen/Basel 2003, 90–102.
- Art. Quirinius, Publius Sulpicius, in: *RGG⁴* 6 (2003) 1871.

2004
- Apokalypsen als Erzählungen, in: *Apokalyptik in Antike und Aufklärung*, hg.v. J. Brokoff / B.U. Schipper, Paderborn u.a. 2004, 105–130.
- Reconstructing Q?, in: *Expository Times* 115 (2003/04) 115–119.
- Der Kompromiß bei Paulus, in: *Im Labyrinth der Ethik*. FS Martin Honecker, Rheinbach 2004, 66–78.
- Das lukanische Doppelwerk als Epochengeschichte, in: *Die Apostelgeschichte und die hellenistische Geschichtsschreibung*. FS Eckhard Plümacher, Leiden u.a. 2004, 253–284.
- 'Ihr sollt aber wissen . . .'. Das Anakoluth nach ἵνα δὲ εἰδῆτε in Mk 2,10–11 parr., in: *ZNW* 95 (2004) 269–275.
- Eine neue paulinische Perspektive, in: *ZNT* 14 (2004) 2–9.
- Neutestamentliche Gesichtspunkte (Replik zu E. Zenger), in: *Einander zugewandt. Die Rezeption des christlich-jüdischen Dialogs in der Dogmatik*, hg.v. E. Discherl u.a., Paderborn 2004, 91–95.

2005
- Christliches Ethos nach der Offenbarung des Johannes, in: *Studien zur Johannesoffenbarung und ihrer Auslegung*. FS Otto Böcher, Neukirchen-Vluyn 2005, 189–209.
- (Herausgeber:) *Studien zur Johannesoffenbarung und ihrer Auslegung*. FS für Otto Böcher zum 70. Geburtstag, Neukirchen-Vluyn 2005 (zusammen mit Friedrich Wilhelm Horn).
- Apokalyptik als Redeform im Neuen Testament, in: *NTS* 51 (2005) 171–191.
- Der Heilstod Jesu als theologisches Argument, in: *Deutungen des Todes Jesu*, hg.v. J. Frey/ J. Schröter (WUNT 181), Tübingen 2005, 297–313.
- Sünde. Neutestamentliche Aspekte, in: *GlLern* 20 (2005) 119–130.
- Escatologia paolina, in: *Protestantesimo* 60 (2005) 91–106.199–221.
- Der Epheserbrief als nachpaulinischer Paulusbrief, in: *Ethik als angewandte Ekklesiologie. Der Brief an die Epheser*, hg.v. M. Wolter (SMBen.BE 17), Rom 2005, 189–210.
- (Herausgeber:) *Ethik als angewandte Ekklesiologie. Der Brief an die Epheser* (SMBen.BE 17), Rom 2005.

2006
- Verstehen über Grenzen hinweg nach dem Neuen Testament, in: *Verstehen über Grenzen hinweg*, hg. v. W. Härle/R. Preul (MJTh 18), Marburg 2006, 53–81.
- The Theology of the Cross and the Quest for a Doctrinal Norm, in: *The Nature of New Testament Theology*. Essays in Honour of Robert Morgan, ed. C. Rowland/C. Tuckett, Oxford 2006, 263–285.
- Reich Gottes und weltliche Macht. Frühchristliche Perspektiven auf Staat und Gewalt, in: *Religion, Politik und Gewalt*, hg.v. F. Schweitzer (VWGTh 29), Gütersloh 2006, 172–184.
- Let no one seek his own, but each one the other's (1 Corinthians 10,24): Pauline ethics according to 1 Corinthians, in: *Identity, Ethics, and Ethos in the New Testament*, ed. J.G. van der Watt (BZNW 141), Berlin/New York 2006, 199–217.

2007
- Art. Schniewind, Julius Daniel, in: *Altpreußische Biographie* V/2, Marburg 2007, 1936–1938.
- Der Reichtum Gottes, in: *JBTh* 21 (2006) 145–160.
- Schriftkenntnis. Anmerkungen zu Joh 20,9, in: *Fragmentarisches Wörterbuch*. FS Horst Balz, Stuttgart 2007, 343–352.

LIST OF PUBLICATIONS: PROF. DR. MICHAEL WOLTER 231

- (Herausgeber:) *Moses in Biblical and Extra-Biblical Traditions* (BZAW 372), Berlin / New York 2007 (zusammen mit Axel Graupner).
- Prophet oder Messias? Einige Anmerkungen zu den Christologien von Lk 24,19–27, in: *Logos – Logik – Lyrik. Engagierte exegetische Studien zum biblischen Reden Gottes.* FS für Klaus Haacker, Leipzig 2007, 170–184.
- Geist und Leib: Aspekte paulinischer Anthropologie, in: *Menschenbild und Theologie. Beiträge zum interdisziplinären Gespräch*, hg.v. F.M. Brunn u.a. (MThSt 100), Leipzig 2007, 33–40.

2008
- Von der Entmachtung des Buchstabens durch seine Attribute. Eine Spurensuche, ausgehend von Röm 2,29, in: *Sprachgewinn.* FS Günter Bader, Münster 2008, 149–161.
- *Das Lukasevangelium* (HNT 5), Tübingen 2008.
- Paulinische Ethik als angewandte Ekklesiologie, in: *Sacra Scripta* 6 (2008) 44–57.
- Die Rede von der Sünde im Neuen Testament, in: *Marburger Jahrbuch Theologie.* XX. Sünde, hg.v. W. Härle/R. Preul (MThSt 105), Leipzig 2008, 15–44.
- 'Paulus', in: *GllLern* 23 (2008) 101–108.
- Probleme und Möglichkeiten einer Theologie des Neuen Testaments, in: *Jesus, Paul, and Early Christianity.* FS Henk-Jan de Jonge (NT.S 130), Leiden/Boston 2008, 417–438.

2009
- C.F. Evans and His Commentary. Preface to the Second Edition (mit Robert Morgan), in: C.F. Evans, *Saint Luke*, 2. Auflage, London 2009, xi–xix.
- *Theologie und Ethos im frühen Christentum. Studien zu Jesus, Paulus und Lukas* (WUNT 236), Tübingen 2009.
- Die Proömien des lukanischen Doppelwerks (Lk 1,1–4 und Apg 1,1–2), in: *Die Apostelgeschichte im Kontext antiker und frühchristlicher Historiographie*, hg. v. J. Frey u.a. (BZNW 162), Berlin/New York 2009, 476–494.
- Taufe als Initiation im religionsgeschichtlichen Kontext, in: *Das Baptisterium am Dom. Kölns erster Taufort*, hg. v. U. Krings/R. Will, Köln 2009, 139–159.
- Jesus as a Teller of Parables: On Jesus' Self-Interpretation in His Parables, in: *Jesus Research. An International Perspective*, ed. J.H. Charlesworth/P. Pokorný, Grand Rapids/ Cambridge 2009, 123–139.
- Art. 'Am ha-Arets. III. New Testament, in: *Encyclopedia of the Bible and Its Reception* 1 (2009) 916–917.
- Jesu Tod und Sündenvergebung bei Lukas und Paulus, in: *Reception of Paulinism in Acts. Réception du Paulinisme dans les Actes des Apôtres*, hg.v. D. Marguerat (BEThL 229), Leuven u.a. 2009, 15–35.
- Die Ekklesia und der Alltag. Der 1. Korintherbrief als Quelle für die Entstehung der christlichen Ethik, in: *ΑΠΟΣΤΟΛΟΣ ΠΑΥΛΟΣ ΚΑΙ ΚΟΡΙΝΘΟΣ. Saint Paul and Corinth II*, ed. By C.J. Belezos, Athen 2009, 837–845.

2010
- 'Für uns gestorben'. Wie gehen wir sachgerecht mit dem Tod Jesu um?, in: *Für uns gestorben. Sühne – Opfer – Stellvertretung*, hg.v. V. Hampel/R. Weth, Neukirchen-Vluyn 2010, 1–15.
- Das Israelproblem nach Gal 4,21–31 und Röm 9–11, in: *ZThK* 107 (2010) 1–30.
- Art. Emmaus, in: www.wibilex.de. *Dass wissenschaftliche Bibellexikon im Internet* (http://www.bibelwissenschaft.de/wibilex/das-bibellexikon/details/quelle/WIBI/zeichen/e/referenz/47884///cache/0126dda127f263da3ae49794b92af909/).
- Art. Zachäus, in: www.wibilex.de. *Das wissenschaftliche Bibellexikon im Internet* (http://www.bibelwissenschaft.de/wibilex/das-bibellexikon/details/quelle/WIBI/zeichen/z/referenz/56002///cache/29a4b6fc63a4a39e8de413c3d1d3a8b1/).

232   LIST OF PUBLICATIONS: PROF. DR. MICHAEL WOLTER

- Primitive Christianity as a Feast, in: *Feasts and Festivals*, ed. C. Tuckett, Leuven u.a. 2009, 171–182.
- Die Entwicklung des paulinischen Christentums von einer Bekehrungsreligion zu einer Traditionsreligion, in: *Early Christianity* 1 (2010) 15–40.
- The Letter to Philemon as Ethical Counterpart of Paul's Doctrine of Justification, in: *Philemon in Perspective*, ed. D.F. Tolmie (BZNW 169), Berlin/New York 2010, 169–179.
- Die Autonomie des Textes gegenüber den Lesern als Anliegen der historisch-kritischen Exegese des Neuen Testaments, in: *Verstehen, was man liest. Zur Notwendigkeit historisch-kritischer Bibellektüre*, hg.v. K. Finsterbusch/M. Tilly, Göttingen 2010, 88–99.
- Zum neutestamentlichen Glaubensverständnis, in: *GlLern*25 (2010) 152–154.

2011
- *Paulus. Ein Grundriss seiner Theologie*, Neukirchen-Vluyn 2011.
- Der heilige Geist bei Paulus, in: *JBTh* 24 (2009) 93–119.
- Was macht die historische Frage nach Jesus von Nazaret zu einer theologischen Frage?, in: *Erinnerung an Jesus. Kontinuität und Diskontinuität in der neutestamentlichen Überlieferung*. FS Rudolf Hoppe (BBB 166), Göttingen 2011, 17–33.
- 'Eschatology' in the Gospel According to Luke, in: *Eschatology of the New Testament and Some Related Documents*, ed. J.G. van der Watt (WUNT 2,315), Tübingen 2011, 91–108.
- The Distinctiveness of Paul's Eschatology, in: *Eschatology of the New Testament and Some Related Documents*, ed. J.G. van der Watt (WUNT 2,315), Tübingen 2011, 416–426.
- Art. Bed. II. New Testament, in: *Encyclopedia of the Bible and Its Reception* 3 (2011) 730–731.

2012
- The Development of Pauline Christianity from a 'Religion of Conversion' to a 'Religion of Tradition', in: *Paul and the Heritage of Israel*, ed. D.P. Moessner u.a. (LNTSt 452), London / New York 2012, 49–69.
- Η ηθική του Παύλου ως εφαρμοσμένη εκκλησιολογία, Δελτίο Βιβλικών Μελετών / in: *Bulletin of Biblical Studies* 27/37 (2009) 120–136.
- Die Rhetorik der Sünde im Neuen Testament, in: *Sündenpredigt*, hg. v. M. Meyer-Blanck u.a. (Ökumen. Studien zur Predigt 8), München 2012, 108–124.
- Η αμαρτία σύμφωνα με την καινή διαθήκη, Δελτίο Βιβλικών Μελετών / in: *Bulletin of Biblical Studies* 28/38 (2010) 65–81.
- Die Auferstehung der Toten und die Auferstehung Jesu, in: *Auferstehung*, hg.v. E. Gräb-Schmidt/R. Preul (MJTh 24), Leipzig 2012, 13–54.
- Alte und neue Perspektiven auf Paulus, in: *Paulus in der Schule*, hg.v. P. Müller, Stuttgart u.a. 2012, 15–29.
- 'Das Geschriebene tötet, der Geist aber macht lebendig' (2Kor 3,6). Ein Versuch zur paulinischen Antithese von γράμμα und πνεῦμα, in: *Der zweite Korintherbrief*. FS Dietrich-Alex Koch (FRLANT 250), Göttingen 2012, 355–379.

2013
- Mt 12,31–32 (Mt 3,28–30/Lk 12,10): ... nur die Lästerung des heiligen Geistes wird den Menschen nicht vergeben, in: *Gottesdienste zum Pfingstfest*, hg.v. H.-H. Auel, Göttingen 2013, 131–142.
- Die Rhetorik des Bösen im Neuen Testament, in: *Rhetorik des Bösen The Rhetoric of Evil*, hg.v. P. Fiddes/J. Schmidt, Würzburg 2013, 23–42.
- Jesus bei Paulus, in: *The Rise and Expansion of Christianity in the First Three Centuries of the Common Era*, ed. C.K. Rothschild/J. Schröter (WUNT 301), Tübingen 2013, 205–232.

INDEX OF AUTHORS

Abaelard, P.   191
Ahlers, B.   212
Albrecht, C.   210
Allison, D.C.   2, 3, 8, 102, 106, 113, 115, 131, 132, 133, 139, 150, 153, 182, 193
Alt, A.   41
Assmann, A.   10, 26, 31, 32, 33, 34, 35, 36, 37, 41, 42
Assmann, J.   10, 26, 27, 31

Bachner, S.   102
Baggett, D.   109
Bailey, K.E.   26
Barclay, J.M.G.   115, 116
Barnett, P.   115
Barrett, C.K.   112, 115
Bauckham, R.   36, 116, 148
Baum, A.D.   36
Baxter, A.   116
Beasley-Murray, G.R.   84
Blass, F. & Debrunner, A.   16
Bockmuehl, M.   132, 134, 139, 142, 148, 151, 152
Borg, M.J.   5, 74, 78, 107, 108, 109, 116
Bornkamm, G.   168
Braaten, C.E.   109
Braun, H.   193, 195
Breytenbach, C.   24, 26, 29, 35, 40, 41, 42, 44, 45
Broek, van den, P.   41
Brown, R.E.   108
Bultmann, R.   4, 14, 21, 22, 23, 27, 49, 107, 167, 178, 193, 195, 196
Burridge, R.A. & Gould, G.   115
Byrskog, S.   46

Carnley, P.   109
Casey, E.S.   26
Charlesworth, J.H.   84, 109
Chancey, M.A.   69
Chilton, B.   88
Claussen, C.   10
Claussen, J.H.   221
Collins, A.Y.   90
Craffert, P.   106, 109, 110
Craig, W.L.   113
Crossan, J.D.   5, 9, 69, 73, 75, 107, 108, 131, 132, 149
Culpepper, R.A.   69, 77, 84, 85

Danz, C.   220
Davies, W.D. & Allison, D.C.   80
Dembski, W.A. & Licona, M.   124
Dijk, van Teun A., & Kintsch, W.   26
Dijk, van Teun A.   35, 41
Dilthey, W.   47, 48
Dodd, C.H.   26, 28, 64
Dormeyer, D.   24
Droysen, J.G.   23, 24
Duling, D.C.   91
Dunn, J.D.G.   7, 10, 12, 25, 26, 27, 34, 37, 44, 50, 58, 59, 61, 63, 69, 74, 77, 83, 85, 108, 109, 115, 139, 140, 144, 146, 147, 148, 150, 154, 180, 195
Dupont-Sommer, A.   81

Ebeling, G.   197
Ehrman, B.D.   106, 107, 108, 109, 110, 132, 133
Engelbrecht, J.   115
Evans, C.A.   76, 88, 89, 102, 107

Farley, E.   162
Fay, B.   105
Fiensy, D.A.   74
Fischer, H.R.   14
Førland, T.E.   119, 120
France, R.T.   90
Fredriksen, P.   73, 74, 108, 109, 110
Freyne, S.   69, 71, 72, 73, 75
Fried, J.   29, 31, 32, 33, 34, 35, 36
Funk, R.W.   107, 115, 116, 117, 132, 149

Gadamer, H.-G.   134, 135, 136, 137, 138, 139, 140, 141, 144, 145, 155
García Martínez, D.   93
Gilderhus, M.T.   105, 106
Gnilka, J.   10
Goertz, H.-J.   8
Goppelt, L.   12
Goulder, M.   115
Grant, M.   115
Gregory, A.   148
Grice, P.H.   42
Güttgemanns, E.   23, 24

Habermas, G.R.   110, 113
Halbwachs, M.   26, 27, 34
Härle, W.   14

INDEX OF AUTHORS

Harnack, von, A. 20, 192
Harvey, V.A. 177
Hays, R.B. 115
Hengel, M. 84
Henning, W.B. 93
Heszer, C. 43
Hooke, S.H. 117
Hoover, R.W. 115
Hoppe, R. 6, 87
Horst, van der, P.W. 92
Hoskyns, E.C. 177
Hurtado, L.W. 112, 116, 126

Jaspert, B. 167
Jenkins, K. 105
Jenson, R.W. 151
Jeremias, J. 72, 80, 98, 163, 191
Johnson, L.T. 4, 12, 13, 109, 131, 132, 134, 139, 140, 153, 173, 193
Joubert, A. 26

Kähler, M. 2, 3, 6, 9, 12, 13, 139, 160, 164, 177, 178, 180, 192, 193
Kansteiner, W. 34, 35, 36, 37
Kant, I. 221
Karris, R.J. 79
Käsemann, E. 4, 21, 22, 23, 29, 167, 193, 195, 196
Keck, L.E. 134, 139, 140, 142, 176
Keener, C.S. 71, 74, 75, 115
Kelber, W.H. 26, 36
Kendal, D. 116
Keppler, A. 33, 34, 36
Kerplin, M. 6, 12
Kirk, A. & Thatcher, T. 34
Klauck, H.-J. 90
Knox, J. 180
Koester, H. 110, 115
Kotansksy, R.D. 90
Kuitert, H.M. 52
Kümmel, W.G. 163

Landmesser, C. 7
Lapide, P. 108, 109, 116
Lategan, B. C. 24, 25, 29
Laube, M. 207
Lessing, G.E. 202
Levene, D. 93
Licona, M.R. 105, 110, 111, 113, 114, 117, 121, 122, 123, 125
Lightfoot, R.H. 21
Lindars, B. 116
Link, H.-G. 180
Lohmeyer, E. 21, 28

Lorenz, C. 8, 102, 106
Lüdemann, G. 108, 109, 115, 116, 133, 149
Luther, M. 191
Lyons, W.J. 146

Malina, B. & Rohrbaugh, R. 78
Marcus, J. 90
Marxsen, W. 23
McCown, C.C. 91
McCullagh, C.B. 102, 120
McIntyre, J. 108
Meier, J.P. 5, 9, 78, 89, 107, 108
Miller, R.J. 108, 119, 120
Minear, P.S. 134
Moeser, M.C. 46
Montefiore, H. 109
Morgan, R. 7, 65, 134, 139, 140, 145, 146, 147, 150, 151, 172
Müller, E.F.K. 191
Murphy-O'Connor, J. 72, 117

Neill, S. & Wright, N.T. 5

Oegema, G.S. 194
Onuki, T. 40

Panneberg, W. 48, 187, 190
Patterson, S.J. 115, 116, 117
Pellegrini, S. 44
Pesch, R. 90
Perrin, N. 29
Placher, W.C. 133, 141, 142
Preisendanz, K. 92
Price, R.M. 110

Quest, K. 117

Ratzinger, J. 13, 151, 190
Reimarus. H.S. 2, 3, 6, 174, 175, 205
Reed, J.L. 42, 43, 69, 73
Rhoads, D. & Syreeni, K. 24
Richardson, P. 69
Ricoeur, P. 26, 28, 30, 31, 32, 34, 35, 36, 50, 52
Ristow, H. & Matthiae, K. 196
Roberts, D.D. 105
Roberts, J. & Rowlands, C. 138, 140
Robinson, J.M. 4

Sanders, E.P. 5, 75, 87, 107, 109
Schacter, D.L. 26, 36
Scheliha, von, A. 220
Schlatter, A. 163, 178
Schleiermacher, F.D.E. 181, 182, 209, 210

INDEX OF AUTHORS

Schmidt, K.L.   20, 41
Schmithals, W.   19, 20
Schniewind, J.   21, 23, 28
Scholtissek, K.   24
Schröder, M.   210
Schröter, J.   8, 10, 12, 13, 23, 26, 27, 28, 34, 37, 39, 44, 45
Schröter, J. & Brucker, R.   195
Schweitzer, A.   2, 4, 49, 192, 194, 199
Segal, A.F.   106
Shanks, H. & Witherington, B.   115
Sherwin-White, A.N.   103
Sibcy, G.A.   123
Slenczka, N.   190, 192, 202
Stagg, E. & F.   82
Stanton, G.N.   89
Strange, J.F.   72
Strauss, D.F.   160, 178
Strecker, C.   10
Swinburne, R.   149

Tabor, J.D.   117
Talbert, C.H.   144
Theissen, G. & Merz, A.   5, 9, 25, 68, 107, 108, 115, 133, 154, 182, 194, 195
Theißen, G. & Winter, D.   22
Toit, du, D.S.   23, 26, 40

Troeltsch, E.   206, 207, 222
Tucker, A.   119, 120
Twelftree, G.   99, 107, 108

Vermès, G.   68, 74, 80, 108, 109, 154
Viney, D.W.   109
Vorster, W.S.   23, 24
Vossler, O.   8

Watson, F.   133, 139, 142, 150
Webb, R.L.   98
Wedderburn, A.J.M.   109, 115, 117
White, H.   8, 102
Wise, M.O., Abegg, M.G. & Cook, E.M.   95, 97,
Witherington, B.   12, 115
Wittekind, F.   220
Wolff, W.   40
Wolter, M.   98, 174
Wrede, W.   20, 21, 26, 27, 28, 38, 43, 44, 46, 47
Wright, N.T.   12, 75, 78, 109, 113, 119, 120, 133

Yeago, D.   152

Zammito, J.   102
Zimmermann, R.   45